TESTED

TESTED

Marshall Test Pilots and Their Aircraft
In War and Peace 1919 to 1999

Dennis Pasco

GRUB STREET · LONDON

Published by
Grub Street
The Basement
10 Chivalry Road
London SW11 1HT

Copyright © 1999 Grub Street, London
Text Copyright © 1999 Dennis Pasco

British Library Cataloguing in Publication Data
Pasco, Dennis
   Tested: Marshall test pilots in war and peace, 1919-1999
   1. Marshall of Cambridge (Firm) – History 2. Test pilots –
   Great Britain 3. Airplanes – Piloting – Great Britain
   4. Test pilots – Great Britain – History 5. Airplanes –
   Piloting – Great Britain – History
   I. Title
   629.1'3252'0922

ISBN 1-902304-35-7

Typeset by Pearl Graphics, Hemel Hempstead
Printed and bound in Great Britain by
Biddles Ltd, Guildford and King's Lynn

To Margaret, for her endless and loving encouragement

Contents

Foreword by Michael J Marshall   6

Preface   7

Acknowledgements and Bibliography   8

Glossary   9

PART ONE – They Flew in World War Two   11

CHAPTER 1   Sir Arthur Marshall, by Dennis Pasco   12

CHAPTER 2   Leslie Worsdell   26

CHAPTER 3   Herbert Tappin   47

CHAPTER 4   Douglas Page   58

CHAPTER 5   The Not Forgotten Ones, by Dennis Pasco   73

PART TWO – Post-World War Two Pilots & Activities   96

CHAPTER 6   A 'Fat Albert' Flight Test, by Dennis Pasco   97

CHAPTER 7   Ron Frost   104

CHAPTER 8   John Preece   113

CHAPTER 9   Colin Rudder   131

CHAPTER 10   Dennis Pasco   150

CHAPTER 11   Tim Mason   173

CHAPTER 12   The Falklands War and Aftermath, by Dennis Pasco 191

APPENDIX ONE

List of Marshall Test Pilots   214

APPENDIX TWO

Special Marshall Designations & Project Numbers   218

Index   220

Foreword

BY MICHAEL J MARSHALL

I am delighted and honoured to write a foreword to this exciting book which represents the bringing together of much courage and a huge range of airmanship skills and expertise based round the Company's seventy years of activities at Cambridge Airport and ninety years since its first foundation in the retail motor business.

It all came together because of the foresight and boldness of my grandfather and the entrepreneurial courage of my father who was born just thirteen days prior to the first flight by the Wright Brothers at Kitty Hawk on 17th December 1903. His flair attracted some keen and enterprising pilots and the Company built up a huge reputation in the fields of pilot training and aircraft repair and modification. This in turn led to even more exciting programmes such as the Valiant TI Rapid Take-Off Procedure and TriStar conversions for launching satellites via Pegasus and the X-34 Rocket.

Life in the fast lane is not without its risk. It has also had its rewards not only through the national recognition under which Leslie Worsdell was awarded the OBE and John Blake, the MBE, but also because of the huge levels of respect and friendship that have been gained during so many hours of flying on programmes which were of importance to the United Kingdom.

All of us in Marshall of Cambridge are grateful for their endeavours and we know that they have enjoyed carrying out their craft with meticulous planning and immeasurable airmanship, skill and courage. This expertise has contributed enormously to the Company's engineering ability.

I am delighted that this book has been put together by Dennis Pasco on behalf of his colleagues. I hope that it will give much pleasure to all members of the families of Cambridge Test Pilots as well as to many colleagues and friends and to the wider community of those who enjoy reading or participating in the magic of aviation, which never ceases to thrill.

The feats of Marshall Test Pilots vividly portray the development of flying from its early pre-World War Two days through to the much more meticulous testing of modern aircraft. Through it all, they show how the call of flying with all its excitement and challenges was always irresistible once the bug had bitten. Flying for all these test pilots was not only a profession in which they took great pride, but also it was one of huge fun and great camaraderie.

Preface

This book is the result of a chance remark by my wife Margaret. While I was writing my autobiography in 1996 she suggested that I should expand it to include the experiences of the longer-serving Marshall test pilots. Seven pilots have contributed a chapter and I am indebted to them for their candid revelations. I hope that the book will reward the reader with an insight to the world of aviation and the significant part played in it by the Marshall Company and its personnel for most of this century.

I have taken 1919 as the starting point in the title of the book simply because it was in that year that David Marshall and his son, Arthur (later Sir Arthur), made their first flight. In addition to the flying careers of the pilots featured in this book I have included a few details of domestic life to give the reader a brief insight to the different backgrounds of the pilots.

Readers will note the different names by which the aviation side of the Marshall Company is referred to in the text. Marshall's Flying School Ltd became Marshall of Cambridge (Engineering) Ltd in 1962 and then Marshall of Cambridge Aerospace Ltd in 1992. The Cambridge Aero Club Ltd was founded in 1934 followed by the University Aero Club Ltd in 1936. Both were wound up in 1939. The Cambridge Aero Club Ltd was revived shortly after World War Two ended. Few companies in the world can look back at so many varied and successful projects as those completed by Marshall of Cambridge Aerospace.

In 1965 single-service ministries, such as the Air Ministry, disappeared with the creation of the Ministry of Defence (MOD).

From its early biplane and fabric-covered aircraft to the present range of Jumbo-jets, Cambridge airport, which started business just days after I was born, is still a worthy place for the air enthusiast to observe and I hope and trust will continue to be so.

Performance details and specifications, wherever possible, have been taken from Pilot's Notes or Flight Manuals. They should not be taken as definitive. For example, all aircraft wingspans and lengths are to the nearest three inches. The information is there to permit the reader to compare easily one aircraft with another.

Finally, I am very conscious of the fact that aeroplanes have never just 'appeared' on the flight line, ready for the pilot and crew to hop aboard and fly off. To the many technicians and boffins, military and civilian, who have worked long and hard to prepare aircraft for me to fly I give my thanks for a hugely satisfying and rewarding career.

DENNIS PASCO
9th June 1999

Acknowledgements

In addition to the pilots who contributed a chapter I thank the following for their help and encouragement:

Sir Arthur and Michael Marshall, Barbara and Derek Birch, John Brownlow, David Bywater, Karl Chapman, Diana Else (who, sadly, died on 1st May 1999), Roderick Else, Silvio and Sylvia Fella, Brian Foskett, Maria Froggatt, Malcolm Gault, Tim Gooch, Geoff Guest, Norman Harry, Peter Hedderwick, Terry Holloway, Keith Ingle, John Kellock, Ken Kitchiner, Alan and Mick Milne, Steve Rolph, Dave Rowland, Dave Ryding, Doug Silk, Marjorie Smythe, John Stephens, Tommy Thompson, Robin Welch, David Whitehead, Paul Willmott and William 'Tug' Wilson.

For their patience and diplomacy I especially thank Gordon Bruce (who also contributed to the script) and Ken Starling who read the text critically. I thank Gerald Coulson, an ex-Marshall employee, for his kind permission to use his painting for the front cover, and Michael J F Bowyer for providing so many fine photographs.

Bibliography

Action Stations series, Patrick Stephens Ltd, Bar Hill, Cambridge, 1979.
Aden, Sir Tom Higginbotham, Constable & Co, London, 1958.
Against All Odds, RAF Association, The Rococo Group, London, 1990.
Air International, Air International Magazines, Bromley, Kent, 1983.
Aircraft of the RAF since 1918, Owen Thetford, Putnam, London, 1967.
Looking for Trouble, General Sir Peter de la Billière, Harper Collins, London, 1995.
Profile Publications, Profile Publications Ltd, London, 1966.
The Spitfire Story, Alfred Price, Arms & Armour Press, London, 1982.
The British Bomber since 1914, Francis K Mason, Putnam, London, 1984.
The Marshall Story, Sir Arthur Marshall, Haynes Publishing, Yeovil, 1994.
Wings, Encyclopaedia of Aviation in Weekly Parts, Orbis Publishing Ltd, London, 1980.
The Public Record Office at Kew.

The origin of photographs is given in the photograph captions. The Shrike-carrying Vulcan on the rear cover is © British Crown Copyright/MOD. Reproduced with the permission of the Controller of Her Majesty's Stationery Office.

If any reader is able to add to the information in the book, please write to me care of The Cambridge Aero Club, Newmarket Road, Cambridge, CB5 8RX.

Glossary

AA	Anti-aircraft.	BST	British Summer Time.
A & AEE	Aeroplane & Armament Experimental Establishment.	CAA	Civil Aviation Authority.
		C of A	Certificate of Airworthiness.
AAR	Air-to-Air Refuelling.	C of AT	College of Air Training.
AC 2	Aircraftman second class.	CAACU	Civilian Anti-aircraft Co-operation Unit.
ADC	Aide de Camp.	CAC	Cambridge Aero Club.
ADF	Automatic Direction Finding.	CB	Thunderstorm.
		CFS	Central Flying School.
AEF	Air Experience Flight.	DFC	Distinguished Flying Cross.
AEO	Air Electronics Officer.		
AFC	Air Force Cross.	DFCS	Day Fighter Combat School.
AFS/AFTS	Advanced FTS.		
AID	Aircraft Inspection Department.	DH	de Havilland.
		DLC	Direct Lift Control.
Anchors	Brakes.	ECM	Electronic Counter Measures.
AOC	Air Officer Commanding.		
		EFTS	Elementary FTS.
ARO	Aircraft Repair Organisation.	E & RFTS	Elementary & Reserve FTS.
AST	Air Service Testing	ETPS	Empire Test Pilots' School.
ASV	Air to Surface Radar.		
ATC	Air Traffic Control.	Fg Off	Flying Officer.
ATPL	Airline Transport Pilot's Licence.	Flt Lt	Flight Lieutenant.
		FIS	Flying Instructor School.
Avtur	Aviation turbine fuel.	Fpm	Feet per minute.
BA	British Airways.	FTS	Flying Training School.
BABS	Beam Approach Beacon System.	G or g	Gravity force.
		GAPAN	Guild of Air Pilots & Navigators.
BAC	British Aircraft Corporation.	GEE-H	A radar navigation aid.
BAe	British Aerospace.	GCI	Ground Controlled Interception.
BCAR	British Civil Airworthiness Requirements.		
		GPR	Glider Pilot Regiment.
		GPS	Global Positioning System.
BEA	British European Airways.	Hack	A 'run-around' vehicle.
BFTS	Basic FTS.	HCU	Heavy Conversion Unit.
BHP	Brake Horse Power.	HDU	Hose Drum Unit.
BOAC	British Overseas Airways Corporation.	HP	Horse power.
		HQ	Headquarters.

HUD	Head Up Display.	RAFVR	RAF Volunteer Reserve.
ILS	Instrument Landing System.	RFS	Reserve Flying School.
		RPM	Revolutions per minute.
IRT	Instrument Rating Test.	SAS	Special Air Squadron.
Knot	One nautical mph.	SEPECAT	Société Européenne de Production de l'Avion d'Ecole de Combat et d'Appui Tactique.
LABS	Low Altitude Bombing System.		
MAROC	Marshall's Orange Crop.		
MBE	Member of the British Empire.	SFIS	Supplementary Flying Instructor School.
Mk	Mark.	Slot	Approved entry or take-off time.
MOD	Ministry of Defence.		
Mph	Miles per hour.	Sqn	Squadron.
NASA	National Aeronautics and Space Administration.	Sqn Ldr	Squadron Leader.
		TACAN	Tactical Air Navigation System.
Nav	Navigator.		
NDB	Non-directional Beacon.	TIA	Transient Ischaemic Attack (Stroke).
OC	Officer Commanding.		
OCU	Operational Conversion Unit.	TRE	Type Rating Examiner.
		TT	Target Towing.
OBE	Order of the British Empire.	UAS	University Air Squadron.
		USAF	United States Air Force.
OLM	Operational Load Measurement.	U/T	Under Training.
		VC	Victoria Cross.
OTU	Operational Training Unit.	VHF	Very High Frequency.
		VLF	Very Low Frequency.
PPL	Private Pilot's Licence.	VOR	VHF Omni Range navigation system.
QFI	Qualified Flying Instructor.		
QRE	Estimated time of arrival (Q code).	V1/VR	Take-off decision(V1) & rotation (VR) speeds.
		UHF	Ultra High Frequency.
RWR	Radar Warning Receiver.	Wg Cdr	Wing Commander.
RAE	Royal Aircraft Establishment.	W/T	Wireless Telegraphy (Morse code).
RAF	Royal Air Force.		

PART ONE

They Flew in
World War Two

Chapter 1

Sir Arthur Marshall

BY DENNIS PASCO

How many Managing Directors would take the wife of one of their employees to the shops on a Saturday afternoon and then drive her home? A customer's aircraft was scheduled for completion on the Monday morning. It was obvious before noon on the Saturday that work was needed that afternoon to guarantee completion on time. One by one Arthur Marshall asked the key group of employees 'Will you work this afternoon?' Only one said 'No.' Asked why, he said 'I have the only car in our household, there is no bus, and my wife has to go to shop in Cambridge today.' 'Will you work if I get the Transport Section to collect your wife, take her in to town, then return her to home?' 'Yes' said the man. In the event, Arthur Marshall collected and returned the lady himself. The customer's aircraft was ready by the Monday.

Born in Cambridge, on 4th December 1903, Arthur Marshall was the first of eight children. Raised in a strict and disciplined regime, Arthur attended infant school from the age of six. By this time, his father, David, had started a motor business in Cambridge. For the naturally inquisitive Arthur, the garage became a favourite place in which to spend time. Education continued at the Perse Preparatory School in Bateman Street, with a move in due course to the big school opposite the Catholic Church. Thereafter, Arthur moved to Tonbridge boarding school, Kent, in 1918. As World War One ended, the Marshall family moved to Elfleda House, on the eastern side of Cambridge. At the same time David Marshall realised that aviation had an important future. For £5 he bought a Handley Page 0/400 twin-engine bomber and a canvas-covered hangar. The hangar was re-assembled in the grounds of Elfleda House. David and Arthur Marshall's first flight was in July 1919 at Brighton. The aircraft was a Fairey IIIA seaplane conversion of a shipborne bomber; the cost was ten shillings (50p).

From Tonbridge school Arthur Marshall went up to Jesus College, Cambridge. There, he gained a full Blue for athletic prowess; in 1924 he was included in the Great Britain team at the Olympic games in Paris. On leaving Cambridge University, in April 1926, Arthur joined the family garage business. His first flying lesson was on 29th June 1927 in a de Havilland (DH) Cirrus Moth of the Norfolk & Norwich Aero Club at Norwich. *Flight* magazine, in reporting that flight, made its first ever reference to Arthur Marshall.

Arthur continued his lessons until the August, flying without his parents' knowledge. Before recommencing the lessons in July 1928, he came clean with his parents. To his surprise, there was no problem and he resumed his flying training at Norwich. His first solo flight came on 3rd July. *Flight* reported the event as 'A splendid show and the landing was a treat to watch.' On 13th July Arthur completed his Private Pilot's (A) Licence test. With his father's enthusiasm for flying rekindled, he approved the purchase of a new DH60 Gipsy Moth. Delivery was scheduled for the end of February 1929. Where would it be kept? An offer was made to the farmer who owned the adjoining Whitehill Farm, which included a 45-acre field – adjacent to the present Cambridge United football ground. The offer was accepted. Sufficient ground was now available to provide landing runs, in all directions, of about 450 yards.

DH GIPSY MOTH. One DH Gipsy I engine of 100HP. Span 30 feet. Length 24 feet. Loaded weight 1,650lb. Cruising airspeed 85mph. The version used by the RAF was of metal construction, but the early Gipsy Moths were made of wood. RAF Central Flying School used them until the early 1930s; 15 and 17 E & RFTS used them from 1937.

Boulton & Paul, of Norwich, erected a hangar in the paddock at Whitehill (the Marshall family changed the name of their home from Elfleda House to Aviation Hall). Access from the paddock to the landing ground was achieved by cutting out part of the intervening hedge. With about forty hours flying under his belt, Arthur collected his brand-new Gipsy Moth, registration G-AAEH, from Hatfield aerodrome. Navigation was simple – follow the road through Stevenage, Baldock and Royston. So as not to encroach on the time spent working in the garage business, Arthur made some practice flights before breakfast. One morning, to save taxiing time, he decided to start the take-off run in the paddock, aiming to pass through the gap in the hedge. Just before reaching the gap, a gust of wind pushed the Moth to the right just as it was leaving the ground. The hedge was missed by the smallest margin. A lucky break and a lesson well learnt.

On 17th March 1929 Arthur and his father set off for Hooton Park, near Liverpool. The weather was poor, with a low cloud base. Within a few miles of leaving Cambridge conditions worsened. Turning back was the only option. Next day the weather was better but, about forty-five minutes into the flight, engine power suddenly dropped from 1,900 rpm to fewer than 1,000. This gave insufficient power to maintain height. Fortunately, a large field presented itself, into which a successful forced landing was made. On the ground, the engine behaved normally. What now? Leaving his father by the aeroplane, Arthur launched into a test flight. Just before take-off speed was reached, power dropped. The take off was abandoned. The field's owner allowed Arthur to make a telephone call to de Havilland, who immediately told him 'Disconnect the fuel pipe, let fuel flow and reconnect the pipe whilst fuel is still flowing.' It worked; the flight continued. Nearing the time that Hooton Park was about due, the weather again deteriorated. Concerned about how much fuel remained in the tank, which held just nineteen gallons, and with visibility down to a few hundred yards, Arthur landed in a field. By chance a man stood in the field. 'Hooton Park?' he answered, 'it's in the next field.' David Marshall walked there, whilst Arthur flew his Moth over the hedge and landed. As time was short, refuelling was left until the next day. Nineteen gallons went into the tank. A close shave, not unknown to most aviators.

With the weather improving, but still not good, the return flight went well until about forty-five minutes after take-off. Just as on the previous day, the engine power suddenly dropped. This time, the field was much smaller – too short for a fully loaded departure. Repeating the fuel pipe procedure recommended by de Havilland, normal power was restored. A co-operative motorist took David and the baggage down the road to a larger field. Arthur took off from the small field and landed in the larger one. With David and the baggage aboard, the flight continued to Cambridge without further mishap. Later on the fuel system was simply modified by increasing the length of the vent pipe on top of the fuel tank.

A couple of weeks later Arthur made a flight to Land's End. He took with him a friend: Frank Morell. Arthur made a successful landing in a field and the aircraft was refuelled with ten gallons of motor car fuel purchased from a nearby garage for the return journey. The flight home was going so well that Frank was quite contentedly reading poetry in the front seat. Suddenly the engine produced a violent and frightening noise. Arthur planned an immediate landing into the only available but very short open space. Not only was the field a small one, it had a hedge at the far end. Arthur was unable to stop the aircraft before reaching the end of the landing run. The left wing of the Gipsy Moth hit the hedge; the aircraft swung round and the right wing dropped into the sunken road beyond. Fortunately the aircraft was not badly damaged and, the following day, the Moth was dismantled and transported to the nearest railway station, and thence on to de Havilland's at Stag Lane. The cause of the problem was identified as too small a gap between a valve cap and its serrated valve cotter. The third lucky escape.

In a speech to the Guild of Air Pilots and Air Navigators (GAPAN) in London on 22nd May 1997, Sir Arthur stated how the official opening of the first Marshall aerodrome came about:

'On a Monday in late March 1929, Sir Alan Cobham was carrying out an aerial survey in the Huntingdon area. His aircraft developed engine trouble, causing him to land in the forty-five acre patch behind the Marshall home. It was just after lunch. Sir Alan asked if there was any chance of getting something to eat. My mother gave him some cold beef from the large Sunday roast joint and some pickled onions. He ate them with gusto. Sir Alan, my father and I talked about the possibility of other people landing on our patch. By three o'clock we had committed ourselves to a grand opening of the forty-five acre field for Cambridge on University May Week Sunday – just a few weeks away. The opening was a great success, with forty-three visiting aircraft and a full military band in an old-fashioned bandstand. The aircraft of John Tranum, the famous wing-walker who always performed without a parachute, had gone unserviceable. Dermot Boyle (later to be Sir Dermot, a Marshal of the Royal Air Force and Chief of Air Staff) was persuaded to stand in and fly my aircraft for his demo.'

After the official opening of the aerodrome enquiries for flying training soon followed. The flying school opened in the October. A second Gipsy Moth, G-EBYZ, was bought. This Moth was the first Gipsy production Moth and, in the hands of Hubert Broad, the famous DH test pilot, won the King's Cup Air Race. One of the first three pupils was Norman de Bruyne, the junior bursar of Trinity College. He went on to design and build his own aircraft, the Snark – a famous machine, which was eventually bought by the Air Ministry for wing airflow research. Leslie Worsdell was once taking off in one of Norman de Bruyne's aircraft when the fuel flow became intermittent and he had to abandon take-off, finishing up running into a ploughed field on the edge of Coldham's Lane. Norman became the inventor of synthetic glues and honeycomb construction. Without Norman's glues the famous Mosquito could not have been built. Aged 92, Norman died in March 1997.

Both the flying instructors who taught on the Moths were on temporary employment. They were ex-RAF commissioned officers, and they instructed in their spare time on Sunday afternoons. To join in with the flying instruction, Arthur needed to obtain his Commercial (B) licence. He passed the general flight-test and a qualifying cross-country flight in January 1930. Having had G-EBYZ fitted with elementary night flying equipment Arthur passed the night flying test at Croydon on 20th January. In February the remaining two cross-country flights were conducted. During the first one, from Croydon to Lympne, Lady Luck appeared again. The weather en route deteriorated, with cloud making visual navigation a near impossibility. At precisely the right moment a gap appeared. There below, in clear white letters on the aerodrome, was the word LYMPNE. Arthur's commercial licence was issued on 5th March 1930; that same day he gave his first flying lesson.

A very busy year followed. Arthur flew all but a few of the total instructional flights made by his flying school. In summer, from Monday to Saturday and all day on Sundays, he worked in the garage until the evening, followed by flying instruction. In winter months, the mornings were spent at the garage, with afternoons devoted to flying. On Sundays, after essential garage work first thing, there was more time for flying instruction. During 1933, on a flight from the south of France to Cambridge, poor weather struck again. A lowering cloud base during the approach to Le Bourget threatened the cross-Channel leg. Arthur discussed the options with the captain of an Imperial Airways Handley Page HP 42 aircraft. The captain's plan was to fly at 4,000 feet where he expected to be between layers of cloud. 'Right' Arthur said, 'I'll follow you.' With conditions over England forecast as fine the two aircraft took off. Climb and initial cruise went well. However, before long cloud layers merged. The HP 42, being somewhat faster than the Puss Moth, soon disappeared from sight. As the Moth approached Le Touquet, with ground out of sight, the remaining fuel quantity looked low. Suddenly the clouds parted; directly below was Le Touquet. Arthur spiralled down and flew at low level to Lympne.

The Whitehill site contained about four, quite small, hangars, and was a magnet for aviation-addicted schoolboys. By 1935 the recently appointed chief engineer was Stephen Wilkinson. He was a god to those serving under him. Tommy Thompson, at the time still a schoolboy, recalls his introductory chat from 'god' when he was first allowed inside a hangar. 'This is a propeller, this is the fuel cock and these are the ignition switches. If you touch any of them you will walk straight out on to Newmarket Road. Is that clear?' Arthur, too, kept a close eye on airfield activities. The grass surface was sacred. From a distance one day, Arthur spotted that Tommy had drained some glycol liquid onto the grass. Shortly afterwards Tommy was on the receiving end of a short sharp lecture from a more senior god. As an example of good instruction leading to greater things, Tommy became an engineering apprentice with the Company from 1938 to 1945 and retired from the position of Chief Surveyor of the Civil Aviation Authority (CAA) Airworthiness Division in 1984. Until April 1999 he was still helping the Company as a part-time flying instructor with the Cambridge Aero Club.

All through the 1930s flying instruction activity steadily increased. Arthur decided, in December 1935, to recruit additional instructors. Again quoting from the speech to GAPAN in May 1997, Sir Arthur revealed how this scheme came about:

> 'Before and during the war RAF civil contractors undertook Volunteer Reserve elementary flying. With the expansion pre-war there was a very big shortage of flying instructors, with the only source of supply being ex RAF. So we decided to train our own from scratch, from the age of eighteen, to be passed out by the CFS as advanced instructors on Tiger Moths, Harts, Hinds and Battles within a total time of eleven to fourteen weeks. When war broke out we had thirty-five flying instructors, nearly half of whom had been trained in this

way. This scheme, which became known as the Marshall Ab Initio Flying Instructor Scheme, made a big difference to the number of pilots trained by my Company and available for the Battle of Britain. War was declared on Sunday 3rd September 1939 and on Monday September 4th we started an intensive but unsuccessful campaign for our Ab Initio Flying Instructor Scheme to be adopted by the RAF. With the fall of France we felt it did not matter who we offended, and we made direct approaches to the Air Minister. This resulted in Guy Garrod being appointed as the first Air Member for Training in July 1940 with the request that he should see me immediately after he had taken office. He took office on the Monday and we met on the Wednesday. After many meetings and further trials, including ab initio training of pupils over air crew age, our scheme was finally adopted with the establishment of five Supplementary Flying Instructor Schools (SFIS), one of which was at Cambridge, in May 1941. Had our scheme been adopted when war broke out, there would have been no shortage of pilots for the Battle of Britain. Leslie Worsdell, who was the first recipient of the Guild's Clem Pike Trophy for "the most praiseworthy contribution to the maintenance of high standards of flying instruction and safety" in 1963, was our first Ab Initio Instructor Apprentice in 1936. This award is not an automatic annual award but is only presented as and when there is a worthy recipient. Herbert "Tap" Tappin was another of our Ab Initio instructor pupils in 1938. He instructed with the RAF Volunteer Reserve (RAFVR) at Oxford. Two of his pupils there had transferred from the Oxford University Air Squadron (UAS) to the RAFVR for advanced training. They were Leonard Cheshire VC, a famous Bomber Command pilot and founder of the Cheshire Homes, and Foxley-Norris, a Battle of Britain pilot who later became an Air Chief Marshal. Tap transferred to Cambridge at the outbreak of war, and one of his pupils later became the most successful and most decorated RAF fighter pilot, Johnnie Johnson. Leslie and Tap both had very distinguished RAF operational careers during the war.'

In 1937 the new aerodrome, near Teversham corner, was under construction. Which was just as well because, flying a twin-engine Monospar, Arthur had just got airborne from the Fen Ditton site on an easterly heading, when both engines lost power. Throttling back immediately, Arthur landed on the new aerodrome. By the time the new aerodrome was officially opened five hundred pilots had been trained. With quantity the quality is sometimes lost but not at Cambridge. The Aero Club had earned the reputation of being the finest flying school in the country.

The new aerodrome was officially opened on 8th October 1938. Typically, for the time of the year, there was a stiff south-westerly wind blowing. After three speeches from the assembled dignitaries, Dr Norman de Bruyne proposed a toast to the Cambridge aerodrome, to which David Marshall responded. Sir Kingsley Wood, Secretary of State for Air, then formally declared the aerodrome open. Three Hawker Harts of the Reserve Squadron took off, and nine Avro Tutors of the Cambridge UAS opened the air display with a demonstration of squadron drill. Three Spitfires of 19 Sqn from RAF Duxford, led by Sqn Ldr H Iliffe Cozens, then gave an exciting display of formation flying. The three Harts roared in and performed their formation display followed by a spirited solo display flown by Leslie Worsdell in a Hawker Hind (L7206) of the Reserve Squadron. With light rain now falling, the Cambridge Gliding Club completed the air display with winching and aero-tow demonstrations.

HAWKER HIND I. Two-seat light bomber and trainer. One 640HP Rolls-Royce Kestrel V. Span 37 feet 3 inches. Length 29 feet 6 inches. Loaded weight 5,300lb. Maximum speed 185mph at 16,400 feet. Climb to 6,500 feet four minutes.

1938 was a year to remember. Flying took place on every single day, including Christmas Day and Boxing Day. Both David and Arthur Marshall had the habit of dropping in at any hour of the day or night to see how things were going. The workforce, many of them ex-Service personnel, got used to being kept on their toes by seeing Arthur Marshall call in after an evening's social event. About a quarter of the technical staff were apprentices, which for some was a seven-year stint. A number of Company employees joined the RAFVR at the age of eighteen. Some of them learned to fly. Among them was Peter Else who had been the very first Marshall engineering apprentice.

In 1939, with war approaching, the second hangar was completed at the Teversham site. In August of that year the Air Ministry made Marshall responsible for refurbishing, modification and rebuilding the Armstrong Whitworth Whitley, a twin-engine bomber. At that time nine squadrons of Whitleys, and eight of Wellingtons, represented the might of Bomber Command, however pathetic that may seem now.

ARMSTRONG WHITWORTH WHITLEY V. Long-range night bomber. Crew of five. Two Rolls-Royce 1,145HP Merlin X engines. Span 84 feet. Length 70 feet 6 inches. Loaded weight 33,500lb. Maximum airspeed at 16,500 feet 230mph. Cruising speed at 15,000 feet 210mph. Range with 7,000lb bomb load 470 miles. The Mk III, powered by the Armstrong Siddeley Tiger engine, was the only Whitley to have a ventral 'dustbin' gun turret. A hole was dug into the floor of 2 Hangar at Cambridge to accommodate the installation of the Frazer Nash turret. The turret was placed in the hole, the aircraft was pulled across the top and the turret was then hauled up to mate with the Whitley. Railway sleepers, still there, covered the hole. Marshall fitted radios, hydraulics and modified the bomb-door opening mechanism. The original rubber bungee 'opening' device failed to work properly every time – it relied on the bombs' weight forcing open the doors when lowered onto them. The replacement mod was a mechanical device operated by the bomb-aimer. Leonard Cheshire earned a DSO in November 1940 while flying a Whitley on a bombing raid on Cologne. The Whitley served with the RAF in a number of roles until the end of the war, although it was phased out at Marshall's in 1944.

Peter May, an ex-RAF pilot, had joined Marshall's Flying School as a flying instructor in 1935. He was well known as one of the Hendon Display Team. On the establishment of the RAFVR School at Cambridge he became chief flying instructor. With Peter, Arthur collected the first Whitley from Shawbury on 2nd September 1939. On 3rd September Neville Chamberlain announced that England was at war with Germany. Flying instruction was to continue throughout World War Two. Cambridge aerodrome was to become home, usually temporary, for a wide variety of aircraft.

Cambridge UAS closed down for flying at Duxford that September. However, to secure its share of the high calibre young men still flowing to the University, the Air Ministry re-opened the squadron in October 1940. Flying training was not a feature of the new syllabus, but over the Christmas vacation in 1940 selected pupils were allocated to 22 Elementary Flying Training School (EFTS) for flying experience. In the period 1942/43 the Air Ministry introduced air experience training for UAS members in Tiger Moths based at Cambridge. Additionally, as much navigation training as possible was practised in an Airspeed Oxford. The almost daily routine was for the Oxford, with three cadets aboard, to fly up to Liverpool, fly out to sea to do a 'square-search' and then land at Speke. After a refuel the Oxford flew back to Cambridge.

No 4 SFIS operated from the southeast side of the aerodrome, flying the Miles Magister and Master. Each year the school received a visit from the CFS flying instructor examiners who would sometimes arrive in Spitfires and Hurricanes. Apparently involved in developing a dive-bombing sight in conjunction with Cambridge University Laboratories was a Royal Navy Barracuda, probably on attachment to the EFTS. This aircraft, a dive-bomber built by Fairey Aviation, was picketed close to where the helicopter school currently operates, east of 1 hangar. An observer noted that the Barracuda's target area appeared to be on the Gog Magogs golf course. A Barracuda unit severely damaged the German battleship *Tirpitz* in a dive-bombing attack on 3rd April 1944.

From June 1940 two squadrons of Westland Lysanders were attached to Cambridge, as were four Royal Navy Blackburn Roc fighter aircraft, which acted as escorts to the Lysanders. One Lysander task, until August, was to patrol virtually the whole of the north Norfolk coast at night on the look-out for any signs of German surface incursions. The Airport Hotel, the present Airport House, became the Officers' Mess, and tents were erected on the Teversham side of the aerodrome to house airmen of the Lysander and Roc units.

A very unexpected, and large, arrival came one night in the shape of a Short Stirling. Apparently the pilot homed onto the Cambridge night lighting system and, mistaking it for another airfield, touched down very late and ground-looped at the end of the landing run. Tommy Thompson recalls another unannounced visitor. Out on the airfield one night, he was suddenly bundled to the ground by a Flight Sergeant who was shouting 'Get down.' Seconds later an unlit Vickers Wellington passed over the airfield and crashed in the field opposite Teversham school.

Marshall also had the contract to service the forty-two Anson aircraft of 3 Air Observers' School at Halfpenny Green, then known as RAF Bobbington. Before operating the Anson, the school used the unpopular and under-powered Blackburn Botha aircraft. When these aircraft were suddenly grounded, forty-two Anson units were each ordered to send one aircraft to No 3 School. Predictably, the aircraft sent was not going to be the best one on their inventory! RAF pilots flew the Avro Ansons, one of whom, Gordon Clark, was an ex-Marshall apprentice. It was difficult to keep the Ansons serviceable and their flying commitment was very heavy. Day and night, the aircraft flew to the Isle of Man to drop practice bombs. They then did some gunnery practice while over the Irish Sea before returning to Halfpenny Green.

A huge variety of aircraft types were serviced and repaired at Cambridge during the war. They included the Albemarle, Anson, Gladiator, Hart, Hind, Mosquito, Oxford and Typhoon. After an aircraft was repaired, it had to be flight-tested. One take-off in a Whitley bomber was, fortunately, on a northerly heading. Mr A N Charles, the engineer on board, was making his first flight. Having made a mental note of the instrument readings on take-off and while passing over the top of 1 hangar, he looked out of his window and was horrified at what he saw. He immediately drew Arthur's attention to the fact that the starboard engine was engulfed in flames. Arthur was already dealing with the engine's failure. Its northerly take-off direction headed the stricken Whitley straight for Waterbeach, just five miles to the north. Happily, the airfield had opened for operations in January 1941. Wellington bombers were the first to use it, with Stirling four-engined bombers arriving later that year. Although aircraft at Waterbeach were using the opposite direction for landing, the light wind allowed Arthur a swifter option of an emergency landing straight ahead. Who in their right mind wants to extend a flight with an engine ablaze? Responding to Arthur's shouted instructions the engineer lowered the undercarriage, set the flaps to the landing position and prepared for an immediate evacuation after landing. On landing, a Stirling bomber was just touching down at the other end of the aerodrome, and was now heading straight at the Whitley. The pilots of both aircraft followed the book and avoided a collision by each turning to starboard. No sooner had the Whitley stopped than the fire crew was at the scene, rapidly dousing the engine blaze. Arthur was taken to the Control Office and after a short delay rejoined his engineer at the aircraft. From there the two aviators travelled by road back to Cambridge. The action had not yet finished, however. No sooner were they back at Cambridge than the pair was off on a short but hectic flight in an Oxford. The pilot enjoyed that flight but the engineer did not, stating that his stomach was no longer his own.

Flight test commitment was, at times, heavy. In the first eighteen months of the war Arthur shared the task with Peter May. In December 1941 Peter was posted away. Always resourceful, Arthur Marshall was able to return an ex-RAF pilot, Leslie Scatchard (featured in Chapter 5), to flying duties.

Boeing Fortress I, AM 531, arrived in early March 1943, another first for Cambridge. It needed some minor repairs and maintenance, and was scheduled for test on Monday 8th. On Sunday 7th, Arthur received a phone call 'The Fortress is ready for flight.' He had not even had time to sit in the cockpit! Grabbing the Marshall Chief Engine Mechanic, Jack Burnett, Arthur climbed aboard. Together they took off from a very soggy aerodrome with the Fortress just clearing the hedge alongside the Teversham Road. After that short flight the necessary rectification was completed swiftly, with a second flight taking place the same afternoon but this time with Arthur's wife and the Chief Cambridge resident Inspector of the Air Ministry Aircraft Inspection Directorate aboard. Airborne time for the two flights was one hour.

BOEING FORTRESS I. Heavy bomber. Four Wright R1820, 9-cylinder engines. Crew of six to ten. Span 103 feet 9 inches. Length 67 feet 9 inches. Loaded weight 45,450lb. Maximum airspeed 320mph at 20,000 feet. Range, with bomb load of 2,500lb, 2,100 miles. Entered service with Bomber Command in 1941. Not successful as a bomber with the RAF, it was transferred to Coastal Command in October 1942.

On 2nd May 1944 Arthur added the Hawker Typhoon to his list of military aircraft. Early that year the Air Ministry had introduced a new procedure. Hitherto, Marshall nominated its own test pilots and was responsible for their performance. The Air Ministry now required test pilots to undertake a technical exam and flight test on each new type of aircraft, such as the Typhoon fighter-bomber. Arthur travelled down to the Hawker factory, at Brockworth (Hucclecote), Gloucester, for his checkout. Two more local flights on 31st May added one hour and forty-five minutes Typhoon expertise. Arthur then flew the first test flight at Cambridge, in a IB,

JR 511. The flight lasted twenty-five minutes. In July JR 511, after modifications at an RAF Maintenance Unit, went to 137 Sqn. A powerful aircraft, the Typhoon was fun to fly but needed care on the take-off run. The huge power output, if applied too rapidly, could cause a massive swing to the right.

HAWKER TYPHOON IB. Single-seat fighter-bomber. One 2,200HP Napier Sabre IIA, 24-cylinder engine. Span 41 feet 6 inches. Length 32 feet. Loaded weight 13,250lb. Four 20mm cannon plus bombs or rockets under the wings. Maximum airspeed 410mph at 19,000 feet. Climb to 15,000ft six minutes.

At the end of one air test in a Whitley, having arrived overhead the aerodrome, Arthur turned to his observer and said 'Who are all those people down there looking up at us?' 'They are employees' replied the observer. 'I hope they have all clocked out,' replied Arthur. 'I don't know' said the observer, 'but for God's sake get your hands back on the stick or we'll crash.'

The first step towards Air Traffic Control (ATC) on the aerodrome came towards the end of the war. A control van was positioned at the downwind end of the field from where the occupant used Very Lights, flares shot out of a large pistol, to prevent circuit traffic taking off and landing when test aircraft were doing so. There was little in the way of aircraft radio use and weather forecasting was still rudimentary. Immediately after the war ATC officers were trained at Watchfield, near Swindon. The holder of ATC licence number one, Geoff Baker, came to work at Cambridge.

Marshall was allotted a number of battle-damaged Dakotas for repair immediately after D-day, 6th June 1944. When the first was ready for return to service, Arthur telephoned the Ministry of Aircraft Production for delivery instructions and allocation of an approved pilot. 'Have you flown twins Arthur?' said the voice. 'Yes, Monospar in the 1930s, Oxfords, Whitleys, Albemarles, Flying Fortress and Mosquito.' 'Right' said the voice, 'You, Arthur, are the approved pilot.' Arthur's logbook shows Dakota KG 441 delivered to Blakehill Farm, near Cricklade, on 10th June 1944.

Come Victory-in-Europe day Marshalls made available timber from a number of redundant Oxford airframes for Cambridge's bonfire on Midsummer Common and similarly for VJ Day a few months later. Arthur Marshall's final military test flight, of twenty-five minutes, was in Dakota KG 604 on 2nd April 1946. By that time Leslie Worsdell had completed his RAF service and was back at Cambridge.

DOUGLAS DAKOTA I. Medium-range transport and glider-tug. Crew of three. Two 1,200HP Pratt and Whitney Twin Wasp R-1830 engines. Span 95 feet. Length 64 feet 6 inches. Loaded weight 25,000lb (overweight limit 31,000lb). Maximum airspeed 230mph at 8,500 feet. Cruising speed 185mph. Range 1,500 miles. Could carry 28 troops with kit. About 1,900 were supplied to the RAF under Lend-Lease and the type served with the RAF from 1942 to 1970. Until the late 1970s the Company operated two Dakotas from RAF West Freugh, Scotland, for anti-submarine sonobuoy testing.

In 1974, for services to the RAF, Arthur Marshall was made a Knight of the Realm. Sir Arthur continued to fly his Citation, initially sharing with one of his professional pilots – usually Bob Smythe. Later on Sir Arthur would sit in one of the passenger seats. He still, however, took a close interest in piloting activities and would often appear just behind the pilot's shoulder to check on how things were going. Woe betide the pilot if he forgot to provide Sir Arthur with a radio log and route map. His final flights at the controls of his Citation G-BFRM were with the author over the Easter period 1st, 3rd and 4th April 1988. (The last two letters of the Citation's registration were chosen to honour Rosemary Marshall).

At Christmas 1989, Sir Arthur handed over responsibilities of Chairman and Chief Executive to his son, Michael Marshall. The Marshall shareholders elected Sir Arthur as Honorary Life President of the Marshall Group.

Michael Marshall first flew in a Puss Moth and later in a Miles Falcon that his father was flying to visit the Marshall-run EFTS at Clyffe Pypard during World War Two. On one occasion a pair of Spitfires came up to inspect. Luckily the pilots recognised the Falcon as friendly and flew off. Michael learned to fly with the Marshall Flying School from 1948, making his first solo flight shortly after his seventeenth birthday. He went on to fly DH Chipmunks with 22 Reserve FTS before starting his National Service with the RAF in 1950. After entry at Padgate, followed by square bashing and basic military training at Digby, Lincolnshire, a Handley Page Hastings took him to Canada for training at the Canadian FTS at Gimli, Manitoba. During an eleven-month course he flew the Harvard and gained his RAF wings in December 1951. After an acclimatisation course at Feltwell, Norfolk, he started a trend for Marshall test pilots by being posted to Valley, then the home of 202 AFS, to fly dual in the Meteor 7 and solo in Vampires. First solo in a Vampire came on 10th April. The events of 1st May 1952 are best described in Michael's own words.

> 'I had a very lucky experience when my engine flamed out during the course of aerobatics with the result that I did a tail slide and ended up in a very unpleasant spin from which the Vampire, with its very small tail fin was somewhat unwilling to recover. And of course in those days there were no ejector seats. I remember calling "Mayday Mayday" as I tried to get out of the spin but when the aircraft failed to respond I decided to climb out. I jettisoned the canopy, unstrapped from the seat and started to climb out. However, my parachute got caught on the back of the seat and I remember being straddled with the

top half of me out of the aircraft. Fortunately, possibly due to a combination of me being partly out, coupled with the denser air as we came down from 18,000 feet to something below 8,000 feet, the aircraft came out of the spin in a fairly steep dive. My flying helmet flew off, but I managed to put my right leg round the control column and bring the nose up, reduce speed and then was able to climb in. I had another go at re-starting the engine, but failed and by this time I was pretty low and was fortunate enough to be able to land wheels up in a tiny ploughed up field near the village of Bryngwran.'

'As I was not strapped in and had no helmet my forehead was cut as it hit the top of the instrument panel, and I remember bleeding badly, jumping out of the aircraft and going to a nearby farmhouse. They kindly let me have a bucket of cold water to wipe away the blood and lent me a bicycle on which I went downhill a short way to Bryngwran village post office where I dialled 999 and soon the RAF ambulance and medical officer arrived to retrieve me. The OC Flying, Wg Cdr Manns, told me that he wanted to award me a Green Endorsement in my logbook, but the bureaucratic rules stood in the way. They tried to persuade me to sign on and make the RAF my career – but I had other commitments.'

'I found that I had damaged my back, so I had a few weeks at Headley Court physiotherapy and rehabilitation centre, after which I returned to Valley to complete my training.'

Michael was not eligible to join the Cambridge UAS but he enlisted in the RAFVR and gained a flying instructor's licence on Chipmunks. In 1955, having joined the Company, he very nearly made a test flight in a Vampire T11. Unfortunately the flight was cancelled, and due to other Company commitments his currency on the Vampire lapsed.

From 1955 onwards Michael frequently flew in Auster G-AIGM. Two memorable flights took place in 1958 and 1959. Firstly he took a friend down through France and Spain to Portugal and back, and then he took another friend to Tit Melil, near Casablanca. There were no navigation aids or radio, just maps, pencils, paper and a lot of luck, without which no pilot survives forever.

In the 1960s he made a number of flights in the Company Piper Apache, and on one occasion had to return to Cambridge on one engine. In 1972 Michael took a lease for his family on a cottage on Osea Island, which had a small landing strip alongside. After some research, Leslie Worsdell and Michael decided that the right aircraft for the job was a MS894A, better known as a Rallye Minerva. This resulted in the acquisition of G-AZGL, in which Michael has now accumulated over eight hundred flying hours. He has flown his family to Sardinia and several places in France, and he still retains the aircraft. The Minerva is unspinnable but with the stick fully back and no power it performs what is known as a descent parachutal with about forty knots of forward speed. Its normal cruising speed is almost one hundred and twenty knots with over five hours' endurance and a safe range approaching five hundred miles.

During his time with Cambridge University Michael got in to the University Boat Race crew for the Centenary Race in 1954. That event entailed a remarkable five-day flight in a BOAC Argonaut to Dusseldorf, Rome, Nicosia, Damascus, Basra, Karachi, Bombay, Colombo, Singapore, Saigon (then in French Indochina), Hong Kong, Okinawa and Tokyo.

Chapter 2

Leslie Worsdell

'A Royal Air Force examiner carried out the final handling test in the 1930s; my examiner had a silver Tiger Moth. The test started with a "blind" take off (under a special hood), and then continued by flying a steady heading for a given length of time. At the end of the half an hour or so the RAF chap said "Take off the hood and tell me where you are." I just looked over the side, and having lived and flown in Cambridgeshire all my life, I said "That's St Neots down there and that's Eaton Socon over there." He thought I was a brilliant navigator! I had not even looked at my map. So, I got my commercial (B) licence. After qualification as a commercial pilot and flying instructor, work began in earnest at the Cambridge Aero Club, owned by Marshall.'

Born in January 1917 at Huntingdon, Leslie Worsdell attended the local primary school until 1928. Having gained a scholarship he then moved to Huntingdon Grammar School. That same year the Worsdell family moved from Brampton to Earith. Leslie's father, with his brother, ran a road haulage business. After the move the business was named A V Worsdell & Son, Leslie being the son. On attaining the age of seventeen, Leslie, for his first job with his brand-new driving licence, drove a five-ton truck to London loaded with meat.

The extensive grounds of the family home contained remains of a World War One aircraft. Leslie worked on the remains and connected up the flying controls to the joystick and rudder pedals. He could then sit in the pilot's seat and imagine himself airborne and his mother realised he had a very keen interest in aviation. She heard on the wireless one day that the RAF was recruiting boys over the age of seventeen into the Reserve; they would be taught to fly. At the Air Ministry in London, he sat facing five senior and stern looking RAF officers. Asked 'What do you know about the flying controls of an aircraft', Leslie was able to respond in great detail – thanks to his 'garden' aircraft. He was selected.

At Hatfield, in 1935, he learned to fly Tiger Moths. When a notice appeared in the *Cambridge Daily News* saying that Marshall of Cambridge was looking for young men to join the Company as apprentices to learn to fly, to obtain commercial licences and instructor certificates, Leslie applied. With sixty Tiger Moth hours already in his logbook, he was snapped up. The final part of the course was a qualifying cross-country flight. Even in those days, with rudimentary weather forecasting, the weather sometimes-poor en route, no radio in the aircraft, and no Air Traffic Control, that flight was a long one. Leslie's was a flight from Cambridge to Cardiff, then along the south coast to Lympne, in Kent, and back to base. After qualification as a commercial pilot and flying instructor, he began work in earnest at the Cambridge Aero Club, owned by Marshall.

DH TIGER MOTH. Two-seat trainer. One 108HP DH Gipsy Major engine. Span 29 feet 3 inches. Length 24 feet. Loaded weight 1,775lb. Maximum airspeed 107mph. Cruising speed 90mph.

In 1991 Leslie recorded details of his flying experiences with the Sound Archives, Imperial War Museum. Both have kindly agreed to the use of the recorded material that now follows.

At thirty shillings (£1.50) an hour, most of the students of the Cambridge Aero Club were the wealthier undergraduates of Cambridge University. Air Charter work was largely in a Puss Moth or Leopard Moth. One flight was from Gatwick to Wales, on 27th August 1938, with a Lord and his Lady. For the return flight, the engine would not start; one magneto was defunct. Efforts to solve the problem failed. A night stop was necessary. I rang Mr Marshall to acquaint him with the problem. His advice was to get a motor car alongside the aircraft and run a wire from one plug of the car to one plug of the Leopard Moth engine. Then, keep swinging the propeller until everything coincided and the engine starts – an original sort of 'jump start' indeed. With a forecast of good weather at Cambridge – although very cloudy in Wales – I finally set off, albeit with only one good magneto. The route stayed cloud covered, so I flew above the cloud. I had foolishly taken off without a watch, and the aircraft, a Leopard Moth, had no watch, either. I estimated my position by calculating time gone based on fuel used. When the fuel gauges were looking pretty empty I thought it was time to come down below cloud. I had no idea where I was. I started a very slow descent through cloud. At about 1,500 feet, I broke clear of the cloud – only to see myself surrounded by a mass of red lights! Despite a low fuel reading, I pushed the throttle hard open and climbed back into the safety of the cloud. I went on for about another ten minutes before my shaking hands and heart eased off a bit. After flying further east, I descended through cloud a second time. Recognising Sywell aerodrome, Northampton, and still feeling frightened, I decided to land, get the magneto fixed, and refuel. The red lights that I saw were on the radio masts at Rugby – they were about 1,250 feet above sea level. I was quite lucky!

The present Cambridge airport site came about because Cambridge City Council wanted to build houses on what was then Fen Ditton aerodrome, now Whitehill estate. Marshall sold Whitehill and bought land close to Teversham for a new aerodrome. The boundaries of the two sites were only a few hundred yards apart, so when it was time to move, October 1937, it was a flight of only a few seconds into an easterly wind, at a height of about fifty feet. The official opening of the aerodrome was in October 1938, and included a display – the first time in public – of the Spitfire, from 19 Sqn, Duxford.

At the outbreak of war, September 1939, I was called up and given the rank of Sergeant pilot. At the Initial Training Wing, at Cambridge University, we spent much of our time being drilled in groups of about one hundred through the streets of Cambridge. We also received a few airmanship lectures. As an already experienced flying instructor it was not unsurprising that the RAF posted me to the CFS at Upavon, Wiltshire. There were three young pilots from Marshall's; the others were all experienced RAF pilots. At this time I had about 2,000 flying hours. We were taught to instruct on the Avro Tutor and the Airspeed Oxford. From Upavon I was posted to a service flying training school at Grantham.

My task at Grantham was to convert pilots from the Tiger Moth to the Avro Anson. After two months I was posted back to CFS at Upavon to teach pilots to become flying instructors. I was also promoted to Acting Pilot Officer, RAFVR. Despite applying to be posted to an operational unit, I stayed at Upavon until January 1942.

The demand for instructors was insatiable; the work was hard, with intensive spells of flying on Oxfords, Harvards, Masters and Tutors. One day, in a Tutor, I was teaching my four students how to restart the engine in flight – dive, pull out into a climbing turn – using the hand operated flight starter. I demonstrated the technique to my first student over the practice forced landing field – just in case. I stopped the engine, stating 'If we haven't started the engine on reaching 2,000 feet we'll do a forced landing.' The engine did not start. We did a forced landing. The engine started normally on the ground, so I carried on with my second student. The same thing happened again. The afternoon was a repeat performance of the morning. By now I was getting known as the instructor who could not start his engine in flight. To my relief the groundcrew found a fault with the in-flight starter.

AVRO TUTOR. Two-seat trainer. One 215 to 240HP Armstrong Siddeley Lynx IVC engine. Span 34 feet. Length 26 feet 6 inches. Loaded weight 2,450lb. Maximum airspeed 120mph. Climb to 5,000 feet six minutes. Cruising speed 105mph at 1,000 feet. Replaced the Avro 504K trainer in 1932.

In January 1942, the Chief Flying Instructor was posted to Chivenor – the Beaufort aircraft coastal Operational Conversion Unit (OCU). He was horrified to find that none of his instructors was formally qualified. He arranged for me to be posted to his unit on the understanding with the Air Ministry that after a tour of operations not lasting more than three months

I would be posted back onto his staff. The Beaufort Mk I had a maximum airspeed of 265mph and fairly unreliable (Taurus) engines. The big end had only two bolts holding it onto the connecting rod. If one bolt failed the whole engine just fell to pieces. It needed lots of skill to fly on one engine – a not uncommon event. I was given the most senior staff pilot as my instructor; he flew me on one conversion trip. That night he was on the night flying detail. He had an engine failure and flew into the hills that are along one side of Chivenor aerodrome. One night we saw four aircraft fires on nearby hills. Torpedo dropping training was carried out from Abbotsinch aerodrome, now Glasgow airport. We flew there from Chivenor.

Dummy torpedoes were filled with sand and painted bright orange. Our first 'dummy-dropping' flight was in Beaufort N1179, on 5th May 1942. Having climbed to 2,000 feet, we headed for the coast. About halfway to the coast, the navigator piped up 'Skipper, the jettison bars of the Mickey Mouse are at Jettison.' (The Mickey Mouse was a bomb selector device, mainly clockwork, part electrical, designed to permit the dropping of sticks of bombs in sequence or all together. If in trouble, you could press the Jettison bars and away the bombs went). Without thinking, I said 'For Christ's sake put them back to Safe.' He did. On we went, reached the coast, and saw the target ship steaming along. We made our recognition orbit and got into the attacking position – about sixty degrees to the bow of the ship, sixty feet above the sea at an airspeed of 120 knots. We ran in. When I thought we were at 1,000 yards from the target, I pressed the bomb release. The torpedo was expected to go down with a big splash. The observers on the ship would know from the splash and the angle of entry whether I had made a good attack. The photo taken from the nose of the aircraft would also show whether I might have hit the ship. The rear gunner was briefed to watch for the splash as we passed over the point of entry of the torpedo. 'I can't see any splash; I don't think you dropped it.' 'Of course I did; I nearly pushed the bomb button off!' He was quite adamant that nothing had happened. In the midships of the aircraft sat the wireless operator. He could look through a hole to see if the torpedo was in place. 'No, the torpedo has gone', he said, 'it's not there.' We flew back to base, puzzling over what could have happened.

We landed, taxied to our dispersal point where we noticed the OC waiting – with a couple of military policemen in attendance. As I got out of the Beaufort the OC shouted 'Flying Officer (Fg Off) Worsdell, you are under open arrest.' I said, 'What have I done?' 'You dropped your dummy torpedo in the middle of such and such a village.' Apparently, this orange thing had descended out of the sky and fell, fortunately, into the village green just as the village policeman was cycling by on his patrol. He recognised a Beaufort when he saw one, and he knew where it had come from. He rang the airfield, and that is why I was put under open arrest. I explained what had happened, that approximately in the position of the village the Jettison bars were seen to be in the jettison position, and I had ordered them to be put back to Safe. The OC sent for an armourer. He found that an electrical connector, with about twenty-one pins on it, had been fitted the wrong way round. It should have gone in one way only, but by forcing it in the wrong way round it was possible to push it home. It was the first time I came across Murphy's Law (. . . if you could possibly fit something the wrong way round, it would one day be done). This had happened. We should have seen before take-off that the Jettison bars were in the wrong position. Anyway, no harm was done, and I was released from open arrest.

After completion of the torpedo training, I was posted to the north of Scotland. From there we flew Rover patrols – looking for shipping on the Norwegian coast. After just three days I was posted to Lyneham, Wiltshire. From there I was sent to Bristol's to collect a brand new Beaufort II fitted with Pratt & Whitney engines. On 2nd July 1942 I set off in Beaufort DD898. Our destination was a Beaufort squadron in the Middle East, via Gibraltar. At Gibraltar we met up with a Beaufort flown by a South African pilot who was also on a delivery flight. He said that his aircraft was unserviceable, but I suspected he was really waiting for someone else, so that he did not have to fly alone.

BRISTOL BEAUFORT II. Torpedo-bomber. Crew of four. Two Pratt and Whitney R-1830 S3C4G Twin Wasp engines. Span 57 feet 9 inches. Length 44 feet 3 inches. Maximum airspeed at sea level 265mph. Approximate range 1,450 miles. Service ceiling 22,500 feet. Maximum loaded weight 21,000lb for take-off and straight flight only; for all permitted manoeuvres the weight limit was 18,500lb.

We took off quite early the next morning for Malta and managed to land between air raids. We met up with some crews we had trained with at Chivenor, and we all had a very good party that night. The OC of 39 Sqn wanted to impound my aircraft, but I said I was going to stick to my orders and deliver the Beaufort to Egypt. At 0300 the next morning we got up, and set off at 0400. All went well until we were about half way between Crete and the North African coast. We carried additional fuel in a long-range tank, which was installed in the bomb bay. The general principle was to use that fuel first. When the time came to change tanks, I used to climb up to about 2,000 feet do a quick change over, make sure the engines went on running on the main fuel supply, and then drop back to our transit altitude of fifty feet above sea level. I told the South African pilot that that was my plan. I climbed, did the fuel changeover, and dropped back to sea level. He did the same shortly after; he was, in fact, flying just ahead of me. I watched him pull up, stay there for a minute or so, then descend – but he just continued straight into the sea. We got there a few seconds later. There was a wheel floating, a dinghy, but no sign of survivors. We could see the trail of the aircraft through the clear blue Mediterranean Sea; there was a big trail of bubbles going down to the seabed. We started to circle, and then I climbed to 2,000 feet to send out an SOS, hoping that someone would come out and have a look. We, of course, were drawing the attention of ourselves to the enemy, so we wanted to get out of there pretty quickly. Having concluded that we could do no more we dropped back to fifty feet and continued on to our destination: an aircrew reception centre at Heliopolis.

The first thing I did was to follow up the accident to my colleague. However, the local Air Ministry said they were not going to risk any more aircraft in that area so there was no further action taken. I was asked what I thought had happened. Two alternatives, I think. One was that we were tired, after some long days, a big party the night before, up before the crack of dawn and he may have misjudged his height at sea level. But since he went in so smoothly I got the impression that he fell asleep and went straight in.

It was a quite complicated situation in Egypt at that time. Nobody seemed to know the location of squadrons. Someone found what was called 39 Sqn in Egypt; there was also a 39 Sqn in Malta. A month later I was posted to the Malta squadron. I was involved in three attacks on Italian shipping. In one attack I was leading a flight of three Beauforts, following two other flights of three. For some reason we went inland, before attacking a freighter of about 6,000 tons. It was steaming fairly close to the coast, so we were attacking from land to sea. We were the last section to attack. Just as we got to the 1,000-yard position the ship exploded. I had to go straight on, flying through all the debris – it was quite a spectacle, bits of flaming boarding, chicken houses, I do not know what sort of things, passing in front of me, behind me, on each wing tip. It was quite a spectacle. I took my torpedo back to base. They were brought to the island by submarine from Gibraltar. We did not waste them; they were worth their weight in gold. When we got back to base, I started 'shooting a line' that my prized moustache was nearly burnt off by the flames as I flew through them!

During September targets seemed to be scarce; the 6th was an exception. We were told of four motor vessels, protected by ten destroyers and fifteen enemy aircraft. We sent out the full squadron of twelve torpedo aircraft, escorted by twelve Bristol Beaufighters. The Beaufighters' task was to climb up ahead of our attack, dive in on the targets and shoot off their enormous cannons to neutralise enemy defences, whilst we sneaked in underneath to drop our torpedoes. We were reasonably successful. One ship went to the bottom and one was damaged. Three enemy aircraft were claimed as destroyed, and I think we lost four of our Beauforts. No Beaufighters were lost. Several of us were awarded the DFC after that affair.

Life in Malta was not that comfortable. Our meals were mainly bread – rationed to about five slices a day – lots of jam, bully beef and fresh tomatoes. We lived on that for weeks at a time. My very first meal was interrupted by an air raid. The four Maltese waiters, in white jackets, just dived straight out of the net-covered windows. There was a deep shelter just outside. We all trooped off and joined them. There was very little beer available. Some Maltese pubs had stocks of rum – sold to them by the submariners who had saved up their rations. We could hire horse-drawn garries, but they would not move after dark.

A lot of time was spent on standby, where we were called at 0200 or 0300 hours. The flight leader and his navigator would go to be briefed, and the rest of us would go to the main mess room to hang about, with all our flying kit. We played darts, shove halfpenny and cards. By 0400 we were all very bad tempered – it is not the best time to be playing cards. We all hoped that the ace photographic chap, Adrian Warburton – OC of 69 Sqn – would come back and announce that he had found a target, tell us its position and what it was, so that we could go out and hit it. If not, we would carry on with a two-hour standby.

In October, we went back to Egypt for training and to support Montgomery. The Germans were trying to get one more tanker into Tobruk. It had been spotted, and it was a case of going out to find it. My squadron went out, with me leading part of it. That is, until enemy fighters attacked. We broke up in some disarray. We saw some shipping, but by this time I was out of position as a leader. In any event, I saw that the targets were barges, and our torpedoes, set to run at about nine feet, would have passed underneath. We went back to base, never having sighted a tanker. I believe torpedo-carrying Wellingtons sank it that night.

In November 1942, I volunteered to take half a dozen Beauforts back to Malta, because it was believed that more targets would appear. I stayed until the February, chiefly mining harbours around the Cape Bon area of Tunisia. There were a few torpedo attacks at night. The mining attacks were rather nasty, because it meant flying into well-defended harbours. We lost two or three of my detached flight. A meteorological phenomenon known as St Elmo's fire troubled us at times. An electrical discharge built up around the aircraft. A flickering blue light travels around the propeller tips, or it starts off on any projection around the aircraft. Very quickly the whole aircraft can become bathed in this shimmering blue light – very eerie. It's very frightening, because you imagine that you are sitting there as an absolute sitting target, visible for miles. In fact, they probably could not see you from a hundred yards.

Eventually, our Beauforts were equipped with ASV: air-to-surface radar. We got no training on it, but picked up the skills as we went along. If a target was picked up, a green blob appeared on the screen. We knew that there was a ship going between Sicily and Cape Bon. So, on the night of 21st January 1943, we went looking for it in DD 898. We found this 'blob' and started to look at it from a distance. A second blob appeared, probably a destroyer, just about where we wanted to drop our torpedo. We thought we might use it as a pointer for homing in. I calculated a timed circuit to get into the right attacking position. As we started the run-in the destroyer started to fire at us. We kept going. Suddenly, 'Bang.' The rear gunner shouted, 'I've been hit.' He was blinded. I broke away because we were no longer in the right dropping position. I said 'Never mind, you'll have to put up with it. We're going in to have another go.' There was some protest from the crew. As we started the run-in, the wireless operator (still the same crewmember who was with me when we dropped the dummy torpedo in Scotland), shouted, 'Your torpedo's not there. There's nothing to throw at them.' We broke away. I had not pressed the drop button. The aircraft was out of trim because the trim wires had been shot away, and the rear gunner was still exclaiming that he could not see. Very likely I had pressed the button involuntarily. We set off for Malta. After shutting down in dispersal, we inspected the aircraft. Two strop ends were still hanging in the hooks. A shell from the destroyer had severed the strop, allowing the torpedo to drop without us knowing. The rear gunner was okay. The shell that had hit the rear of the aircraft had struck armour plating and thrown up great quantities of sand collected in Egypt. The sand went into the gunner's eyes temporarily blinding him. This was our last operational mission in the Med.

I came back to England in February 1943. Posted to Headquarters (HQ) Coastal Command, at Northwood, my job was to brief the Beaufighter squadrons, which were then forming the 'big wings.' Their task was to attack shipping off the Dutch coast. The crews were new to the game. In addition to that task, because I was probably the most experienced instructor in Coastal Command, I was sent to North Coates to investigate the reason for so many swings on take-off and landing. Pleasingly, there was a dual controlled Beaufort Trainer available. Hitherto, I had had to stand behind the pilot, giving instructions, hoping that they would be correctly carried out. After I had flown with each pilot, they all gathered in the station cinema. The station commander, a Group Captain, stood up and said that he hoped that I had the answer to the problem. So I said, 'Yes, gentlemen, the answer is quite simple. Your reactions are too slow.' They were furious, and would have thrown oranges and apples at me if they had been available. I explained the principles of flight to them. With the relationship of the centre of gravity well behind the main wheels, as soon as a swing started, and the centre of gravity moved outside the wheels, the body of the aircraft just kept moving further into the swing. The answer was to kill the swing immediately it started, by swift application of rudder. I heard no more about it.

In September 1943, I was posted to East Fortune, near Edinburgh. I was OC the operational flight, where we were teaching the new crews how to use the Beaufighter operationally – including the early rocket firing trials. Our rockets were not live; they had a solid concrete warhead. We needed some targets. Someone towed up a barge, and moored it on a sandbank in the Firth of Forth. I went off with a couple of other aircraft to show them how to do a rocket attack – which I had never done myself anyway. The mission went wonderfully well. The three of us blew the barge to smithereens! We were convinced that, given live warheads, we would be much more successful than using torpedoes.

During this time I had received letters from Arthur Marshall, saying that on my demobilisation, he wanted me as his chief pilot. I said that I had hoped that I would go back to Marshall's. He followed this up by saying that if I made application for premature release, to go back to Marshall's as chief test pilot, he understood that it would be approved. The Company was doing a lot of test flying on repaired aircraft. The test programme was bigger than Arthur Marshall and his assistant could handle, and he wanted me back. I made some preliminary enquiries, and it looked as if my application would succeed. It did not, and I was posted back into Training Command. East Fortune was a very nice posting, and my wife and I did not want to leave. However, I was posted to another training unit, and then, in April 1945, to Church Lawford, near Rugby, as OC a testing flight. Church Lawford was established as a new 'straight through' training unit, with Harvards. There would be no Tiger Moth or Magister flying beforehand. The Harvard was to be the first aircraft that trainee pilots set foot in. It was quite a big beast. How were we going to know which pilots were going to make it, and which ones we ought to turn off at a reasonably early stage? It would be a lot more expensive to train pilots on the Harvard, compared to the Moth or Magister. The Empire Flying School and the Royal Canadian Air Force had evolved schemes that broke the flying exercises down into component parts, with a mark to be awarded – good, fair, poor, or points out of ten. It made it possible to work to a common standard. I liked the idea. With the OC and the chief instructor we developed a system whereby five of us could test one student, and get within about 1% of each other in assessment. It was a successful scheme. On 31st October 1945, in Harvard FS825, I made my last flight with the RAF. I was demobilised on 5th November, and on 7th November I reported for work at Marshall's.

My brief was to get the aerodrome, and myself, licensed. Hitherto, the aerodrome had not been requisitioned. It had been taken over by Marshall's in a RAF capacity; it was merely approved to fly military aircraft. A licence was needed to permit civil flying to proceed. I succeeded with both tasks. The ban on civil flying was due to be lifted on 1st January 1946. We needed aircraft to fly. Arthur Marshall had located a Tiger Moth, which had been dismantled and stored. He managed to get this aircraft, G-ACDG, ready to fly by 1st January 1946. I made the very first post-war instructional flight in it that day. The mayoress of Cambridge, Lady Bragg, was the student. There was a queue of people waiting to learn to fly at £5 per hour. Cambridge Aero Club was the first club in the country to start operating after the war.

I was appointed chief test pilot. Mosquitoes and Dakotas were the first to be test flown. I also flew charter flights. One such flight, in a Proctor, G-AHBI, was very exciting. I was called to the Czechoslovakian embassy, in London. I was sworn to secrecy, and was asked to fly to Prague to collect a passenger. Game for anything, I went to Prague, via Cologne, on 29th

May 1946. I taxied in, to be met by the marshaller. He said 'Ah, Marshall, welcome to Prague.' 'How on earth', I said, 'do you know where I am from?' 'Because it is written on the side of the aircraft, and I was at RAF Bottisham, Cambridge, during the war.' What a small world! He was marvellous. He took me to the RAF liaison officer. That officer arranged a room for me in his hotel, and said he would take me to my contact the next day. He took me to a cabinet in the corner of his office and opened the door. One half was full of the most exquisite Czechoslovak glass; the other half was filled with bottles of whisky. 'We'll take one of those, it'll get us anywhere, and this bottle will pay for your hotel bill.' 'Where does all this stuff come from?' I said. There was a flight once a week into Prague, from somewhere in Germany, I think. The crew would take out glass, which they sold in England, and brought out the whisky to Prague, which the liaison officer sold. He was making an absolute fortune.

The next morning he took me to the contact address, and left me to it. This rather small door opened. As soon as I started speaking English I was pulled inside. None of them spoke English. They were eating a cold lunch, and offered me the same. They just carried on talking amongst themselves. One of them took me back to my hotel. 'The next day, we go,' he said. The next day I was taken to an address, and met a very tall, gaunt man. He spoke no English, and not much Czech. We went in a ramshackle taxi to the airport, got aboard, started up and took off. The weather was appalling; every cloud seemed to be stuffed with mountains. We landed, I think, at Croydon, on 1st June. It turned out that this man was a Czechoslovakian scientist, being actively sought by the Russians. The British, or maybe the Americans, wanted him also. We succeeded.

PERCIVAL PROCTOR. One 210HP DH Gipsy Queen II engine. Span 39 feet 6 inches. Length 28 feet 3 inches. Loaded weight 3,500lb. Maximum airspeed 160mph at sea level. Cruising speed 140mph at 3,000 feet. Range 500 miles.

In June 1947, a number of reserve flying training schools were contracted out by the Air Ministry to train, and keep trained, pilots from the last war. We had one such school at Cambridge: 22 RFS. I was the chief flying instructor. The aircraft used was the Tiger Moth. The school also had two Ansons for navigation training. In August 1950, Chipmunks replaced the Tiger Moths. That December we flew the first Vampire. It is worth pointing out that Marshall's, in World War Two, was the largest civilian maintenance unit in the country. After the war ended, Arthur Marshall had to make a decision as to the future direction of the company. Using the skilled labour in the hangars, repair work started on London Transport buses and other vehicle work. On the aircraft side, he decided to carry on with aircraft repair work. To the aircraft manufacturers, he said that 'We don't want to build aeroplanes, we would like the work that you don't really need.' For example, with the Vampire, after a goodly number had come off the production line, 'You get on with the next generation, and leave the earlier ones to us. We can design, modify – the whole lot.'

With the Vampire, advice about operating the aircraft off grass areas was hard to find. We discovered that Vampires had been flown from the grass airfield of Newton, near Nottingham. Someone told me that the important thing was to get the nose-wheel off the soft ground as quickly as possible on the take-off run. So, taking the longest run available, I applied the power, let the brakes off and held the stick right back. The nose-wheel dug in quite firmly at first, but as elevator control came in, the nose lifted. I popped the stick forward, to keep the nose-wheel just off the ground, and flew away. I made many test flights on that aircraft, VZ 840, before it was ready for collection. Every time it stalled, one wing dropped viciously. We had to build up the profile of the wing until it stalled wings level. Then came the day, 21st June 1951, when the RAF ferry-pilot came to collect the Vampire. He was a Flight Sergeant and had done quite a lot of Vampire flying, but he said 'I have never flown off grass before, what's to do?' I told him the technique, 'Get the nose-wheel off the ground as quickly as possible, pop the stick forward, hold it just clear of the ground and fly away.' He looked a bit doubtful; so was I.

When he taxied out, I followed him in a car, and sat behind him under the hedge to watch his take-off. There was a grass cutter working away, hundreds of yards to the starboard side, so I thought there's no problem there. He applied full power, let the brakes off, held the stick hard back, and he held the stick hard back, accelerated, and still he held the stick hard back. Eventually, he flew out of the ground, and immediately stalled. A wing dropped, and struck the ground. The Vampire spun round and slid backwards towards the grass cutter. Realising the danger, the driver leapt off his tractor, still running, and ran out of the way. There was no collision. Unfortunately, the Vampire that I had lovingly flown thirteen times to get it right, now lay in a crumpled heap in the middle of the aerodrome. It was one of the reasons we decided that we had to go to a hard runway. Work on it started in 1953 and was completed in 1954.

That year we were flying Venoms, Beaufighters, Brigands, Sea Hornets, Viscounts and Valiant bombers. Because the runway construction at Cambridge was not complete, we hired a hangar at RAF Waterbeach. From there, Gordon Hubbard, the deputy chief test pilot, carried out a flight test in a Venom. The flight involved a climb to 45,000 feet, a dive down to 5,000 feet, a climb up for a stall, then back in to land. At this time the Venoms did not have ejector seats fitted. There were, occasionally, problems with engine starts. The engine would sometimes flood with fuel. With fuel and ignition switched off, we would then spin the engine to eject the unburned fuel and vapour. Gordon Hubbard, the pilot, started the engine on the second attempt, took off, and climbed away. The next we heard was a radio call to say that he was over Hull at 39,000 feet. He had had a fire warning, and shut down the engine. He intended to glide back to Waterbeach, over one hundred miles away, for a 'deadstick' landing. I was a bit concerned about this, because, at 6,000 feet long, the runway was barely long enough for such a landing. He made a perfect approach and landing. The aircraft was examined; signs of burning were found.

DH VENOM FB1. Single-seat fighter-bomber. One 4,850lb thrust DH Ghost jet engine. Span 41 feet 9 inches. Length 31 feet 9 inches. Loaded weight 15,400lb. Maximum airspeed 640mph. In RAF service from 1952 to 1962. In 1953 DH contracted with Marshall to build the last 84 Venoms for the RAF. The Venoms arrived in kit form and were built on a production line in 4 hangar, on the north side of Newmarket Road. The completed aircraft were then towed across the road for flight preparation.

I had been a bit concerned for Gordon, because the theory in those days was that if a fire warning light came on and stayed on, even though it might have been a false alarm, it was best to abandon ship. As the aircraft had no ejector seat, turning the aircraft upside down, pushing the stick forward, and being thrown out achieved ejection. The tail booms would, hopefully, not smite one. Gordon said 'There was a strong wind blowing from the west, and I reckoned that if I had thrown myself out at 39,000 feet, I would have been blown into the North Sea. The sea is cold, and I don't like water. I reckoned that I could get the aircraft back on the ground safely.' There was nothing much to be said to that.

A week later, exactly the same thing happened to me, in the same place! I took the same actions, stop-cocked the engine, and set heading for Waterbeach. I was very tempted to go over the side, but I thought just the same thing. I thought 'If Gordon can do it, so can I.' I, too, arrived safely back at Waterbeach. The aircraft had suffered a lot of burn damage. Had I not stop-cocked the engine, the aircraft would undoubtedly have broken up and my situation would have been very serious.

I sent a pretty strong signal to the Ministry of Defence (MOD) about the two events. I explained what had happened, and suggested that the answer was to drill some holes in the engine casing. This would allow excess fuel to drain away after a wet start, rather than to rely on the slipstream to suck the fuel out. We had no way of knowing why this thing should suddenly burn at 40,000 feet. A month or two later, a notification in *Flight* magazine said that a RAF pilot at Gütersloh, Germany, had been awarded an Air Force Cross. Why? Because he had successfully landed a Venom after a fire warning at 40,000 feet. We felt a little resentful over that.

In 1955 we were helping Vickers to deliver their Viscounts to Canada and the USA. To increase my experience in the Viscount, I went along as co-pilot in CF-TGT, a Canadian-registered aircraft. With Captain Marsh in the left-hand seat we left for Prestwick, near Glasgow, on 3rd August. From there we flew to Keflavik, in Iceland. The next day we reached overhead

Narsarssuaq, on the southern tip of Greenland. Being above cloud, and unable to make radio contact with ATC, we had to return to Keflavik. Narsarssuaq, in World War Two, was one of a series of staging posts between North America and the British Isles. It was known as Bluie West One. The lives of many aircrews were lost there, attempting to approach in poor weather. Situated at the top of a coastal inlet, aircraft could only safely approach in good weather. Adjacent high ground required, especially, a relatively high cloud base. To get below the cloud, the normal technique was to home to a radio broadcasting station, known as a non-directional beacon (NDB). This NDB was several miles away from the airfield, at the mouth of the inlet. Further care was needed after passing the NDB. The inlet split into two. Taking the wrong course invited disaster, as it led the aircraft up a route too steep and narrow to escape. Prudence, therefore, demanded satisfactory weather at Narsarssuaq, and sufficient fuel to reach a diversion airfield.

VICKERS VISCOUNT Type 810. Passenger transport aircraft. Four 1,990BHP Rolls-Royce Dart Mk 525 turbo-propeller engines. Span 93 feet 9 inches. Length 85 feet 9 inches. Loaded take-off weight 72,500lb. Maximum cruising airspeed at 20,000 feet 355mph. Range with maximum payload 1,585 miles at 333mph.

On 9th August the weather forecast was satisfactory for the flight, with cloud expected, but not too low to stop us getting in. Just as forecast, we arrived above cloud, and thus needed to fly an instrument approach. The descent through cloud towards the NDB went smoothly. On reaching the beacon, however, a nasty shock. The cloud base was below 'minimums.' We needed to break below cloud at 1,250 feet, I think. At that height we were still completely enshrouded. No choice now, on with the power, climb, and set heading for Søndre Strømfjord. Heading north, we checked and rechecked the fuel situation. We should just make it, but with just enough for one attempt at landing. Nearing Søndre Strømfjord, we descended at just three hundred feet per minute. The weather there was also right on minimums. Should we not see the airfield, that rate of descent would, we hoped, permit a safe forced landing on the icy surface. Lady Luck smiled. We saw the runway dead ahead, and landed. On landing, all four fuel-low warning lights illuminated. Just one hundred and fifty gallons remained in the tanks. In a large aircraft, that is next to nothing.

In 1956 we were doing a lot of Valiant flying and started to do work on Canberra bombers for English Electric. On one day I flew six different types, including a Tiger Moth and a Valiant. In those days we did not need to do a formal course on the aircraft before we flew it. Nowadays, you need a three-hour brief before being allowed to sit in the thing.

In 1959 we started work on the MA 4 project. It came about because of work being carried out by the Cambridge University Engineering

Laboratory on boundary layer control. The boundary layer is that layer of air closest to the wing. It 'sticks' to the wing, and is stagnant. It slows down the air above it for quite a distance. The theory was that if the stagnant air could be taken away, or be made to move, the aircraft wing would behave as if it were much cleaner. The aircraft would then fly faster on the same power or at the same speed on less power. Initial experiments took place, with Dr Head in charge, with a sleeve attached to the port wing of a Vampire, a Mk 3, registration VT 858. (Herbert Tappin and Gordon Hubbard did most of the flying on that aircraft). The sleeve was porous, still Vampire shaped, about seven inches thick. There were various galleries, fed by a tube to the aircraft engine. The result was that the boundary layer air was sucked away. It became a test pilot trick to fly the aircraft level, with the stick held central, and to pull the lever that operated the suction. The aircraft then immediately did a smart roll to the right because the left wing now produced so much more lift than the right wing. This encouraged the University and MOD, or whoever, to go ahead with a larger scale project. We were tasked to modify an Auster, the original Mk 7 prototype: VF 665. The Marshall designation was MA 4.

MA 4. One Gipsy Major VII engine. Wingspan increased to 40 feet 6 inches from the original 36 feet. Length 23 feet 9 inches. Alterations to the original Auster design led to a weight increase from 2,160lb to 2,850lb.

Gordon Hubbard flew the Auster from Rearsby to Cambridge on 6th September 1955. An extensive redesign included a new mainplane (wing), fuselage, an all-moving tailplane and rudder. A plywood sheath, drilled with thousands of very small holes, which in turn were covered by 'Japanned' silk doped on top, covered the wing. Fuselage members were strengthened, and a new undercarriage and propeller were fitted. Containing eleven gallons of Avgas, the main fuel tank was ahead of the pilot, at the rear of the engine compartment. The cabin interior was redesigned and additional instruments were fitted, for use by the observer. Ailerons could be 'drooped' in flight to provide additional lift; when drooped they became extensions of the flaps. When that happened there was no aileron control. There was a set of triangular plates inset in the wing. Operated by a lever, the plates could be raised through the wing's surface to act as spoilers on the same basis as some gliders are controlled in roll. A 60hp Budworth jet engine drove a suction pump, which pulled in the boundary layer airflow through the rows of bleed holes. It was installed behind the crew compartment; the jet efflux was below the fuselage. A spin recovery parachute was installed in a canister at the rear of the aircraft. Initial flight tests of the MA 4 revealed a poor rate of climb. Various modifications were made to improve things. The wing profile was changed in 1964, which improved handling and led to lower stalling speeds. For boundary layer research purposes most of the stalling was done with the engine at full power. The Ministry of Aviation owned the aircraft and Cambridge University Engineering Laboratory conducted the research programme.

I did nearly all the flying on this aircraft, and I well remember the first flight on 28th February 1959. I had made two or three fast taxi runs. The aircraft just left the ground on each run, and I put it back on the ground because we were fast running out of aerodrome. I thought it was now safe to attempt a full take-off. The aircraft left the ground easily, but then I had to push the stick fully forward to hold the flying attitude steady. I used the tailplane trimmer to change the angle of the tailplane. This allowed me to fly safely, but only just. I was pleased to be able to get the aeroplane around the circuit at 500 feet and get it back on the ground. My fear was that I would run out of elevator control during the landing. Fortunately, I landed safely, except that I failed to keep the aircraft straight. It caught me out many times, and I remembered what I had told the Beaufighter pilots some years earlier! It was an absolutely vicious aeroplane to keep straight during the landing run. Much of the flying was done at, or near, the stall. Stalling speed for a normal Auster was fifty-nine knots, but the MA 4 would stall at about thirty-nine, a big drop. However, at this low speed, the nose attitude was very high, about forty-five degrees. There was no forward view at that attitude; I just hoped no one got in front of me. The spoilers did not work very well. They worked better on one wing than the other. In order to get true airspeeds, we trailed a 'bomb', a remote, static, measuring device. The observer let it out. The cabin was very cramped. With my 'bonedome' on, I could just sit in it without my head touching the canopy. The observer sat facing the rear. He, too, was cramped.

The test programme ran until 1966. I had a spell of leave coming up, so I briefed and passed the aircraft over to another test pilot: Brian Wass. While I was away the aircraft came out of servicing, and Dr Head wanted to get on with the next phase of tests. Brian took the MA 4 for its 140th flight on 8th March. He flew out towards Linton, near where he lived, south east of Cambridge. Last seen spinning inverted, the MA 4 crashed into a field. Both occupants were killed. The investigation into the accident failed to reveal the cause. That was the end of experiments with the MA 4.

For Company communications work, Arthur Marshall first bought a Piper Apache, then replaced it with a Piper Aztec. In addition, he bought a Beechcraft Queenair. This was a larger aircraft, with eight seats, and had a good range. I went to the works, in the USA, with the ferry pilot, who was an employee of the UK distributor. On collection of the Queenair, G-ASDA, we first flew to Boston. There, the long-range fuel tanks were fitted. Next stop was Goose Bay. To my surprise, we took off from Boston with the extra tank empty. This meant that we were not going to test the tank system until we were over the Atlantic en route for the United Kingdom. I was horrified. I could object, but I was only the co-pilot. I could either get out and walk, or go along. We reached about fifty miles off the southern tip of Greenland, at 10,000 feet, when both engines stopped. The silence was enormous! I jumped out of my seat and rushed back to try all the tanks in the fuselage. Unfortunately, the fuel tanks had been fitted partly under the floor. We had no access to the tank filler caps. I rushed forward, and was satisfied that, from the condensation marks on the outside of the tanks, at least one tank was full, and two were rather low. I decided to turn off the interconnecting taps between the two tanks that were nearly empty. Immediately, and to our immense relief, the engines fired up. This was my first flight across the Atlantic in a small aircraft.

BEECH QUEENAIR. Two Lycoming IGSO-480 turbo-propeller engines each of 340HP. Span 46 feet. Length 35 feet 6 inches. Loaded weight 8,000lb. Maximum speed 240mph at 12,000 feet. Ferry range 1,650 miles.

Around this time we were having a very interesting time, flying so many different types of aeroplanes. While I was at Vickers, learning how to fly the Valiant, I was still doing quite a lot of work back at Cambridge. Brian Trubshaw, the Vickers chief test pilot, said that I must have the most interesting test-flying job in the whole of the aircraft industry. Manufacturer's test pilots flew only about three types of aircraft a year. I flew many more.

The first Vickers Valiant, WZ 368, arrived at Cambridge 30th January 1956. Because there was not a suitable tug available the pilot taxied the aircraft straight inside 10 hangar. In April 1962 we tried out a trial installation on a Vickers Valiant, WP 209. This was at a time when the four-minute warning (of incoming ballistic missiles) was taken quite seriously. Fighter Command aircraft were all organised so that the pilots were in their aircraft, close to the take-off point, and had only to start engines, taxi a few yards, and get airborne swiftly. The Air Officer Commanding (AOC) the Group that operated the Valiants wanted the same capability as the fighters. He tasked Marshall to find some means of getting the aircraft off the ground more quickly than the current fifteen to twenty minutes. Our engineers came up with some quite ingenious devices.

Under the wings, well off the ground, were two pitot tubes each about two to three feet long. Each tube had a protective cover placed over it after each flight. The cover prevented ingress of moisture and insects, either of which could effect the instruments dependent on the pitot pressure supply. A ladder was needed to reach the tubes, for removal of the covers before flight. Also, there was an opening for what was called a 'Q'-feel. This was a device to make the hydraulically operated flight controls feel heavier as airspeed increased. Starlings would often build nests in the opening, so it had a cover over it, which also had to be removed before flight. Engines had to be started one by one. Each start would place a heavy discharge load on the ground support batteries, slowing down the rate at which all four engines could be started. All these processes took time to complete. The solutions were ingenious.

The solution for the pitot head and 'Q'-feel covers was to spring load them. Tapes were attached to fittings on the ground. As the aircraft taxied forward, the triggers and springs were pulled, the covers shot forward, and the aircraft was clean. For the engines, the ground power unit connector was moved under the fuselage and turned round, to face aft instead of forward. Heavy-duty starter generators were connected to the new entry point, and placed behind the aircraft. By a suitable system of elastics and levers, as the aircraft moved forward, the ground power unit was automatically disconnected. A spring-loaded flap would then close over the electrical entry point.

We did several trial starts with the new installation. The co-pilot and I would sit in the aircraft, all strapped up – as if on immediate stand by – with vital-actions completed up to 'start engines.' When the 'Get airborne' call came, we would start the engines, taxi out and take-off. One day, the AOC said he wanted to come and see what he was paying for. So he came to me for a briefing. I said 'Well, Sir, there is your slit trench. You are going to be sitting there, and you will get the four-minute warning. The crew will be in the aircraft where we won't get the warning, because for some reason we can't be on the radio. You will say, over the intercom, four-minute warning, go! We will carry on.' He said, 'When do you want me to say the word?' 'Whenever you like', I said. 'You can sit us there for as long as you like; an hour or more if you wish. It is a demonstration of its effectiveness.' 'No, no, no, I understand, I'm with you.' I said I would tell him when we were at readiness. Almost immediately he said 'Four-minute warning, go!'

With that, we started all engines simultaneously, increased power (against regulations) to speed up the engine start, released the brakes, started taxiing, turned on the short loop, then on to the runway, and took off. By five hundred feet, we had raised the undercarriage, and turned downwind. We then lowered the undercarriage, put down some flap, turned onto final approach, and landed before the four minutes were up. We thought he would be terribly pleased, and we would be issued with medals. We taxied in, grinning all over our faces, to be met with this very irate Air Marshal. 'I've never seen anything so dangerous in all my bloody life. How did you know those covers would come off?' 'Well, someone would have told us if they had not come off, and we can see the pitot covers from the cockpit.' 'You can't see the 'Q'-feel cover, because that's in the fin.' 'No, quite right, Sir.' 'Well, don't you ever do that again, or I shall withdraw my aircraft from Marshall.' So that was another unsuccessful demonstration.

VICKERS VALIANT B1. Heavy bomber. Crew of five. Four 10,000lb thrust Rolls-Royce Avon 201 jet engines. Span 114 feet 3 inches. Length 108 feet 3 inches. Loaded weight 140,000lb. Maximum bomb load 21,000lb. Service ceiling 54,000 feet. Maximum airspeed at 30,000 feet 567mph. Maximum range 4,500 miles. Entered RAF service in 1955. The last Valiant in to Cambridge was WZ 379, a B (PR) Mk 1, 10th June 1964. It flew out on 21st July. After the discovery of major airframe fatigue in August 1964 the Valiant was withdrawn from RAF service and scrapped in January 1965.

I also flew as co-pilot to Brian Trubshaw (Vickers) for the initial air-to-air refuelling and the initial rocket assisted take-off trials. The Company carried out routine maintenance and many modifications, including the trial installation of the Blue Steel 'stand-off' bomb.

In 1957 we decided to widen and lengthen the Cambridge runway, which was then eighty feet wide and 4,465 feet long. This gave us a problem, because we had about ten Valiants in our hangars at the time. To widen the runway would require a big hole to be excavated alongside it. The hole would then need to be filled with rubble, with a layer of concrete on top. I went to the boss of the test flying units in the Air Ministry and put to him our predicament. Would he mind if we went on flying his Valiants whilst the runway work proceeded? It would mean that, on take-off, there would be only ten feet clearance of the right wing tip from the concreting machinery on the right-hand side, and two feet clearance between the left undercarriage wheels and the grass. He was not very pleased at the prospect. However, I made it plain that we had to take action. From Vickers there was a threat that they would prohibit the operation of the Valiant from our runway – known as the bootlace, narrow and short. He relented, but said 'I tell you what, Worsdell, if you prang an aircraft in that hole, I'll come and have your guts for garters.' 'Sir', I said, 'if I finish up in that hole, they'll be there for the taking. You'll be welcome.'

Before the first take-off with the restricted width clearance, I did some practice runs. By keeping the nose-wheel on the third bitumen strip from the left-hand edge of the runway I knew that I had adequate clearance for the wing tips. I briefed my co-pilot: 'What you must not do is look out of the right-hand side when we go past that concreting machine.' Gordon could not resist. As we went along the runway, bearing down on the machine, his eyes stuck on the thing. 'Oh my God, my God, Aaaaah! Missed it', he said.

We widened the runway to one hundred and fifty feet and lengthened it to 5,220 feet. It was just as well. One day, a Viscount had a flap problem. One flap failed on its mountings, ran up and in while on an approach into Manchester airport, and the aircraft crashed. All Viscounts were grounded while modifications were carried out. Vickers produced the modifications and undertook some of the work, but Marshall had the majority of Viscounts to modify. We were called upon to go to London Heathrow to collect the aircraft, and deliver them to Cambridge. The approach and landing had to be done with the flaps left in the 'up' position, which entailed a much longer landing run. We were asked to do the flying because it was felt that the ordinary airline pilot had never carried out such a task. Neither had we. I sought advice from Brian Trubshaw, the chief test pilot of Vickers. All he said was 'Don't scrape the tail end.' We found that it was no particular problem. We collected all the Viscounts from Heathrow, repaired them, and took them back. The runway was finally lengthened to 6,447 feet in 1972. We could then operate VC-10s. (The same runway today serves Boeing 747s).

In 1965 we discovered that the CAA was going to issue a tender for the pilot training of Air Traffic Control cadets. The training would have to be done in cabin aircraft equipped with radio. Our Tiger Moths would not comply with the CAA requirements. Arthur Marshall agreed that we should make a competitive bid, to secure the contract. The bid was successful. Initially, we hired Cessna 150s, as new ones would not have been available in time. In due course we purchased new models and sold off the Tiger Moths.

In 1965 the Government announced its intention to purchase, in batches, Lockheed C-130 aircraft from the USA. Arthur Marshall foresaw that business was to be had here. Based on our previous experience with the RAF, he realised that the first wave of people trained to look after the new aircraft would move on in just a few years. This would leave gaps in the knowledge of their replacements. A sounder approach would be to appoint a civilian company to provide continuous servicing support. He began talks with MOD. Officials there were not enthusiastic. However, at his own expense, he sent engineers out to Lockheed to learn as much as they possibly could about the maintenance of the C-130. The Ministry eventually concluded that Arthur Marshall was right. However, the contract should go out to open contract, not just be given to one company.

The tender's requirements were not as extensive as we knew would be encountered once the new aircraft was in service. We put in two tenders. One based on the Ministry's stated requirements, and one based on what we knew to be the more extensive requirements. The Ministry realised that Arthur Marshall and his team knew a lot more about the new aircraft than they themselves did. The contract to support the C-130, therefore, came to us on 14th April 1966. This meant that co-pilot Doug Page, two flight engineers and myself went to Sewart Air Force base, in the USA, for training. We first completed a very impressively organised ground training programme and then moved on to simulator training. A Major and a Sergeant gave us a briefing and then practice at handling the aircraft systems and dealing with emergencies. We loved it. On completion of the course, had we been RAF crews, we would then have completed the flying phase of the training. However, the RAF would not pay for the flying training. Instead, we went to Lockheed's factory, at Marietta, Georgia. There, we spent two weeks starting and stopping engines and doing ground tests, but did no flying. We returned to Cambridge, to await delivery of the new aircraft. The British government ordered three batches of C-130s:

twenty-four in June and another twenty-four in October1965, with a final batch of eighteen in March 1966.

LOCKHEED C-130 HERCULES C1. Long-range tactical transport. Crew of four. Four Allison T56-A-15 4910BHP turbo-prop engines. Span 132 feet 6 inches. Length 99 feet 6 inches. Maximum take-off weight (normal) 155,000lb. Max overload weight 175,000lb. Cruising speed 374mph at optimum altitude. Range, with 20,000lb payload 4,800 miles. Can be considered as a 'fives' aircraft: cruises five nautical miles high at five nautical miles per minute and uses five thousand pounds of fuel per hour. Entered RAF service in 1967.

The aircraft were flown to England in the 'green' (unpainted) state, with the first one, XV 177 arriving at Cambridge on 19th December 1966. They contained a selection of radio and navigation aids, and came to us for painting and installation of the British military equipment. A RAF crew came to Cambridge to test fly the first aircraft. I accompanied them, because of my greater knowledge of the Cambridge and East Anglian area. The tested C-130, named Hercules for the RAF, then went to Boscombe Down for official acceptance trials. From there it went to the RAF for squadron use. We then did our conversion flight training. We each did half a dozen circuits and landings, some stalls and three-engined approaches. From then on we carried out the full flight testing of each new aircraft. Additionally, and more interesting, the Company modified XV 208 to become the W Met Mk 2 version. This would enable the aircraft to take air samples for meteorological and pollution purposes such as over Kuwait after the 1991 Gulf War. The most obvious, visual changes, were the long nose probe and the addition of a radar dome on top of the fuselage. In early 1971 we carried out quite a few flights to establish the 'before-modification' performance criteria. Two years later, on 21st March 1973, we started the after-modification flight tests.

It was interesting that there was very little difference in performance from the pre-modified aircraft. One requirement was for engines-off approach and landings at maximum landing weight. This was a most unusual requirement, especially with engines-off. We needed to do six landings to satisfy the test requirements. Having given it some thought, I decided that we needed to arrive over the end of the (suitably long) runway at RAE Bedford, at 2,000 feet. We would then close all four throttles to the zero-torque setting, dive almost vertically down at the landing threshold and, at exactly the right time, pull out of the dive in to a three-point landing. Nearing the runway, the remainder of the crew was shouting out their concern at this dive-bombing approach. To their relief, and mine, the landing worked beautifully. We managed to complete all six landings without mishap. Subsequently, we discovered that the seemingly suicidal approaches were unnecessary.

Another unnecessary test came our way. We were tasked to determine
the stalling speed at full power and maximum weight. I got to within about
twenty knots of the expected stalling speed. At this point, the aircraft nose
was so high, because of the high engine power, that I was really frightened.
If one wing had dropped at the stall, we would flick over into a spin.
I chickened out. In the post-flight debrief I said that the high-power stall
test was not safe. Some years later, I met the Lockheed chief test pilot.
I told him that I was very surprised that the C-130 was not put on to the
British civilian register. He said that Lockheed had wanted to do that, but
for one thing. The CAA had insisted that stalls at full power had to be
demonstrated during the flight tests. He said that he had tried a full power
stall, and frightened himself so much that he was unwilling to continue
such tests. I wish I had known that at the time.

In 1977 I found myself under increasing pressure to retire from active
flight-testing. The MOD thought that the civilian test fliers were getting
somewhat over age. I retorted that when John Cunningham retired, I would
retire. The reply was 'Well, he is five months younger than you are. When
he gets to sixty, he will retire.' I gracefully retired from test flying.
I continued to fly the Company twinjet Citation, and the Aztec, a twin
piston engine aircraft. However, the administration of Cambridge airport
took more and more time. The frequency of my flights steadily declined. In
1981 I took the Aztec to Renfrew, in Scotland. For the return flight, the
weather turned sour. The cloud base dropped to about four hundred feet.
I no longer held an Instrument Rating, so I was required to fly clear of
cloud. With that cloud base I was looking at a dangerous flying situation.
I decided that now was the time to stop flying.

Chapter 3

Herbert Tappin

My interest in aviation goes back as far as I can remember, before my schooldays. I recall stating during French conversation that I wanted to be 'un aviateur', probably hoping my flying would be better than my French. In Southampton we were surrounded by aircraft activities. There were the heavies of those days, the Vickers Virginias from Worthy Down, but mainly flying boats from the Supermarine Works on the River Itchen and those from Calshot, on the Solent.

Calshot was the base of the RAF High Speed Flight, formed in 1927 to fly the Schneider Trophy aircraft. Flt Lt Webster won the 1927 contest at just over 280mph. Flt Lt Kinkead, on 12th March 1928, flew a Supermarine S5 in preparation for an attempt on the world air speed record. Ill with malaria, he set off from Calshot during the late afternoon in conditions that were less than ideal. The sun was low on the horizon, it was hazy and, with almost no wind, the sea was like a millpond. Flying just a few feet above the sea he died when his S5 hit the mirror-like surface of the Solent. Flying a Supermarine S6, Fg Off Waghorn won the 1928 race. After the race Flt Lt Orlebar set a new air speed record. The high spot for me was a place on a barge that was towed from the Supermarine works to a position in the Solent. This gave me a close up view of the final Schneider Trophy race in 1931. Flt Lt Boothman won the race, and the Trophy for Britain, in his S6B. After the race Flt Lt Stainforth twice set a new air speed record, pushing it to 407.5mph. I think my place on the barge cost me 1/– (5p). Other names from that era were Atcherley and d'Arcy Greig. A younger member of the Orlebar family, Chris, came through Hamble in the 1960s on his way to British Airways. He added to the family's high-speed history by becoming a Concorde pilot. Still on the Schneider Trophy subject, in the early post-1945 years I probably realised a boyhood dream when I found a Supermarine S6B in the corner of a hangar at Eastleigh Airport. It was dusty but it looked complete, and I was able to squeeze myself into the cockpit and try to visualise what it was like to fly.

I was born in Sholing, Southampton, in Hampshire, 12th June 1918. My mother was Emily Martha Tappin (née Cotton). My father, Charles Edward Tappin, was a turner (engineer) by trade. He worked on heavier machinery whilst employed by John I Thornycroft, shipbuilders and commercial vehicle manufacturers. Subsequently he moved to Southern Railway, mainly concerned with the maintenance of their cross-channel passenger ferries, which plied between Southampton, the Channel Islands, St Malo and Dinard.

My health was not good in my early years and my mother spent much time nursing me through various illnesses. As my school years started, the situation improved and continued to do so. My first school was Porchester Road Infants School, followed by Sholing Boys School. There I gained a scholarship to Itchen Secondary, now Grammar, School (co-educational), where I gained my Oxford School Certificate (Hons), with Matriculation Exemption. My father and Headmaster wanted me to continue with my education. I enjoyed my school days, and for a while continued with Commercial subjects, but felt I wanted to start earning a living and paying my way at home. Games were not a strong point, but I took part in most and for a while ran the Old Boys football team and played regularly for them. I left school to work for the Southampton Corporation Electricity Dept, in the meter test room, then at the Ordnance Survey Office, which was based in Southampton.

In the late 1920s and early 1930s I spent much time either walking or cycling to Hamble, the home of the Hampshire Aeroplane Club. The Club later moved to Eastleigh, to be replaced by Air Service Training (AST) with their Atlas, Siskin and various other aircraft. Avro, Armstrong Whitworth and Fairey Aviation also had bases at Hamble. A pilot who lived locally and whose activities I followed closely was Australian born 'Bert' Hinkler. He had flown in the 1914-18 war and was a test pilot with Avro for some years. He made a number of record-breaking long-distance flights in light aircraft, but was killed when he flew into high ground in Northern Italy when attempting another long distance flight. It was at Hamble in the AST days that I had my first flight. I was attending an Empire Air Day and I heard that there were free flights available, so I spent most of the day trying to locate the man with the tickets. I was successful. He was Sqn Ldr Jenkins, the Chief Instructor of AST, and I was given a generous flight in an Avro Cadet flown by a senior AST student. I am uncertain of the year, but I little realised that within a year or so I would myself be flying an Avro Cadet in a formation display of nine aircraft at the Empire Air Day of 1938 at Hamble.

AVRO CADET. Two-seat trainer. One Armstrong Siddeley Genet Major of 135HP. Span 30 feet. Length 24 feet 9 inches. All-up weight 1,860lb. Maximum airspeed 113mph. Cruising speed 100mph.

I had throughout been looking for ways of getting into aviation. I felt my prospects of a Short Service Commission in the RAF were not good, but a strong attraction was an apprenticeship at Halton. This would have given me a sound engineering training, with the prospect, but no certainty, of being selected for pilot training at a later stage. This was not to be, as my father was initially reluctant. When he finally agreed I had missed the age limit by days. However it all worked out well, as in early 1937 the RAFVR was formed and one of the first Schools to start operating was No 3 E &

RFTS run by AST at Hamble. My application to join was successful and I was among the first reservists to start flying in April 1937 on the Avro Cadet, which was an excellent training and acrobatic aircraft. I spent every available evening and weekend at Hamble flying the Cadet, Avro Tutor, Hawker Hart and Miles Magister. In my first year I completed around 200 hours flying. I qualified for my Flying Badge, or Wings, on 25th May 1938.

In August 1938 I replied to an advertisement in either *Flight* or *Aeroplane* for trainee flying instructors at Marshall's Flying School at Cambridge. I was successful and moved to 26 E & RFTS at Kidlington, Oxford, where the instructors were Flt Lt E B Grace (Chief Flying Instructor), Flt Lt Alan Mills and Sgt Jack Bentley. Alan Mills gave me an instructor's course in November and December 1938. After a successful test at CFS, Upavon, I started instructing on 30th December 1938. From that date to September 1939 we flew quite hard on the Hawker Hind and Miles Magister, on occasions totalling 100 to 120 flying hours in a month. Some of our trainees at that time were members of the Oxford UAS, among them being Leonard Cheshire and Christopher Foxley-Norris, who were both to become renowned in the RAF during 1939 to 1945 and beyond.

September 3rd 1939 brought the outbreak of hostilities with Germany and the School at Kidlington was closed. The school's aircraft were dispersed to other units and the staff moved to 22 EFTS at Cambridge. Planning at that time was difficult to understand. Many training schools were closed and training capacity reduced. Aircraft and instructors at Cambridge were very much under-employed, yet many VR pilots with varying experience were sent to Initial Training Wings in Cambridge and other places to march the streets and take part in other basic service activities. Things were speeded up after a few months, but much time and opportunity was wasted. Many of our early trainees did make it to the Battle of Britain, but with far less experience than they might have had. Two of them were mine: J A Hughes-Rees and J E Johnson. Both went to Spitfire squadrons. Hughes-Rees did well and later received the DFM. He was then commissioned, after which he served in the Mediterranean area, where he died of polio in 1943. 'Johnnie' Johnson was not so fortunate with his postings, which were initially outside No 11 Group of Fighter Command, the highly active area. He was troubled by an old rugby injury to his shoulder. This was put right, and in the ensuing years he became a foremost leader, destroying thirty-eight enemy aircraft. He ended the war years as a well decorated Group Captain and left the Service later as an Air Vice-Marshal.

Life was pleasant at Cambridge. Four of us, flying instructors, shared Tudor House on the main street of Bottisham, a few miles east of Cambridge. A rented house, it had been converted from three cottages. It was better known as 'Hangover Hall.' Whilst enjoying life at Cambridge and appreciating the importance of the work I was very conscious of our immediate situation. We had a Lysander squadron with us. They had been withdrawn after action in France. We had seen fringe activity during the Battle of Britain, and realised, but probably not fully, how stretched Fighter Command and other services had been. Additionally, our own Tiger Moths had been fitted with bomb racks for use against possible invading forces. We were in fact called out one night in response to an alert, but spent it sleeping on the hard floor of the Instructors' Room.

Throughout this time my family was in Southampton, and had a very uncomfortable time. The town had been heavily bombed and the Supermarine Works, the birthplace of the Spitfire, which was within a mile of our home, was totally destroyed. I, with others, wanted to move onto operational flying, but this was resisted because of the importance of training new pilots, and possibly a shortage of flying instructors. It was not until April 1941 that I obtained a posting to 52 (Hurricane) Operational Training Unit (OTU) at Debden. After five weeks and about sixty hours flying on Miles Masters and Hurricanes I was posted to 3 (F) Sqn at Martlesham Heath, near Ipswich, flying the Hurricane IIC armed with four 20mm cannon. The Squadron Commander was Sqn Ldr N A 'Digger' Aitken who I was to meet again, in 1943, when he was Station Commander at Bradwell, in Essex, and I was there with 157 Sqn. About this time the Germans attacked the Soviet Union, so there was very limited activity over Western Europe. The bulk of our activity initially was covering merchant shipping convoys off the coast of East Anglia. We were called on at times to take part in fighter 'sweeps' over the near continent, or to escort small bomber formations, usually Blenheims, but on one occasion four-engined Stirlings. There was little or no reaction from the Luftwaffe. We then moved to Hunsdon, in Hertfordshire, and became more involved with night work, part of which was to co-operate with Douglas Havoc night fighters. These aircraft were fitted with a powerful searchlight, instead of guns, in the nose. The plan was that the Havoc would intercept enemy aircraft, using its radar equipment, then use the light to illuminate the target so that the escorting Hurricane could move in and use its guns. This originated at a time when desperate attempts were being made to strengthen our night defences, but it had little chance of success and was eventually abandoned.

HAWKER HURRICANE IIC. Fighter-bomber. One Rolls-Royce Merlin XX of 1300HP. Span 40 feet. Length 32 feet 3 inches. Maximum take-off weight about 8,000lb. Maximum airspeed 340mph at 22,000 feet. Four 20mm Hispano or Oerlikon cannon fitted in wings. Carrying two 500lb bombs, maximum airspeed about 180mph. Climb to 20,000 feet (clean) about 7.5 minutes. Experience in the Battle of Britain showed that the penetrative power of the rifle-calibre Browning machine-guns was inadequate. Hawker submitted a tender to the Air Ministry to arm a Hurricane with four 20mm cannon. The Air Staff initially took no action. The Mk IIC was built in the greatest numbers, and entered RAF service in May 1941. Thousands were sent to the Soviet Union. The Hurricane was withdrawn from front-line RAF service in northern Europe by mid-1944. The Battle of Britain Memorial Flight maintains a MkIIC, LF 363, in flying condition.

More successful was a night-intruder Flight, which was set up at Manston in Kent. For this the Hurricane was fitted with long-range drop-tanks and we could operate for about three and half hours over France, Belgium and Holland, mainly around airfields. Initially, the Germans were very helpful with their generous use of airfield lighting and aircraft navigation lights, much to their cost. In March 1942 I became a Flight Commander with the Squadron and my main duties were at Hunsdon. I was only able to carry out a small number of these operations, which were fairly uneventful. However, the Flight destroyed or probably destroyed, twenty enemy aircraft, and damaged a similar number. In addition they had considerable success against locomotives, road transport and shipping, but it did cost us six pilots and aircraft. As a further variation from our night duties we were called on to attack shipping when the *Scharnhorst* and *Gneisenau* left Brest and made their dash through the English Channel. We also gave low-level support to the Army during the Dieppe Raid in August 1942.

The *Scharnhorst/Gneisenau* incident took place in February 1942 when we were operating at night. We were stood down during the day but received an urgent call from Operations at North Weald to provide aircraft to attack 'shipping.' The OC and both Flight Commanders could not be located and I found myself to be the senior pilot available. I located a further seven pilots and we set off in two sections of four aircraft each, heading for Manston in Kent where we were to rendezvous with a Spitfire escort. From Manston we headed east over the southern North Sea, flying at sea level in indifferent weather with limited visibility. Nearing the estimated target area and the limit of our range we found two destroyers. We attacked them with our cannon fire through a fair amount of light flak. We then returned to base, all intact apart from a sizeable hole in the leading edge of my port wing.

The Dieppe raid in August 1942 was a very different operation. There was a great deal of planning involved, but Squadron and Flight Commanders were not briefed on the target or the form of the operation until the evening before. We had, in June, moved to Shoreham on the South Coast, but were recalled to Hunsdon after an uneventful stay. We returned to Shoreham in mid-August and the operation took place on the 19th. It turned out to be quite a busy day.

We set off before dawn. On leaving Beachy Head we headed for Dieppe and could see ahead of us a curtain of tracer, so things had obviously started. Our task on this first trip was to harass the enemy guns in the beach area as the Allied troops in their landing craft covered the final part of their journey onto the beach. There was a good deal of smoke, which had been laid by our own aircraft, and a fair amount of light flak. On my second run

I was hit in the port wing. There was a strong smell of fuel and the port gauge went to zero, but otherwise things seemed pretty normal. On inspection back at Shoreham we found that the port fuel tank had been blown open by a direct hit. We lost one pilot and two aircraft on this first trip. Most if not all aircraft had some form of damage, but the ground crews produced a full complement of aircraft for three further sorties. These were less hectic, but on the final trip of the day we did lose the OC, Sqn Ldr A E 'Eddie' Berry, a New Zealander. We spotted some Focke-Wulf 190s crossing left to right ahead and slightly above us. Warning was given and there was ample time to take action, but there was broken cloud about and somehow he must have failed to sight them. Two days later the Squadron returned to Hunsdon. In September I was posted to 534 Sqn at Tangmere for a final effort with the Searchlight Havoc (Turbinlite), but after a short while the project was abandoned.

I was then posted, in January 1943, to 157 Sqn (Mosquito Night-Fighters) at Castle Camps, once more close to Cambridge. The OC was Wg Cdr V J 'Pop' Wheeler who had an MC and Bar for service with the army during 1914-18 and a DFC and Bar from current activities. He was a great character and after being taken off operational flying with Fighter Command he dropped a rank and flew Lancasters with Bomber Command. He went missing after about five trips. Things were still quiet with defensive work and we began to look at intruding again. We were initially restricted because of the highly classified Airborne Interception radar equipment carried. This was overcome and life became much more interesting. Later the restriction on the earlier type of radar was eased and we were able to make deeper penetrations into hostile territory in support of Bomber Command operations. We also worked from Predannack in Cornwall, with Coastal Command, as long-range day-fighters over the Bay of Biscay, to counter Ju 88 fighters, which were harassing our anti-submarine aircraft. On occasions we were also able to deal with heavier German aircraft operating against our own shipping. On these operations we destroyed five Ju 88s and five heavies (four four-engined, and one six-engined flying boat). Our own losses were four aircraft and three crews.

I left 157 Sqn in March 1944 on posting to 51 (Night-Fighter) OTU at Cranfield, near Bedford, as Wg Cdr Flying. We were equipped mainly with Beaufighters, plus a few Beauforts and later some Mosquitoes. I spent the bulk of my time there as OC Twinwood Farm, the satellite airfield. A regular user of Twinwood was Glenn Miller who was stationed nearby with his orchestra, and it was from there that he set out for Paris and disappeared. I liked Glenn Miller's music and was pleased to attend what was possibly the first concert with his full orchestra in this country. The setting was, for me, ideal for the occasion, in an aircraft hangar at the US Air Force base at Thurleigh, quite close to our own Station. He also brought a smaller orchestra to us at Twinwood and gave us an open-air performance. Apart from our own activities there was much going on in the area, with almost daily formations of American B17s assembling for their daylight raids, and returning in not such tidy order. In June came the invasion of Normandy and the Germans launched Vls ('Doodlebugs', ramjet-powered pilot-less bombs) against southern England. Again we were away from it all. My two old squadrons were both in south-east England, 3 Sqn with Tempests and 157 Sqn with updated Mosquitoes, both chasing Vls by day and night, with some success. I did manage to visit them both, at Newchurch and West Malling respectively, for a closer look at what was going on.

I left Twinwood Farm in January 1945 when I was posted to the Mediterranean area, to command 108 Sqn (Beaufighters) in Greece. We flew out from Lyneham in a Vickers Warwick to Naples, then on to Athens by Dakota, only to be told on arrival that the squadron was to be disbanded. However, we did fly a few flag-waving sorties. There had been internal strife in Greece, and Crete was still partially occupied, but things were generally quiet. I then returned to Southern Italy, still accompanied by my navigator Flt Lt I H Thomas who had been with me since I started on the Mosquito. After short visits to transit centres at Bari and Taranto, I went to 334 Wing at Brindisi as Wg Cdr Flying. This was a Special Duties Wing, in which 148 Sqn, equipped with the Halifax, was at that time operating mainly over Yugoslavia. They also had two Lysanders that I spent some time flying, but there was no call for their operational use. Again this was a short stay. No 256 Sqn (Mosquitoes), with the Desert Air Force in Northern Italy, had lost their OC and I was posted in to take over. I was pleased to be going back to the Mosquito, and joined the squadron at Forli, between Rimini and Bologna, on 28th March 1945. No 256 had been a Night-Fighter squadron, but with the lack of hostile air activity they, as part of 322 Wing with four squadrons of Bostons, became involved with interdiction work from dusk to dawn. This was low-level work and was quite intensive and the Germans were still accurate with their light flak. One morning we had three aircraft return for single-engined landings. I was one, having been caught by a single machine-gunner that put a bullet through the cockpit via my trouser leg into the starboard radiator. We lost several aircraft, but it all ceased on 5th May and things seemed strangely flat. After a short period of uncertainty the squadron moved further north to Aviano, close to the Dolomites.

With time and the freedom of movement we were able to enjoy visits into the mountains, to Venice and other places of interest. Hostilities in the Far East came to an end in August and in September the squadron moved to Ballah, by the Suez Canal in Egypt. For the first time I was living under canvas, but it was warm and, apart from the sand, quite pleasant. I had been very lucky with my stations and accommodation since 1939, having had only one period in huts. During my time in Italy with 256 Sqn I lived in a comfortable caravan. Otherwise I lived in permanent buildings. Probably the best of these was at Hunsdon, where I had spells with both 3 and 157

Sqns. There we lived in 'Bonningtons', which had been a large family house, but had become a very pleasant Officers' Mess. Apart from that, the station utilised all available land to grow garden produce that not only raised funds for welfare, but also produced a supply of fresh vegetables for the whole station, and helped to maintain a high standard of catering throughout.

I left Ballah and the Squadron in December 1945 to return to England for release. We travelled in the USS *Medina Victory* from Port Said, through the Mediterranean, via Malta, to Toulon, then by rail to Dieppe. From there it was an overcrowded ferry, SS *Dinard*, to Newhaven, finally by rail to the Release Centre at Hednesford in Staffordshire.

I was home for Christmas, and in the New Year settled down to work to obtain my Pilot's B Licence, before starting back to work at Cambridge with Marshall's Flying School. I arrived in mid-February to find things well under way after a prompt start on 1st January with a number of Tiger Moths for instructional flying, and a Proctor for charter or instruction, with more aircraft coming along. In March, my first full month, I flew more than ninety hours so there was plenty of activity and it was all very refreshing. It was significant that in the ensuing months as aircraft repair and modification work ran down, the hangars began to fill with London Transport buses for refurbishment, and with other projects. They were never allowed to be empty and idle, and eventually when aircraft work began to re-establish itself, aeroplanes came back to their rightful place.

I spent the following fifteen years at Marshall's, a period full of interest and variety. I was largely involved with flying training and charter work. On the charter side, with our Proctors and Rapides, we had a variety of work to start with. Travel was difficult and some fascinating trips, mainly to Europe, came up. Gordon Hubbard, who had been with the Company since pre-war days, led the field with a trip to Cairo in the Proctor and a trip to Johannesburg in a Rapide. Later we built a good connection with the horseracing world, mainly from Newmarket, and rather specialised in this type of operation. On the training side with the Tiger Moths, many ex-service people, male and female, who had not had a chance to fly in the services, came along to fulfil their ambitions. On the professional side we had some ladies from the Air Transport Auxiliary who were working for their Professional Civil Licences; they were experienced on a variety of types and were very good.

I enjoyed flying some of the many aircraft types that passed through the Works at Cambridge, from the Valiant, Viscount, Ambassador, Brigand, Varsity, Valetta, Vampire, Venom, Canberra and others, down to the M L Utility. This unusual aircraft had an inflatable wing, which I would say was more stimulating than enjoyable. Perhaps the most active time with test flying was when we had an assembly line of Venom 1s and 4s, and later when we were updating Vampire T11s by fitting ejector seats, new canopies and revising the instrumentation. The test schedule on the Venom involved a climb to 40,000 ft, then a descent to check limiting Mach numbers at numerous levels, with a high speed run at low level. In addition we carried out trim, handling and stall checks. The Venom 1, with its spring-tab ailerons, presented problems at high Mach numbers, particularly with wingtip tanks fitted. The Mark 4 that followed it had powered ailerons that eliminated this and made it a much nicer aircraft. The test schedule for the Vampire T11 was similar, but with the addition of spinning in each direction. It had an interesting spin but was quite positive on recovery. Test flying requirements were very varied. Civil aircraft, mainly the Viscount and Ambassador, sometimes called for a comprehensive schedule. This was particularly so in the case of two Viscounts that were both seriously damaged in take-off accidents, one at Blackbushe and the other at Heathrow. The recovery itself was a major operation, but both were brought back to Cambridge by road, rebuilt and returned to service. We also maintained and overhauled our own smaller aircraft: Rapides, Tiger Moths and Austers, as well as those of a number of private owners, which enabled us to sample a variety of light aircraft.

Throughout my time at Cambridge we kept up a training programme with our Tiger Moths and Auster. This was mainly Private Licence work with occasional calls for Professional Licence training and Flying Instructor courses. This remained fairly consistent, but was boosted in the school holiday periods by a regular intake of Air Training Corps cadets for Flying Scholarship training to Private Pilot Licence (PPL) standard. This was generally completed in two weeks. In 1997 I was pleased to meet several of these cadets at a Guild of Air Pilots function. They had carried on from the ATC to enter the RAF and were by then retired senior officers.

Charter work with DH Rapides and Percival Proctors started in 1946 as previously mentioned. The Proctors were phased out, but Rapides increased to four in number, mainly carrying up to eight passengers. There was sometimes a variation in load, such as an engine for a BRM racing car to Southern France, a funeral party plus coffin to Southern Ireland or, for a period, flowers from the Isles of Scilly to the mainland.

In January 1961 I left Cambridge to join the newly formed College of Air Training (C of AT) at Hamble. British European Airways (BEA) and British Overseas Airways Corporation (BOAC) formed the College, with the Civil Aviation and Education Authorities also involved. The C of AT was created in 1960 from AST, which had many years experience of training pilots and engineers for Commercial Aviation world-wide. Pilots from the late 1940s and early 1950s were coming up to retirement in fairly large numbers, and the supply of ex-service pilots was limited. The object was to take young men with the right qualifications from schools and universities, and train them from scratch to Commercial Pilot Licence with Instrument Rating standard. After graduation they could go to an airline and train on the type of aircraft they would be operating. It worked very well and had considerable influence on the policy of pilot training. We had our own selection board, based on RAF selection principles, which produced a supply of high quality, well-disciplined cadets. It was pleasing when in 1997 the students from those early courses held a reunion to celebrate the fact that they had all retired after highly successful careers with BEA, BOAC and finally British Airways.

I had been with Marshall's since 1938, apart from a short break from April 1941 to January 1945, during which I was in fairly close contact. They were interesting and enjoyable years and I gave up a great deal in moving to Hamble, but it had its compensations. The working pattern was different, and I was, after all, back on familiar territory. The airfield was still grass, the hangars were still the same, with a few small additions. The main Administration and Mess buildings were unchanged, as was much of the other accommodation. Much of the residential accommodation for students was replaced and added to by first-class brick buildings. In subsequent years there were also members of the staff who had been there during my 1937/38 years. They including Mr Abbott, a flying instructor who was, by then, involved with cadet selection, and Peter Duff-Mitchell, who had been a civilian student and a member of the RAFVR.

I started flying at the College in February 1961. The early intakes of cadets were only a few months into their two-year course, so it was basic instruction on the Chipmunk, mixed with some selection flying with new applicants. Cadets later converted to the twin-engined Piper PA23-Apache, on which they did their night flying, airways and instrument approach work. This was supplemented by a considerable amount of work on two Flight Procedure Trainers, which were fixed-base, but equipped as four-jet aircraft on which airways flying and terminal procedures could be simulated. This later proved to be a great asset during a cadet's transition onto actual airline work.

The cadets also undertook a comprehensive syllabus of all related ground subjects to Airline Transport Licence standard. The results were then 'frozen' until they had accumulated sufficient flying experience to hold the senior licence. We also had a very good Liberal Studies Section, so the cadets had quite a full two years, but even so this was later reduced to eighteen months.

The Chipmunk we all enjoyed, but it had its limitations, weather-wise and with radio and navigation equipment. We spent some time looking for a replacement. During this time I flew a Chipmunk with a Rover turbine engine, the extremely nice Sia Marchetti SF 260 and others. Most promising was the Beagle Pup, which was being built at Shoreham but it still needed changes to meet our requirements. However, this came to a halt when the Government withdrew its support from the Beagle project. We eventually had to settle for the American Piper PA28 Cherokee, because of availability. My main concern about this machine in a busy circuit was the lack of a clear canopy. There were two mid-air incidents, after which my Marshall time had its influence and we cut away a section of the roof and fitted clear panels. We kept a number of Chipmunks for spinning and aerobatics training, but there was much discussion at that time as to the value of this given the characteristics of modern aeroplanes.

We continued with the Apache aircraft as a twin-trainer for a number of years, but we needed something better and faster for airway work. Again we had to go to America, and settled for the Beech Baron, which had the characteristics of a bigger aircraft, and good single-engine and general performance.

The College kept up a good flow of cadets. A new breed of purpose-trained pilots, they adapted quickly and earned a good reputation for themselves with the airlines. It gave me some satisfaction that I had started at Hamble, moved on to train pilots for the war years, then returned in the '60s to train pilots for more peaceful purposes. It is pleasing to realise that the sons of three RAFVR members at Kidlington in 1938 came through Hamble and had successful careers with British Airways, two of them as Concorde captains.

The grass airfield at Hamble was the one thing that could not be developed. A railway line and roads hemmed it in. This caused us to use some nearby airfields such as Lee-on-the-Solent, Goodwood, Eastleigh and Hurn (Bournemouth). This was in reality, beneficial, as it gave the cadets a wider experience, with considerable variation in ATC, and it eased the congestion in the Hamble circuit at busy periods. The entire Advanced Flight, with its Barons, eventually moved to Hurn.

There was, as would be expected, a close liaison and exchange of information with the airlines. Hamble staffs were given opportunities to sit in on route flying and base training when ex-cadets were undergoing conversion onto their operational type. Among my own occasions were a few days in Malta with the Vickers Vanguard and a short period at Shannon with the VC-10.

I retired from Hamble in January 1972 and initially did some free-lance flying with private owners, followed by some photographic work and pleasure flying from Shoreham. Although there were various opportunities, I found nothing that I really wanted to become totally committed to, so I eventually allowed my licence to lapse. At present I have a current Group 3 medical certificate, but it is unlikely that I will ever make use of it. I will remain ever grateful to the world of aviation, the people I have met and the friends I have made.

Chapter 4

Douglas Page

A pleasure flight from the original Marshall airfield in a DH Moth was my first flight. It was probably in 1933, but the aircraft was certainly one operated by the Cambridge Aero Club. I paid three week's pocket money for the short trip – 2/6d (12.5p). I did not fly again until I began my RAF training. Looking back on my life in aviation it looks almost as if I had made a down payment to join the Marshall Company. Before that special day my first memory of seeing aircraft was probably when I was under five years of age. My sister was wheeling me in a pushchair and I saw an aircraft of the period fly over. The aircraft almost certainly came from the nearby RAF airfield of Duxford, which opened the year I was born.

Having flown three miles north-east from Duxford, now the Imperial War Museum, a crow would be right over Sawston. I was born there in 1919, was educated there, and – apart from RAF service in World War Two – have lived there all my life. My secondary education took place at the new school, known as Sawston Village College, which was a new concept in education pioneered in Cambridgeshire. Living so near to Duxford meant that we could easily walk there from home. During school holidays, two or three of us young enthusiasts would take our sandwiches and drinks and spend the day glued to a spy-hole in the hedge that surrounded the airfield. We watched Siskins, Bulldogs, Avro 504s of Cambridge UAS and sundry other machines of that time. Among the bigger types we spied Valentias, Virginias, Harrows, Hendons and, later on, Whitleys. On a few occasions in 1929 and 1930 we were treated to the awesome sight of the truly immense R101 airship (about 132 feet in diameter and nearly 800 feet long) as it wafted gracefully above us, often flying quite low. At the end of the 1930s we witnessed the arrival of the very latest fighters, the Hurricanes and Spitfires. The sky above us seemed to invite aircraft to fly over. This was partly explained by the fact that some of the pilots lived in nearby villages and would show off their aircraft to their families or girl friends. A brother-in-law was in the RAF as a sergeant pilot, and this helped to maintain my interest in aviation.

As soon as I was released from my reserved occupation I volunteered for aircrew in the RAFVR. It was not for the money; at the time a sergeant pilot earned 12/6d a day, or £4-7/6d (£4-37.5p) a week. A uniform blue shirt cost £1 and a black tie 3/–. At the end of 1941 I was accepted for training, but my call up did not come until March 1942. The RAF put me into the usual route for those destined for Bomber Command by sending me to the brand new Grading Scheme at Sywell, near Northampton. The Grading Scheme was an offshoot of 6 FTS whereby the most likely candidates to make the grade as pilots were sorted out by a short course of about ten to twelve hours flying on Tiger Moths. Those who went solo within that time were invariably posted on as pilots. Those who did not fly solo were sent on navigator or bomb-aimer courses. Having made it to solo I moved up to Wolverhampton, the home of 28 EFTS, to complete my flying course on Tiger Moths. After the war the Boulton Paul Company carried out taxiing trials of the BP 111 delta wing jet at the airfield. As luck would have it, my course ran through the often very chilly winter of 1942/43.

In common with most people who had been uprooted from a fairly peaceful life into a totally different world I found that some things came as a shock. My upbringing had been reasonably comfortable as far as the basics went, but the basics really were basic. We all had to work hard and take orders; discipline came easy to me and I pitied many of my colleagues who managed to just about hold a pen. I felt that my sense of discipline stood me in good stead one dark winter night. Not only was there no moon for a crucial event during my night flying, there was also wartime complete black out. Life was made difficult for would-be RAF pilots as well as for the enemy. Even the airfield lighting was just a gesture; it was as dim as could be. A bat would have been hard pressed to find its way back home. It was March 1943 and my instructor judged that I was fit for night solo. He duly sent me off and I managed to get around the circuit safely, but I touched down a bit too far along the landing run. The Tiger Moth came to a stop so close to the iron railings on the airfield boundary that I had insufficient room to turn it round to taxi back to dispersal. I undid my straps, made sure the engine was ticking over at the slowest possible speed, hopped out, lifted the tail and swung the aircraft round. I carried on as if nothing had happened. On returning to the parking area I was asked where I had been. In a trice I replied 'I was temporarily lost.' This explanation seemed to go down quite well.

By May 1943 I had completed my Elementary Flying Course and moved across to Cranwell, the home of the RAF College. The College had closed at the outbreak of war, to reopen as the RAF College FTS. We were scheduled to stay for about four months. What a luxurious establishment it was, even boasting a swimming pool on camp. I lived in the College and was looked after by a civilian batman. There was even a camp band that played every Sunday evening during dinner. Everything was generally very comfortable and most unwarlike. Learning to fly the twin-engined Oxford in such conditions was like living in a dream world. The dream was shattered when we started to night fly. For this we had to leave the luxury of the College to head for a bleak satellite airfield on the Lincolnshire coast. Life returned to the more basic existence that I had previously experienced. Not only that, but we began to lose the odd aircraft to German intruders. This was an early baptism of fire and a precursor of things to come. In September 1943 I completed the course and was awarded my wings.

No 84 OTU at Desborough, Northants, came as a rude awakening after the five-star conditions of Cranwell. The task of the OTU was to teach us how to handle the Vickers Wellington Mk X, the last of the bomber variants. This was achieved without incident through the winter of 1943/44.

VICKERS-ARMSTRONG WELLINGTON Mk X. Long-range night-bomber. Crew of six. Two 1,675HP Bristol Hercules VI or XVI engines. Span 86 feet 3 inches. Length 64 feet 6 inches. Loaded weight 36,500lb. Maximum airspeed 255mph at 14,500 feet. Range 1,470 miles with 4,500lb of bombs. Climb to 15,000 feet 27.5 minutes. Service ceiling 22,000 feet. Six squadrons of Wellingtons (known as Wimpeys) formed the backbone of Bomber Command's night-bombing force for a long period in the opening phases of the war. Over half the aircraft in the first 1,000-bomber raid, on Cologne, were Wimpeys. Total production exceeded 11,400 aircraft. After the war many Mk Xs were converted to navigation trainers and served until 1953. The RAF Museum at Hendon contains a Mk X. A Mk 1A, N2980, was rescued from Loch Ness in 1985, where it had lain undisturbed since ditching on 31st December 1940. It is being refurbished at the Brooklands Museum, Weybridge, Surrey, not far from where it was built in the 1930s.

At last the magic moment came for me. I had always wanted to fly in Bomber Command, in particular to fly the Short Stirling four-engined bomber. Before I was called up, the Cambridgeshire skies were filling up with more and more Stirlings, which had just become operational with 3 Group, Bomber Command. My posting came through. It was for the Stirling Heavy Conversion Unit, 1651 HCU, at No 32 Base Wratting Common, near Haverhill, in Suffolk, just a few miles from my home. The airfield was originally called West Wickham when it opened in May 1943, but in August it was renamed to avoid confusion with another airfield. At the HCU we formed into crews and learned how to fly and operate the Mk I version of the RAF's first British heavy bomber. The course lasted for six weeks, after which my crew was posted to Tuddenham, Suffolk, to join 90 Sqn. (90 Sqn had been formed two years previously, at West Raynham, to fly the unsatisfactory Boeing Fortress I). My period of serious operations was about to commence.

SHORT STIRLING Mk III. Heavy bomber. Crew of seven or eight. Four 1,650HP Bristol Hercules XVI engines. Span 99 feet. Length 87 feet 3 inches. Loaded weight 70,000lb. Maximum airspeed at 14,500 feet 270mph. The Mk I entered service in August 1940 with 7 Sqn. The first operational trip was not until February 1941. Stirlings usually flew lower than the Halifax and Lancaster due to inferior performance. The Mk III was better, but not much. Lower altitudes made it more vulnerable to enemy fighter attack and bombs from above. Due to its inferior performance it was, from the middle of 1943, progressively withdrawn from main-force bomber operations and used, successfully, for mine-laying operations. Later on it was used to tow gliders and carry passengers within Transport Command.

Nearly 2,400 were built. In May 1947 a Belgian charter operator used twelve Mk V Stirling transports on a passenger service between Blackbushe and Shanghai.

Tuddenham was a station within 3 Group and operations commenced in October 1943 with 90 Sqn flying the Stirling Mk III on mining operations. Mining operations were given the codeword 'Gardening.' The word used for minelaying was 'planting' and the mines themselves were referred to as 'vegetables.' Inevitably, the horticultural oriented officer who thought it all up called the designated mining area the 'plot.' My first flight with 90 Sqn was an air test that lasted one hour and ten minutes. The next flight, for experience, was with a neighbouring squadron. I flew as second pilot on a short night-bombing trip to Louvain, in France. Operations now began in earnest with mining missions to various plots from the Bay of Biscay to the Friesian Islands. Our load on these trips consisted of six 1,500lb vegetables, which we had to drop from 300 to 500 feet above the sea.

It was during this part of my operational tour that I witnessed the first major aircraft incident not attributed to enemy action. On an evening in May 1944 I was waiting in line on the taxiway for my turn to take off on an evening planting mission. The aircraft in front, full of fuel, mines and .303 ammunition for its guns, lumbered down the runway and seemed to take off normally. Having lifted into the air, however, it stayed lower than usual and failed to clear the trees at the end of the runway. It then collided with the branches, which knocked off the tailplane. Transfixed, we watched the Stirling as it continued to climb in defiance of the laws of aerodynamics, wondering what would happen next. The stricken aircraft struggled to about 500 or 600 feet above the ground. Suddenly it nosed over and plummeted down, crashed and exploded. There were no survivors. Now it was my turn to enter the runway, line up and go, straight through the pall of smoke and fire. What a way to start a night mission.

After that unforgettable mining operation, my next three missions changed to dropping supplies to the French Resistance. These missions, in June 1944, were very similar to the planting operations inasmuch as they were done from a low altitude, on moonlit nights and we operated as a single aircraft. Trying to find a meadow in the middle of France was quite a problem! The task called for a flight out at about 11,000 feet until we crossed the enemy coast. We then descended to low level and flew to the Dropping Zone (DZ), hoping all the time that the moon would stay out to assist with navigation. We recognised the DZ by spotting small fires or torches laid out by the Resistance people. I would then manoeuvre the Stirling into position along the flarepath to drop the load. The load was usually six containers, similar to oil drums, suspended from bomb racks. We sometimes carried a few boxes internally as well. These we just kicked through the bottom hatch. The Allied invasion of Europe had just been launched, on 6th June, and the English Channel area was a maelstrom of activity. The following night we launched off for another clandestine supply drop.

We were specially briefed for these trips that should we not be able to drop the load we must bring it home. In addition, if we were to land away from base the aircraft captain had to ensure that the bomb doors were closed before leaving the aircraft. The idea behind this was to keep the loads a secret. On the night of 7th June we were unable to locate the DZ. As briefed, we abandoned the drop and set off for base, climbing to 11,000 feet before reaching the coast inbound. It was a brilliant, moonlit night. Just as we were about to cross the coast I made another of my regular look arounds. Contact! Clear as anything, off to our right and at the same height as us, I spotted a Focke-Wulf 190 fighter. I told my air gunners to keep a sharp lookout but not to fire until the enemy made a move; hopefully, the lone German had not spotted us.

Not so many seconds later all hell broke loose from below. We thought this was light anti-aircraft fire. Our Stirling sustained several hits. The fuselage was ripped open in several places, the gunners' intercom was knocked out and a fire started in the mid-section. Looking over my shoulder I got quite a shock. The fire was right where the fourteen fuel cocks and the oxygen bottles were located. Mercifully, my crew managed to get the fire under control. We then set to and assessed the damage. I sent the bomb aimer back to try to contact the rear gunner. He managed to do that, reporting that when he reached the turret it was traversing rapidly back and forth. The rear gunner, 'Jock', was muttering 'Where is the bugger' or words to that effect. He was probably oblivious to what was going on in the rest of the aircraft.

Assessing the state of the aircraft, our bomb aimer reported that, apart from a large hole in the floor of the rear fuselage, we seemed to be in fair shape. It looked as if we could make it home so I instructed the wireless operator to cancel the SOS that he had previously sent out. As we approached Tuddenham I contacted ATC; they told me that a German aircraft had recently attacked the airfield. Since the intruder might still be lurking, I was told to divert to Newmarket Heath, a grass airfield with paraffin flares to illuminate the landing run. I spotted the airfield, set up for the approach, and judged that it and the touchdown went quite well. Everything then went awry. As soon as the weight went on to the port wheel the Stirling lurched to its left and careered across the grass, making its own way to a standstill. It finished up with the left wing low, but with the undercarriage legs still intact. The seven or eight aircrew clambered out in the dark and, remembering our special instructions, we locked the aircraft up and told the hovering groundcrew not to probe around. We then reported to the 'powers that be' and waited for our transport to arrive. The vehicle duly turned up in the early hours of the morning. In the eerie light of the approaching dawn we hopped aboard and drove over to our sorry looking Stirling to collect our gear. On arrival at the aircraft we nearly collapsed with laughter. All that remained of the bomb doors was the framework. The innards, including our secret cargo, were sitting there for all to see. It turned out that the swing on landing was caused by a damaged wheel and a completely missing tyre. As a matter of interest, the first flight of the prototype Stirling, on 14th May 1939, ended in disaster when one brake seized after touchdown, the stalky undercarriage collapsed, and the aircraft was written off. That trip was my ninth, and last, operational flight on Stirlings. My squadron was re-equipping with the Lancaster Mk III, and our future operations would be with the Main Force of Bomber Command.

AVRO LANCASTER Mk III. Heavy bomber. Crew of seven or eight. Four American Packard-built 1,460HP Rolls-Royce Merlin 28 engines. Span 102 feet. Length 69 feet 6 inches. Loaded weight 68,000lb. Maximum airspeed at 11,500 feet 287mph. Range with 14,000lb bomb load 1,660 miles. The Mk I started operations on 3rd March 1942 by mine-laying Heligoland Bight. One of the great features of the Lancaster was its ability to carry ever-bigger bombs. The heaviest to be carried was the Grand Slam, which weighed 22,000lb. 7,377 Lancasters were built. It continued in RAF service, in the maritime role, until October 1956. In 1998 there were two Lancasters in flying condition, one in England and one in Canada.

The grass airfield of Feltwell lies five miles to the north of Lakenheath. It was there, on 9th July, after a one-hour dual, or instructional, flight, that I flew solo for the first time in the most famous RAF bomber of World War Two – the Lancaster. After a few more solo familiarisation flights we were ready for operations with real bombs in our Lancaster Mk III. Up to now we had flown all our missions on our own. We now had to get used to flying en masse. Being just one aircraft among 600 to 800 others came as quite an alarming experience on a pitch-black night. There were no navigation or other lights on, and few clues as to the whereabouts of our colleagues. Only a very good look out by all members of the crew and feeling the rough air from the slipstream of other aircraft just ahead gave one some idea of what else was about. Once over enemy territory the presence of searchlights, anti-aircraft gunfire, flak, and the occasional machine-gun and cannon fire from enemy fighters added to the eerie and sometimes tense situation. At times as we approached our target I thought it would be impossible to fly through such intense flak and survive. My crew and aircraft, however, always made it. Our aircraft was never seriously damaged; it just picked up a few holes from shrapnel now and again. On one occasion, not discovered until after we had landed from the mission, we had first hand evidence of what our bombers were dropping onto the targets several miles below us. A Flight Sergeant aircraft fitter discovered a 4lb incendiary bomb lodged in the top of one wing, between two of the fuel tanks. Nothing like receiving a bit of your own back!

On 18th July I made my first daylight raid. The target was Caen, France, and our load was eighteen 500lb bombs. We were, we thought, not only going to enjoy the luxury of seeing where we were going, but also what was going on around us. The good news was that we saw no Luftwaffe aircraft at all, whereas at night we had suffered three enemy fighter attacks. Luxury, however, it was not. It was probably the most frightening mission we had yet flown. By night we had got used to flak, searchlights and ground fires. What was going on around us unseen neither concerned nor worried us. Daylight was different; we could see everything. From above we could see bombs falling, we hoped, to miss us. We were lucky; some of our colleagues were not. We saw wings knocked off, engines and tailplanes too. Looking up as we approached the target we got an all-too-clear view of a Lancaster with its bomb doors open, with a front-seat view of eighteen 500lb bombs shortly to make their exit at half-second intervals. With our bomb-aimer calling 'Left, left' we were hoping like hell that the one above was calling 'Right, right.' Our nerves were taut that day! We were very relieved when that Channel crossing was over. We did not know many details at the time, but the raid on Caen was in direct support of Operation 'Goodwood', planned by Field Marshal Montgomery to finally break through German defences into open country beyond. Bomber Command launched nearly 1,600 heavy and 350 medium bomber sorties that day in support of the ground forces.

On 20th September we completed our thirtieth operational flight and we were alive to tell the tale. Our tour was over, but the war was not. For me it was time to say cheerio to my crew and move on to my next posting. I went back to Wratting Common as an instructor. Flying Stirlings once more, I set about learning how to teach others the art of flying a heavy bomber. Because the HCU was about to re-equip with Lancasters the course was a short one, a mere twelve days, with twenty-one flying hours. The HCU duly moved away, but I found myself left behind with a flight engineer and a party of groundcrew. The fitters and mechanics set to and made serviceable the few remaining Stirlings. As each machine was made fit to fly, my job was to ferry it over to the maintenance unit at Woburn Park. By the end of November 1944 we had completed the task. Yet another instructor's course came my way in December.

I headed off to Lulsgate Bottom, now Bristol airport, where 3 FIS was equipped with both the Master and the Oxford. I flew the latter aircraft and stayed at Lulsgate until February 1945 to qualify for my multi-engine instructor's certificate. On completion of the course I set off for Woolfox Lodge, Rutland. The airfield sat just to the east of the Great North Road, the A1, and I rejoined the HCU, now fully equipped with Lancasters. However, hardly pausing to catch my breath and get paid, I was despatched up the A1 to Finningley, Yorkshire. Bomber Command had recently opened the Bomber Command Instructors' School, the purpose of which was to teach instructors in greater depth to do a thorough job. The school was equipped with the Lancaster, Halifax, Wellington and a few Spitfires and Hurricanes for fighter affiliation exercises. The course was scheduled to last six weeks. We studied bomber and fighter tactics, use of radar, the

German air defence system and the means to counter it. Some of the flight manoeuvres we had to perform were really hair-raising; they would horrify us today. I managed to pass the course and added yet another certificate to my growing pile. By now it was April 1945. In May I at last set about teaching others 'how to do it.' The war in Europe ended on 8th May, but of course in the Far East we were still fighting the Japanese. My bombing instructor's tour continued, albeit with several moves of base, until I was demobbed from Swinderby on 29th June 1946, flying right up to the end.

Looking back on my time spent on an operational squadron I should say how important it was to have a very good crew. In that respect I was very lucky, I had one of the best. As far as treatment and living conditions were concerned we did not fare too badly as we, being aircrew, had special rations. This sometimes caused friction between flying and non-flying personnel, but as far as I know it never reached serious proportions.

After leaving the RAF in 1946 I did not fly again until 1952, by which time I was rather fed up with having my feet on the ground for twenty-four hours a day. I heard of a flying job at Cambridge airport, applied for it and was appointed as a staff pilot to fly Chipmunks and Oxfords with 22 RFS.

In the Chipmunks the RFS provided refresher flying for RAFVR aircrew, mostly ex-wartime pilots but there were a few civilians that had joined the RAFVR from Cambridge UAS. We flew Airspeed Oxfords for use by nearby RAF units to help train radar operators in Ground Controlled Interceptions (GCI). After taking off in pairs the radar operators would split us up. One aircraft acted as a raider, the other as an interceptor. Hopefully, the interceptor would then be directed to within firing range of the raider. The interceptions did not always go as planned so some flights got quite exciting.

I carried on with the RFS until it closed and was then offered a place at No 2 CAACU (Civilian Anti-aircraft Co-operation Unit) at the wartime airfield of Langham, on the north Norfolk coast. Marshall operated the unit, which flew Spitfires, an Oxford and some Mosquitoes. Vampires superseded the Spitfires a few months after I joined. We flew both types against light anti-aircraft (AA) guns of the Territorial Army and used the Mosquito to tow targets up and down the coast, day and night, for the heavy AA. This was a boring job as a tow was usually programmed to last four hours. However, if the gunners were on form and shot the targets away, the flight was shorter.

We had exemptions from the low-flying rules when operating single-engine machines and this made the job more exciting, as it meant we could indulge in all sorts of low flying. On one occasion I was batting along in a Vampire at about three hundred knots just above the ground. To my great surprise there was a huge bang, a very loud wind roar and all sorts of rubbish flew past me into the atmosphere. The cockpit canopy had parted company from the aircraft; just the side rails were left, intact. Since there was no ejector seat my immediate reaction was to gain height in case a bale out was necessary, but fortunately I was able to stay with the aircraft.

In February 1955 I returned to Cambridge to resume flying the Oxfords in the GCI role. There were other types of flying available too. In the first two weeks I managed to get a trip in a Valetta as a 'second dickey' (second pilot). The following month I managed a familiarisation flight in an Auster and a Tiger Moth, GCI work in the Oxford, an instrument rating in a Meteor 7 and a flight as co-pilot in a Vickers Viscount. During April I joined in the flight test programme for the Venom 4 and Vampire 5 machines and, later, the Vampire T11. In October I flew as second pilot in a Varsity to the Vickers airfield at Wisley for static vent calibration. I was also instructing on the Tiger Moths of the Cambridge Aero Club.

By February 1956 we were again busy and I made my first flight in a Canberra, from Warton, Lancashire, to Cambridge. In the next couple of months I flew twelve different types including more new ones, the DH Rapide and the Bristol Brigand. The Percival Proctor was the only new type that I flew in May. During this hectic period I had been studying for my professional pilot's licence. Having obtained it I was able to operate the Rapide on a regular basis.

In November 1956 I was loaned to ML Aviation to help out with a new autopilot they were developing. It was to be installed in the new types of aircraft that were to be used as live targets by gunnery and missile units. I was seconded to the Fleet Air Arm base at Brawdy, in West Wales. ML used a Piston Provost fitted with the new autopilot. An operator came along to activate the autopilot controls with which he directed the aircraft to perform various manoeuvres. Sitting there while the Provost flung itself around sometimes filled me with horror before we landed, manually, back at Brawdy. Herbert Tappin came down to take over from me after two months.

In April 1957 I flew forty-seven hours instructing in the Tiger Moth in addition to all the test and charter work. The Company had obtained a contract with BEA for work on the Vickers Viscounts and, having sat the Air Registration Board exams and passed a flight test, I was able to join in with the ferry flights from Heathrow to Cambridge.

At about this time another autopilot trial came along. A Varsity was fitted with a simple system with no auto-throttles, and we carried out some interesting auto-land trials at Bedford. The system relied on cables buried either side of the runway; the cables emitted signals that were picked up by the aircraft. It permitted very accurate lining up with the runway although we flew the landing manually or sometimes carried out an overshoot. We were calibrating the device for the MOD; it gave me one or two moments of apprehension.

By now we had some work to do for BEA on the Ambassador aircraft, so I also assisted in this, making my first flight in G-ALZS with Tap Tappin. During December 1957 the Company provided Vickers with a co-pilot – me – to help ferry a Viscount to Montreal for Air Canada. We set off from Wisley on 18th December for our first stop: Prestwick. On 20th the second phase was to Keflavik, refuel, and then to Søndre Strømfjord, Greenland. During the descent from the cruise I noticed for the first time ever that the air temperature was falling rather than rising. The airfield temperature was −33°C, which is exceedingly cold. With our normal UK winter gear we were ill equipped for such extremes. Worse was to come the next day when we found that one of the engines needed a new part and we would have to stay another two days in the big chill. We left Greenland for Goose Bay and Montreal and arrived with no more trouble. By now it was the day before Christmas Eve and we were anxious to get home for Christmas. We managed to get seats on a Super Constellation carrying Canadian service personnel families to Europe, via Heathrow, to join their men-folk.

Things carried on steadily during the first part of 1958 until the Valiants started to arrive for various trials and modifications. My first flight in this new type was on 12th October, in WZ 379 with Leslie Worsdell. I was deeply impressed by it; the power was amazing, made all the more noticeable because of the low weights at which we were flying. During the later part of that year, and in to 1959, we flew an Auster around the country to take photographs of crop and geological markings and anything of potential historical interest. Our passenger was Dr St Joseph of Cambridge University plus suitable cameras. It was a sometimes interesting but usually monotonous job. On 20th June 1959 I flew an uncomfortable eight hours in the Auster followed two days later with six and a half hours.

Summers were always busy and August 1958 was no exception. I completed nearly seventy-three hours instructing as well as other flying in a Valiant, Canberra and Rapide. In September we frequently used the Rapide to fly American specialists to the Thor ballistic-missile rocket sites in Lincolnshire and south Yorkshire.

Fifteen years after the end of World War Two I made my first flight in a Dakota, G-AMZZ. The Dak had some new radio equipment fitted that had to be tested in flight, and it made a pleasant change to bumble around the countryside in the DC-3. An additional instructing task came my way in that I became involved in giving flying instructor courses using the Tiger Moth. Life at Cambridge was rarely quiet.

In order to maintain our approvals to fly RAF aircraft we had to remain current in instrument flying in jet aircraft. To do this we went to Boscombe Down, which involved an early morning drive down, a practice flight in the Meteor, then, the instrument-rating test, followed by the drive home. At the end of 1960 I was again needed by Vickers to crew a Viscount, this time from Washington DC, USA, to Rome. We routed through Montreal, Goose Bay, Keflavik, Prestwick and Wisley. The aircraft behaved itself and everything went according to plan.

As well as the PA-23 Apache the Company had acquired an Aztec, a more powerful and slightly larger version of the Apache. It was needed

because of the increase in the number of contracts within the UK and
Europe. The Company by now had ten or more pilots, but not all of them
were qualified to fly the faster aircraft. They carried out sterling work on
the civil aircraft side.

In January 1962 four of us took Valiant WP 209 to Bedford for some
flight trials with pre-gassed fuel. Before flowing into the aircraft the fuel
was apparently mixed with nitrogen under pressure. The theory was that the
gas would be released as the fuel was used; it would then fill the airspace
with nitrogen so lessening the danger of fire in case of battle damage. The
year continued with no great excitement but I did fly three new types. First
was the MA 4 research aircraft for laminar flow trials under the auspices of
Cambridge University. We carried a PhD student or observer to take
readings from scores of manometer tubes. The upper surface of the wing
was tufted to make the airflow visible, and the tufts were photographed
from above and behind by a photographer carried in a Tiger Moth. Next
was a Tipsy Nipper – a tiny single-seater with a tricycle undercarriage and
a low-powered Volkswagen engine. It was fully aerobatic but the fuselage
was very narrow. Because the wing was at shoulder height my elbows had
to fit into the wing roots. It was most uncomfortable, unlike the third new
type – the Queenair. That aircraft was an up-market executive machine well
fitted out and capable of carrying six passengers in comfort. During that
year, in a private capacity, I also made several flights in the Wallis
autogyro.

1966 was marred by the sad and unexplained loss of the MA 4 along
with the pilot, Brian Wass, and his observer. An unusual trial came along in
the shape of a Dakota, XA 114, modified for the German Air Force. It had
a large wind-driven electric generator in the nose, intended to provide
power for a mass of radar in the fuselage. The generator made the Dak look
like a tri-motor.

The Company had recently won a contract to paint and undertake the
recurrent major engineering of the sixty-six C-130 Hercules transport
aircraft ordered for the RAF. In the autumn of 1966 I accompanied Leslie
Worsdell to Sewart Air Force Base in the USA to take the ground school
part of the conversion course on to the aircraft. The course was typically
American, intensive and well organised, and we were well looked after.
Although we did not fly the Hercules we were able to sample a simulator
for the first time. What an eye-opener that was after the Link trainer. On our
return to the UK we set off for Boscombe Down to join seven or eight other
'newcomers' on the flight deck of the first Hercules to be delivered to the
RAF: XV 177. After about two and half-hours of getting to grips with the
new machine Leslie Worsdell and I were signed-off as captains. We then
returned to Cambridge to await the test flight of the first Marshall-
completed aircraft. That milestone came along at the backend of April 1967
in XV 179. The three-hour flight, with Bob Smythe along for his first go at
the controls, consisted of operating all aircraft systems in flight, stalling,

cruise and climb performance and general appraisal. All future air tests, unless there was a specific additional requirement, followed the same schedule. Since there were going to be another sixty-five airframes to test, plus the steady flow of Canberras and other types, there would be few idle days ahead.

The same mix of aircraft for testing continued until 1972, during which year the Company acquired a new Kingair C90, G-BAAM, a twin-turbine powered executive aircraft. It was a great advance on the Queenair and a joy to fly. By October 1973 I had not flown a Canberra for a couple of years, so I had to hotfoot it to Boscombe Down to revalidate my clearance to fly. After two flights in WJ 867 with Sqn Ldr Vickers I was able to maintain my Canberra skills when WE 188 needed five, and WJ 630 six, flights to complete their test programmes. With all-out support from BAC Warton, Arthur Marshall had flown to Peru to negotiate an order for six, later increased to eleven, Canberras. Marshall purchased and refurbished redundant ex-RAF B (I) 8s. Redesignated as B (I) 68, the first aircraft did not appear until three days before Christmas 1974. My two flights in G52-2 (a temporary Marshall registration) were the Company's only test flights that month.

ENGLISH ELECTRIC CANBERRA B (I) 8. Two-seat light bomber. Two 7,500lb thrust Rolls-Royce Avon 109 jet engines. Span 64 feet. Length 65 feet 6 inches. Maximum loaded weight 56,250lb. Maximum speed 560mph at 40,000 feet. Service ceiling 48,000 feet. Maximum range 3,600 miles. Four 20mm guns in a gun pack below the fuselage. It could carry tactical nuclear weapons, iron bombs and rockets under-wing, or two 1,000lb bombs internally. First entered RAF service with 88 Sqn in Germany in 1956.

1975 came in with a rush. I had been nominated as the project test pilot for the Peruvian contract and I worked under the supervision of the flight test department of BAC at Warton, near Blackpool. We already had a good relationship with BAC and rarely needed to call on their expertise. Flight-testing went well with just the occasional aerodynamic problem, such as correlating the airspeed indicator and Machmeter readings. This was solved by an alteration to the static plate, which was positioned on the forward side of the fuselage near the nose. Even a very small area of unevenness on the plate could cause instrument under- or over-reading. The problem usually manifested itself at the high-speed end of flight, when we were trying to fly at the highest Mach number. I felt very sorry for the flight observer, usually Dave Ryding, who was trying to write down the figures I was giving him while the aircraft was vibrating madly as I tried to reach .84 Mach. Sometimes an aircraft would not fly laterally level. We generally cured this rolling problem by adjusting the central linkages or tabs but sometimes we had to change the rudder to arrive at a solution. Even that was easier said than done. The Company had acquired a 'basket' of spares but they did not necessarily match individual aircraft. Short Brothers & Harland of Belfast had built some airframes and BAC the others, so there could be small differences between them. We usually managed to get the machines ready for delivery in about ten flights, although one aircraft, G52-5, because of the out-of-trim problems, took thirty-nine.

After each aircraft was passed 'off test', a Peruvian Air Force officer came over and flew with me to accept the aircraft. The Peruvian pilots could not operate the flying controls because the seating configuration required them to occupy the navigator's seat low down in the nose. However, they appeared to be quite happy with my demonstrations and always gave the all clear for delivery. I made the delivery flights with the assistance of a BAC navigator.

We planned to do one leg per day, generally of about four hours airborne time, but in order to keep to schedule on two occasions we managed two legs totalling about seven hours flying. This was very tiring, as we had to do our own pre- and after-flight inspections, refuelling and replenishment of the oxygen system, which was not always straightforward or easy. However, it was an exciting experience, especially when we got a grandstand view of the magnificent snow-capped Andes Mountains. Arriving in Lima on the day that had been planned up to ten days before gave me a big lift and a great deal of satisfaction. To take advantage of the best weather, and mainly to avoid icing conditions, we flew via Shannon, Gander and Jamaica in summer and via Morocco, Dakar (Senegal), Recife (Brazil) and Caracas (Venezuela) in winter. I shall always remember my fifty-ninth birthday, during which I was flying at 40,000 feet across the South Atlantic strapped to a Canberra, waiting expectantly to catch that first, re-assuring glimpse of South America. On another occasion I had to resort to telling a white lie to allow us to continue at the best altitude. We were happily cruising at 40,000 feet when the local air traffic control unit asked us to descend to 20,000 feet. I knew that if we did so the fuel consumption would rise and we would probably not make it to Lima. Knowing that we could not be intercepted by any of the local fighter aircraft I waited for a few minutes, acknowledged that we were now at the lower altitude, and continued to fly at 40,000 feet. It was naughty but necessary.

By the end of January 1976 we had completed and delivered the first eight Canberras, thus ending another busy year, having carried out the entire test flying and delivery in addition to all our other varied flying tasks. It was another eighteen months before the final three Peruvian Canberras were modified, test flown and delivered. The whole programme went well and except for one hydraulic pump failure there were no mechanical or engineering faults. The credit for this must go to the quality of workmanship and attention to detail of the Marshall work force, plus help given by the BAC pilots and navigators.

I continued to fly the wide mix of aircraft at Cambridge until I reached sixty, when the MOD decree banned me from flying RAF Hercules as captain, although I could still act as co-pilot. This did not worry me too much because another challenge had come my way in the shape of the Short Belfast.

The Company, at the end of August 1979, secured a contract to engineer the Belfast in order to comply with the British Civil Airworthiness Requirements so that a cargo company called HeavyLift, which had purchased five of these large and capacious aircraft, could operate them on the civilian register. We were contracted to modify three of them to comply with civil requirements. With the help of the aircrew of HeavyLift, most of who had operated the Belfast in the RAF, I quickly converted to the aircraft. It reminded me in some ways of the Short Stirling that I had flown thirty-five years previously.

SHORT BELFAST C1. Long-range heavy transport. Crew of three or four. Four Rolls-Royce Tyne R Ty 12 Mk 101 turbo-prop engines. Span 158 feet 9 inches. Length 136 feet 6 inches. Maximum loaded weight (civil) 230,000lb. Payload of 22,000lb for 3,600 miles; 77,500lb payload for 1,000 miles. Maximum cruising airspeed at 28,000 feet 345mph. Economical cruising airspeed 315mph. First flight 5th January 1964 from Belfast Sydenham aerodrome. Ten aircraft served with 53 Sqn from January 1966 to September 1976, when they were retired through defence-spending cuts. For civil use Marshall fitted a new suite of avionics, including two Omega navigation aids linked to the flight system and autopilot. The certification programme involved a slight weight reduction, removal of 'military only' items and a stall warning and automatic 'stick-pusher' to assist with recovery from a stall. By early February 1982 the stick pusher trials were judged to be satisfactory: 'Not particularly abrupt but the push is readily identifiable.'

The Belfast was a stable and stately aircraft to fly, although it would really have benefited from more powerful engines. Power-off stalls were quite gentle. It suffered, as did some other turbo-prop engined aircraft of the period, in having a vicious power-on stall. During power-on stall trials in the 1960s, before acceptance by the RAF, it had flipped over on to its back. The CAA ordained that the aircraft should have a stall protection system and that became our major task, which required between three and four hundred stalls to be made at weights of, approximately, 165,000lb, 185,000lb and 230,000lb. In addition we had to make sure that it met the other civilian flight behaviour requirements, so a full flight test programme, except the 'hot and high' case, had to be carried out.

Two or three incidents come to mind when reflecting on the tests. Firstly, we had to adjust the centre of gravity position in flight. We did this by moving some of the 25-kilogram bags of shingle from one pre-determined position in the hold to another – by hand. The penalty for this was that, while carrying out negative-g tests, some of the roller tracking bolted to the floor came adrift with a loud bang, and punctured the fuse-lage in several places. It brought back memories of wartime events in the Short Stirling.

On one flight we were making three-engine climbs out of Bedford, starting at about five hundred feet above ground level with one engine feathered. Like most performance climbs the duration was scheduled for five minutes. Just before that time was up, during which we had flown about fifteen miles, Bedford ATC called us to ask if we were okay. On asking why, they said that they had lost sight of us below the horizon, such was the low rate of climb. Fortunately everything was in order and two of the aircraft are still in service with HeavyLift at the time of writing.

My last flight in the Belfast was on 12th March 1982. With only two years to go to my sixty-fifth birthday, my test flying was almost over. I did, however, manage to make three flights in a Cessna Titan, G-OEMA. The task was to fly the approach at a slightly lower airspeed than normal, touch down at the very beginning of the runway and immediately and firmly apply the brakes. Hopefully, this technique would reduce the landing run sufficiently to allow the aircraft to land legally at one particular, quite short, runway. Results were judged to be satisfactory and the green light was given to the aircraft to operate from the target runway.

I saw out the remainder of my time flying in the Company Aztec and Citation aircraft and, as always, instructing on the Cessna 152s, through which I had met and made friends with many grand people.

Chapter 5

The Not Forgotten Ones

BY DENNIS PASCO

PETER ELSE

It was in early 1977 at Marshall's when I first met Peter. I did not know then that he had been a pilot, yet before I was three years old he must have flown over my house in Kent on many occasions. Whenever I was foolish enough to make a less than accurate statement about the serviceability of one of Peter's aircraft, he would say nothing, give me that knowing look and grunt. I knew then that I needed to go away, check my facts, and come back later.

Born in Newmarket in February 1917, Peter, whose father was a motor mechanic, was educated in the town. After leaving school he worked for Ortona, the local omnibus company, but his mind was set on working with aircraft. On 14th January 1935 he became the first engineer apprentice at Marshall's Flying School. At about the time that the new Marshall aerodrome opened Peter met his future wife, Diana. They married soon after he was called up and on 23rd February 1938 he joined the RAFVR and became a Sergeant U/T (under training) pilot the next day. His basic flying training was with 22 E & RFTS at Cambridge. The FTS operated a number of different types: the Hind, Audax, Hart, Tiger Moth and Fairey Battle. Using kits supplied by Fairey, Marshall had modified the Battles to turn them into dual trainers. On the outbreak of war, the RAF sent Peter to 6 FTS at Little Rissington, Gloucestershire, for advanced training. He had no ambition to go to war in the Battle. His wish came true. Successfully completing the Rissington course, Peter headed north to join 72 Sqn in the Vale of York at the recently completed Church Fenton. There, he initially flew the Battle, Magister and Harvard, but soon converted to the Spitfire I. By June 1940, with over three hundred flying hours to his credit, the RAF had sent him south again. His new station was the grass airfield of Gravesend, Kent, where he was attached to 610 (County of Chester) Auxiliary Air Force Sqn. (The auxiliary squadrons were granted the prefix Royal in December 1947).

Not for the only time in her history Britain was virtually alone, facing the threat of invasion from an enemy across the Channel. German armed forces had invaded Belgium and established an Air HQ in Brussels. It was there that Generalfeldmarschall 'Smiling Albert' Kesselring, presided as commander of Luftflotte (Air Fleet) 2. Luftflotte 3, to the south, had its HQ in Paris. These two air fleets, plus the bomber element of Luftflotte 5 in Norway, were gathering their strength to launch the Battle of Britain as a precursor to operation 'Sealion,' the invasion of England.

Reichsmarschall Herman Goering, C-in-C of the Luftwaffe, was leading a self-indulgent and flamboyant life style at Karinhall, his country estate in Prussia. Facing the rampant German eagle was Fighter Command, led by Air Chief Marshal Sir Hugh Dowding, a most determined and focussed man.

During the thick of the Battle of Britain, Peter was frequently hopping between Gravesend, Hawkinge – a forward base just north of Folkestone – and Biggin Hill, which lies about sixteen miles north of Gatwick airport. The second phase of the Battle of Britain ran from 8th to 23rd August. In this period the Luftwaffe continued its assault on RAF airfields and also attacked the radar chain. August 15th – a day of fine weather – turned out to be the heaviest day for fighting so far. Fighter Command launched nearly 1,000 sorties. Combined British and German losses amounted to over one hundred aircraft.

On 20th August in Spitfire Mk1, P9496 (Sqn letters DW-L), having first flown from Biggin to Hawkinge, Peter patrolled the Dover area and landed back at Biggin after an eighty-minute flight. The weather was cloudy and windy, turning to rain. Airborne for the third time he landed at Hawkinge after fifty-five minutes. The next day in a different Spitfire, X4011, Peter made four flights, landing at a different airfield after each sortie. His final flight that day was the twenty miles between Gravesend and Biggin, which took only ten minutes, flown in the dark. Although Peter was having a busy time there was a lull in air activity from 20th to 23rd August due to a spell of poor weather. The third and most critical phase of the Battle ran from 24th August until 6th September.

On Sunday 25th August, just one month after he had destroyed a Messerschmitt 109 off Folkestone, Peter took his faithful P9496 the fifty miles to Hawkinge and then flew it back again. The day started fine but turned cloudy, and the Germans launched a huge raid against targets along the south coast during the afternoon. In the evening another heavy raid approached Dover but 11 Group's fighters repulsed them. In retaliation for a German raid on London eighty-one RAF aircraft bombed Berlin that night.

At first light on 26th August German reconnaissance aircraft were active across southern England, gathering information to assist their commanders to finalise plans. The day started quietly for Peter with a twenty-five minute hop to Hawkinge. The Germans, however, launched another big raid that seemed to be targeting Biggin Hill. Before long Peter was airborne on patrol, landing back at the forward base within the hour. Having had an early start to the day, he probably had visions of a breather and a bite of lunch. However, the order to scramble came too soon and Peter was airborne again in P9496, just before noon, climbing rapidly east over the English Channel to intercept an incoming German raid. After penetrating a layer of cloud Peter spotted the enemy and immediately launched into the attack. He manoeuvred himself on to the tail of a Messerschmitt 109 and pumped a burst of machine-gun fire into it. A shout from a fellow Spitfire pilot warned him of an enemy fighter on his own tail but the call was a fraction too late. Peter felt his Spitfire receive a hit and saw the instrument panel disappear in a sea of flames. He turned the Spitfire upside down in order to bale out but another burst of enemy fire hit his left arm, leaving it shattered. The enemy shells also splintered and shut the Spitfire's hood. Peter was unable to recall exactly how he left his mortally damaged Spitfire, but escape he did. At more than three miles above the English Channel, he tumbled over and over, heading for the cloud below. With his left arm useless, Peter used his right hand to beat at his parachute pack fearing that it was smouldering. His right arm then became trapped in the parachute harness so that he could not reach the ripcord to release the parachute. If ever there was a time to pray this was it. Peter prayed and the parachute opened. At this stage he was still above cloud. On breaking cloud he located himself about ten miles southwest of Dungeness, drifting with the wind towards the English coast. By good fortune the wind floated Peter across Folkestone and deposited him with a thump on to the airfield of Hawkinge, just two hundred yards from his take-off point not that many minutes earlier. At the Kent and County hospital, in Canterbury, surgeons removed most of his left arm.

Two years after Peter's involuntary departure from 610 Sqn the Marshall connection with that unit continued. Johnnie Johnson took command of 610 and led it in to battle as top cover for the raid on Dieppe in August 1942.

Gravesend airfield now lies underneath a housing estate. A plaque on a nearby sports centre commemorates the wartime activities of the airfield. Hawkinge is home to a Battle of Britain display of replica RAF and Luftwaffe aircraft.

SUPERMARINE SPITFIRE 1. Single-seat fighter. One 1,175HP Rolls-Royce Merlin XII engine. Span 37 feet. Length 30 feet. Loaded weight 6,275lb. Maximum airspeed at 19,000 feet 355mph. Climb to 20,000 feet seven minutes. The Mk1 was initially fitted with eight .303in calibre Browning machine-guns; some Mk1s later had two Hispano cannon fitted. Some 20,400 Spitfires of twenty-two different marks were built. The final, Griffon-powered, Spitfire, a Mk 24, came off the South Marston production line in February 1948. The Hong Kong Auxiliary Air Force flew Mk 24s, which had a maximum permissible weight of 12,150lb, until April 1955.

Peter then spent some time at Halton, from where he was discharged from the RAF and rejoined Marshall as an inspector on 15th April 1941. He became the deputy Chief Ground Engineer in March 1943, and, with the assistance of a special add-on left arm made by his fellow workers, was able to return to flying. He used his skills to test fly aircraft like the Tiger

Moth, Falcon and Auster. In the Auster, Peter flew from the right-hand seat. The sole task of the person in the left-hand seat was to operate the flap lever, which was located high on the left-hand side of the cockpit. Peter ceased flying in October 1946.

It was about that time that Leslie Worsdell test flew a Spitfire that was the first private-owner conversion of the famous wartime fighter. The Spitfire, a Mk IIB P-8727, was registered G-AHZI and had been flown into Cambridge by its owner, M L Bramson, at the end of July 1946. The military-only items were removed and some ballast was added to compensate. The civilianised Spitfire was expected to fly in the cruise at just over 200mph, returning a fuel consumption of about thirty gallons an hour from the 86-gallon fuel tank. Named Josephine, the aircraft crashed on take-off from Kastrup, Copenhagen, in April 1947.

During the filming of the Battle of Britain Peter climbed into the cockpit of a Messerschmitt 109 for the first time. The hood of that machine was rather heavy and difficult to close. Peter got one finger of his right hand trapped by the hood. 'Look at that' he said to a colleague, 'after twenty-eight years they're still having a go at me.' In May 1974 Peter became Marshall's chief engineer of light aircraft. For services to the RAF, Cambridge UAS and the Air Training Corps Air Experience Flight (AEF), Peter was awarded the Queen's Silver Jubilee Medal in 1977. Aged seventy, he retired in April 1987, having served fifty-two years with the Company. Peter enjoyed four years of retirement before he died on 19th April 1991.

PETER MAY

Before coming to Cambridge Peter May had been a top-grade A1-flying instructor in the RAF and a member of the renowned Hendon Display Team – the Red Arrows of the day. Having just completed his RAF service, he signed up for a one-year contract to instruct flight trainees of the Chinese Air Force. That contract was not due to start for a few months, so in May 1934 Arthur Marshall engaged him as a temporary flying instructor. At the end of a busy summer he travelled to China, where he was granted the rank of Colonel by the Chinese. During his year in China Peter also instructed budding pilots in the art of gliding. That was to have unforeseen consequences some eight years later. Peter rejoined the Cambridge Aero Club at the end of summer 1935.

At Cambridge Peter usually wore plus fours and favoured a very long non-uniform coat. Full of fun and bright ideas, he greatly enjoyed parties, at which he would often play the washboard. Indeed, had he not opted for a flying career it was more than likely that he would have gone on the stage. He enthusiastically supported Arthur Marshall in his move to train his own instructors. Peter was a disciplinarian, enterprising and popular with students. If he discovered oil on a doorknob he would direct a loud shout of 'Twit' at the offending mechanic.

In 1938 Marshall started up 22 E & RFTS and Peter was appointed the new Chief RAFVR Flying Instructor. The following year he was awarded the Air Force Cross for services to RAF flying training. On 27th August 1939 the government grounded all civil aircraft. This meant that on 2nd September, Rosemary Marshall and Doreen May, Peter's wife, had to drive Arthur and Peter the one hundred and thirty or so miles to Shawbury to collect the first Whitley bomber for the recently awarded servicing and up-dating contract. At eleven o'clock the following morning the Prime Minister announced to an expectant nation that Great Britain was now at war with Germany.

On 1st January 1940 all EFTS flying instructors, with the exception of Chief Flying Instructors, were mobilised as sergeant pilots. Peter became OC of the EFTS in the rank of Wing Commander, but remained on the Company payroll. He assisted Arthur Marshall with test flying Gladiators that had flown in from France with ammunition still loaded in their guns. The aircraft were not worked on until armourers from 54 Maintenance Unit arrived and disarmed them. After a Heinkel 111 bomber overflew Cambridge aerodrome, Peter persuaded Arthur Marshall that, if necessary, the two of them could get airborne in the armed Gladiators to patrol and take on the Germans. The idea was that they could take to the air to protect the airfield – to encourage workers to work on during the air raid warning period. This deterrent was activated three times in August 1940. In the absence of radios the signal to land was to watch for the local buses to start moving again.

GLOSTER GLADIATOR. Single-seat fighter. One 840HP Bristol Mercury engine. Span 32 feet 3 inches. Length 27 feet 6 inches. Loaded weight 4,750lb. Maximum airspeed at 14,500 feet 253mph. Later models were armed with four Browning machine-guns. It was the last of the RAF's biplane fighters and entered service with 72 Sqn in February 1937. It featured in the Battle of Britain but served mainly overseas where three examples became famous as 'Faith', 'Hope' and 'Charity' – defenders of Malta.

Other visitors received a more enthusiastic welcome. Spitfires from Duxford, usually late on a Wednesday afternoon, would fly over and beat-up Cambridge aerodrome at low level. They would arrive in formation, then split up for individual low passes before forming up to return to Duxford. Not letting the Spitfires have all the fun Peter would often give a very polished aerobatics display over the aerodrome on completion of an air test. With Tap Tappin aboard, he came close to flying a Boulton Paul Defiant night-fighter. Unfortunately an unserviceable magneto put the kibosh on that flight.

In December 1941 the Japanese attacked Pearl Harbor, Malaya and Hong Kong. That month, because of his gliding experience, Peter was posted to Brize Norton to help manage the rapid training of glider pilots. During 1942 the Heavy Glider Conversion Unit formed at Brize to teach Army pilots how to handle the Horsa glider. A hefty machine, the Horsa was not the easiest of aircraft to master. There were frequent accidents and night flying was a real challenge. Peter was a great success and got his students quickly on to night flying. On 26th October 1942 Peter arrived at Netheravon to take command of 296 Sqn. Who better to take over a squadron with the motto Prepared for all Things? The following day the squadron moved to Andover. Equipped with the Whitley the squadron had been engaged in glider towing since June. On 30th October Peter flew his first mission to drop pamphlets on Paris. Despite the low ebb of British fortunes that year, action was well under way to create an invasion force of parachute-dropping and glider-towing aircraft. The Armstrong Whitworth Albemarle was earmarked for both roles. On 27th January 1943 Peter brought the first one in from Netheravon to start the squadron changeover to the new machine.

ARMSTRONG WHITWORTH AW 41 ALBEMARLE. Designed as a bomber, the Albemarle was modified to become a transport and glider tug. Crew of four. Two 1,590HP Bristol Hercules XI engines. Span 77 feet. Length 60 feet. Loaded take-off weight 36,500lb. Maximum airspeed at 10,000 feet 265mph. Recommended cruising speed in RAF service 145mph. In addition to the invasion of Sicily, the Albemarle took part in the Normandy and Arnhem operations in 1944.

The first two Albemarles to make an operational sortie headed out across the Channel on the night of 9th February. One, heading for Lisieux, turned back with technical problems. In the other one, P1446, Peter dropped the latest edition of pamphlets onto the citizens of Rouen. Ten days later, in the same airframe, Peter was en route to drop a more explosive load. He was unable to locate the target and had to turn back. In early April, with a party of squadron aircrew, Peter enjoyed a short break from the rigours of training when he was presented to King George VI at Netheravon. On 13th April, again in P1446, judgement and good luck at last combined for Peter. With his right hand poised on the bomb release switch at the bottom of the throttle quadrant, he waited for the executive word from the bomb aimer. It came, and he unleashed his first load of bombs onto Europe. The target was Conde sur Huisne.

June 1943 was the wettest for many years in England. It also saw Peter make an experimental tow of an American glider, the Waco CG-14A, known to the British as the Hadrian. That same month a Dakota, in twenty-eight flying hours, towed a Hadrian across the Atlantic from Montreal to Britain.

In May the Combined Chiefs of Staff had agreed on the final plan for the invasion of Sicily. Attention was now turning towards the

Mediterranean. No 296 Sqn, along with 295, started its move to the Mediterranean theatre by deploying to Froha, in Algeria. From there on 20th June, during Exercise 'Eve', Peter led twenty-two aircraft to Thiersville, each of them towing a Waco glider. Four days later he led his squadron to the advanced base of Gourine II, in the Kairouan area of Tunisia.

The Supreme Commander of the allied forces was General Eisenhower. His air forces included 600 first-line aircraft on Malta alone, a far cry from 23rd April 1942 when the Governor of that cruelly besieged island reported that its serviceable fighters numbered just six. Facing the allies were the forces of Italy and Germany, under the C-in-C Mediterranean, Field Marshal Kesselring.

The invasion of Sicily was set for the second week in July, to take advantage of a favourable moon. It began with an experiment, in that this was the first time in history that a self-contained unit, complete with engineers, anti-tank artillery and ammunition was to be committed to battle from an airborne assault. The British First Air Landing Brigade would be dropped in the sector of the 8th Army, and the 82nd (US) Airborne Division in the American sector.

After dusk on Friday 9th July over one hundred American Dakota aircraft and thirty-five RAF Albemarle and Halifax aircraft, each towing a glider, took off for their drop zones. Peter May led the British aircraft, flying in his faithful P1446. The route took the RAF aircraft, flying at low level, around Malta then north to Cape Passero on Sicily. General Alexander, Eisenhower's deputy, was at Cape Delimara, the south-eastern point of Malta, to watch the airborne armada pass. One task for the British troops in their Horsa gliders was to capture the Ponte Grande viaduct, which lay between the British invasion beach and the enemy forces in Syracuse. The weather that day had taken a sudden turn for the worse. A storm swept across the allied naval armada and created near-impossible conditions for the aircrew. The wind, aloft and on the surface, was strong and gusting. Half the gliders were dropped onto the sea; few on board survived. Only twelve gliders, all British, landed anywhere near their targets. Peter had taken off from Gourine at 1925 hours. Having dropped what is believed to have been the first glider to land on Sicily, he landed back at Gourine at 0040. Fewer than a hundred men succeeded in capturing the Ponte Grande viaduct. Only two hundred and fifty Americans, out of a force of 3,000, landed in the right place. On the following Monday the *Daily Mail*, which then cost one old penny, reported that the first of the airborne troops had landed just after 2200 hours. Despite the inauspicious results further airborne assaults were scheduled.

The Americans launched their next airborne assault on 11th July, this time losing some twenty-five aircraft to 'friendly' fire from some of the 2,500 ships of the allied navies. On the night of 13/14th July the British mounted their second airborne assault on to the eastern side of Sicily.

Nearly 2,000 troops were dropped by parachute or glider. The targets included the vital Primosole Bridge near Catania. By a remarkable co-incidence the Germans had parachuted a machine-gun battalion into the same area just before the British arrived. Barely two hundred British troops reached the bridge. They overpowered the guard, removed the demolition charges and then defended against the German paratroops. About sixteen British aircraft were shot down in the assaults and fifty were damaged.

Originally scheduled for June, Operation Chestnut called for Special Air Service Regiment troops to be inserted behind enemy lines by submarine. Their task was to disrupt communications and cut the Catania to Messina railway line. Now rescheduled for the night of 13th July, the twenty troops were to be dropped from two RAF Albemarles. Peter May, again in P1446, led the two aircraft. Flt Lt Philip Smulian AFC, one of the first Marshall ab initio flying instructors, was captain of the second Albemarle. The two aircraft took off at about 1930 hours, flew successfully to the target area and dropped all their troops. Sadly, Peter's aircraft was shot down between Malta and Catania by 'friendly fire.' All on board were killed. The Americans awarded Peter their DFC for outstanding leadership. The experience gained by the allied forces in the invasion of Sicily went a long way to ensuring the success of the invasion of mainland Europe the following year.

LESLIE JOHN SCATCHARD

The host of spectators at the official opening of the new Cambridge aerodrome on 8th October 1938 were thrilled by the display put on by the pilots of 19 Sqn flying the RAF's newest fighter – the Spitfire Mk I. Blissfully unaware of the event, and its subsequent significance to his later life, Leslie Scatchard was performing south of Grimsby for just one spectator: Flt Lt Bradley, his RAF examiner. Having flown solo for the first time on 14th September, he was flying the same aircraft, a Miles Magister trainer, L8207 of 25 E & RFTS, for his second aviation milestone, the intermediate flying test. He passed, and his reward was a third sortie that day, his first ever instrument training flight.

MILES MAGISTER I. Two-seat elementary trainer. One 130HP DH Gipsy Major engine. Span 33 feet 9 inches. Length 24 feet 9 inches. Loaded weight 1,900lb. Maximum airspeed 132 mph at 1,000 feet.

Born in Grimsby on 27th January 1916, Leslie was educated there and was an early recruit to the local RAFVR training scheme based at Waltham, Grimsby Municipal Airport. On 11th February 1939 he reached ninety flying hours in the Magister, passed his second flight test and made his first flight in a Hawker Hind: L7207. The outbreak of war in September terminated Leslie's course. Still seven months away from the award of his flying badge, he moved to 3 EFTS at Hamble to fly the Avro Cadet on a Special Instructor's Course of thirty flying hours. The course lasted ten days. Despite the demands of the war and the clear need for more pilots, he spent the next four months at Hastings undergoing the rigours of basic service training at 3 Initial Training Wing.

In March 1940 a 'new' type beckoned – the Fairey Battle. No 12 Service FTS operated the trainer version at RAF Grantham (changed to Spitalgate in 1944). Leslie made his first flight there in P6627 on 9th March and, despite poor weather, made his first solo on type on 18th March. One of the many things he practised in the Battle and in the Link trainer was the ZZ approach. A civilian procedure, it was adopted by the RAF early in the war. On days when the pilot of a radio-equipped aircraft found himself returning to base above cloud he was given Direction Finding (D/F) assistance to locate the aerodrome. With the local barometric pressure set on the altimeter, he descended to a given height and, when heard overhead by a body in the watch office – the forerunner of ATC – the radio call 'Motors overhead' was made. The pilot then turned the aircraft away from the aerodrome. After a given time he reversed course and, with continued D/F assistance, descended to the minimum safe height as he headed towards the aerodrome. The ZZ signal indicated that altitude and course were correct. The QGH procedure – controlled descent through cloud – later replaced the ZZ approach. Of interest, the QGH became defunct in early 1999, with Cambridge being the last civil aerodrome in the country to offer it. On 5th May 1940, after seven landings under the guidance of Sgt Strause, Leslie carried out his first solo night flight, making four landings in Battle P6677. He was awarded his flying badge on 9th May.

As if to celebrate, the Germans launched their offensive in the West the following day. At 0545 on 11th May Luftwaffe bombers gave the RAF a fine exhibition of the use of tactical air power at the French airfield of Condé-Vraux. Twelve Dornier Do 17s swept across at low level, destroyed five Blenheim Mk IVs and rendered the remainder of 114 Sqn's bombers unserviceable in the ten-minute raid. It was to this unit that Leslie would eventually be posted.

Remaining at Grantham he continued with the advanced flying course. Formation flying, air-to-air work, air-to-ground gunnery and bombing training were practised with some urgency. On 4th June the Germans captured Dunkirk. Leslie, in Battle P6751, made his second solo night flight. The French surrendered to the Germans on 22nd June; at Grantham Leslie made his last flight of the course. With an 'above average' flying assessment he then moved to 17 OTU at Upwood, Cambridgeshire, to convert to the Blenheim bomber.

He made his first flight in a Blenheim, K7089, on 19th July, flew both the Mk I and IV versions and completed the course on 25th August 1940. With the Battle of Britain at its height, Leslie joined 114 Sqn at Oulton, near Blickling Hall, Norfolk, the recently opened satellite airfield of

Horsham St Faith (now Norwich Airport). His first operational flight was on 9th September during which his aircraft, N3617, received a few hits. Flying the same aircraft two days later, with Sgts Love and Parsons as crew, he took off at 2025 on a single-aircraft sortie to attack shipping off Flushing, in the Netherlands. At 2103 he dropped a stick of bombs from 4,500 feet and flew unscathed back to Oulton.

BRISTOL BLENHEIM Mk IV. Three-crew light bomber. Two 920HP Bristol Mercury XV engines. Span 56 feet 3 inches. Length 42 feet 9 inches. Loaded weight 14,400lb. Maximum airspeed 265mph at 11,000 feet. Armament five .303 machine-guns; 1,000lb bomb load internally and 320lb externally.

His fifth operational sortie came on 24th September. Six Blenheims of 114 Sqn took off from Oulton at 1213, coasted out over the still-familiar lighthouse at Southwold and headed south for the English Channel. Cheekily minesweeping within sight of observers in Dover was a gaggle of German 'R' boats. Spotting the five targets, the Blenheims jostled into position and unloaded eighteen 250lb and twelve 40lb bombs. No hits were observed. All six aircraft landed at 1400.

Leslie's last operational sortie in September was again in N3617, six hours to Wilhelmshaven and back. Another long flight kicked off October, a five and half-hour sortie to Narvik, in Norway. He made his first flight over Germany proper on the night of the 3rd, flying as co-pilot to Sgt Staples in Blenheim N3704, to Borkum. Three days later, back with his usual aircraft and crew, Leslie took off from Oulton at 1213 and headed straight for Den Helder, about forty-five miles north of Amsterdam. The crew failed to find their target – a ship – but located another one nearby. Despite some light tracer and shells from a 'pom-pom' gun, Leslie pressed home his attack, released a stick of 250lb bombs and had the satisfaction of seeing a direct hit on the ship's stern.

A raid against Ostend on 21st October, in N3617, turned out to be Leslie's last operational flight. Armistice Day 1940 saw him make his final two Blenheim flights, both of them being air tests to check the fuel system. Prescient flights indeed. On 14th January 1941, with 620 flying hours in his logbook, he was discharged from the RAF on medical grounds.

Shortly afterwards Leslie joined Marshall's Flying School as an armament instructor. It was not his first contact with Cambridge. Flying Magister N3790 on a solo navigation exercise, he had called in on 17th July 1939. As 1941 progressed so the number of RAF aircraft for repair at Cambridge increased. Peter May was less available for flight tests because of the ever-increasing number of pilots under training, so Arthur Marshall decided that a full-time test pilot was needed. The Chief Ground Instructor encouraged Leslie to apply for the position. After a test flight with Mr Marshall and an Air Ministry medical, he started in his new role on 12th

July, carrying out four air tests. That same day, after their surprise attack on the Soviet Union three weeks previously, the Germans dropped bombs on Moscow for the first time. On 18th July Leslie made his first flight in a Whitley, a Mk V, P4962. The month ended with nineteen air tests completed in nine days: five Oxfords, five Harts, four Gladiators, four Audaxes and one Whitley.

The pace continued through the next four months, with a rare 'away day' to Aston Down on 15th November to deliver a Whitley V, P5003, assisted by Cyril Cooper and Jack Burnett – an ex-heavy weight boxer. The Oxford was the most commonly tested aircraft. Test flights rarely exceeded thirty minutes from take-off to touchdown, but with pre- and post-flight activities the working day frequently stretched to twelve hours.

Oxfords and Whitleys dominated 1942, with a monthly average of tests exceeding forty-five. Even in winter, with poorer weather to contend with, the high rate continued. On some days Leslie flew as many as seven aircraft. Also during 1942 he married Jean, a cousin of Peter Else.

Leslie's New Year started briskly on 2nd January with one Whitley and five Oxford flights. In the hangars work started on Mosquitoes HJ 945 and 946, the first of ninety-eight Mk IIs for conversion to NF (Night Fighter) Mk XIIs. The pendulum of war now started a steady swing in favour of the Allies. The bomber version of the Mosquito struck Berlin for the first time on 30th January. On 11th February Leslie made his first two Mosquito flights, in HJ 946 and HK 110. When the Company had completed the airframe conversion, which included the removal of the four machine-guns and the fitting of a new nose, the first two aircraft went to the Royal Radar Establishment at Defford to have the still-secret radar – AI Mk 8 – fitted. (In 1944/45 Bob Smythe flew HK 110, and four other Mk XIIs tested by Leslie, in combat in Italy). By the end of February Leslie had flown ten different Mosquitoes and established a new monthly record of sixty-four tests. Good going for the shortest month of the year.

There was no let up through spring of 1943. The knowledge that some aircraft he had so recently tested were being put to good use was no doubt encouraging. While Leslie relaxed on the evening of 14th April, after four Oxford tests that day, crews of 85 Sqn, flying their Mk XII Mosquitoes, shot down two Dornier Do 17s in the vicinity of Colchester. May saw Leslie pass 1,000 flying hours and set a new record of eighty-five tests in one month. By now single-engined aircraft were rarities, with just the occasional Gladiator to break the dominance of the Oxford, Whitley and Mosquito. Leslie made the majority of flights on his own, although he normally took Cyril Cooper or Jack Burnett along in the Whitley. Occasionally he carried an Air Training Corps cadet for the experience, as on 21st May with Cadet Flight Sergeant Northfield. On 11th June, he tested two Mosquito XIIs, HK 190 and 199, accompanied by a Lieutenant Pitman and Sgt Nointy, both of the United States Army Air Force. These flights took his tally of Mk XIIs to fifty.

Marshall modified at least one Mosquito, a Mk XVIII, to carry a 57mm six-pounder Molins anti-tank gun, and fourteen B IVs to carry a Highball bouncing bomb (a smaller version of the dam-busting bomb). The war ended before the aircraft could be committed to operations.

Unfortunately records are not available for Leslie's post-July 1943 flying. He would certainly have flown most of the Mosquito NF MK XVII conversions from the Mk II and further conversions of Mosquito bombers to carry 4,000lb bombs. He added the Avro Anson, Dakota, Tiger Moth and Auster to his repertoire. The Albemarle was his least favourite aircraft. From March 1944 he enjoyed testing the fastest aircraft of them all, the Hawker Typhoon. From time to time he ended a flight with a spirited low pass just above (some would say between) the hangars before pulling up for a quick circuit and landing.

In early 1945 a local aviation enthusiast was watching a Typhoon approaching Cambridge to land. 'Good grief,' he thought, 'that looks a fast approach.' It was. The unknown pilot had been unable to throttle the engine fully back. He halted the heavyweight fighter-bomber just before the hedge on the far boundary. Marshall technicians wheeled it into a hangar for investigation. A screwdriver, loose in the engine compartment, had prevented the throttle from closing properly. Using this incident as a Flight Safety message, the Company posted a notice, typed in red ink, around the works. It said, forcefully, that anyone working on aircraft needed to own up and say something as soon as he was aware of a missing tool. The consequences of not doing so could be the loss of an aircraft and all on board.

It is likely that Leslie finished the war with some 2,200-flight tests to his credit – a magnificent achievement. In Sir Arthur Marshall's words, 'Leslie was a very good, hard working test pilot and nobody could have done better.'

With the war over, he retired from flying and moved to Grimsby. After a year spent unemployed he secured a job in the chemical industry with the Laporte Company; he died on 7th November 1995.

ROBERT SMYTHE

One of the highlights of my childhood was the ferry ride across the River Thames at Woolwich, outer London. The open engine-room with all the polished brass rods and knobs pounding noisily up and down produced a unique and unforgettable oily smell. Bob Smythe was born in Woolwich on 27th January 1922. His father had moved from Belfast for employment at the Woolwich Arsenal. By the time he was eighteen, Bob was no stranger to the punishing effects of the destructive weapons that could be released from the air.

Starting on 7th September 1940 Hitler's bombers unleashed the Blitz on London. For fifty-seven consecutive nights his Luftwaffe bombers rained a deadly mix of high explosives, incendiaries and parachute mines onto

England's capital. Bob helped out the defences by joining the air raid wardens as a messenger boy. By this time, he was into his second year of studies for the National Electric City and Guilds course. He terminated his studies in August 1941 and volunteered to join the RAF as aircrew.

Sent to the USA for pilot training, Bob's first flight lasted thirty minutes. It was in a Stearman PT17 trainer at the US Army Air Corps training school at Tuscaloosa, on 20th December 1941. There was no holiday for student pilots that Christmas and training continued apace. Bob achieved his first solo flight of three circuits on 8th January 1942. That year saw him serve at no fewer than eight different air bases, finishing up at Gunter Field in Alabama. After serving there for just seven months as a flying instructor, it was time to leave the USA to return to Europe. Another year passed before Bob completed the four courses that took him to his first operational squadron, 604, a Beaufighter night-fighter unit based at Scorton in Yorkshire.

Bob's nomadic life continued. Before 1944 was over, he had served on sixteen different units, each at a different location. He spent Christmas 1944 with 256 Sqn at Falconara, Italy. Converting to the Mosquito, Bob saw out the end of the war in Italy, remaining with the same Squadron. Not every sortie was without incident. Headquarters 232 Wing, RAF, in its write-up of 19th March 1945 included this report:

> 'Following daylight attacks by D.A.F. (Desert Air Force) Fighters, 256 Sqn went streaking across the waterways at dusk in search of prey. Two barges were located and shot-up by Flt Lt Smythe, who experienced intense light anti-aircraft fire at one point and his Mosquito was hit in two places, one cannon shell tearing a chunk from the leading edge of his wing, a second passing through the fuselage almost severing control cables. Despite this damage, Flt Lt Smythe flew the aircraft [a Mk IX, LR 461] safely back to base. Mosquito aircraft went off at dawn in search of road and river movement but returned without having had any joy. So ended a varied night.'

Four days later the same diary reported more activity and excitement:

> '47 aircraft took off in the continuing good weather on sorties covering the greater part of eastern Italy. Excitement was provided, however, by, and for, Flt Lt Smythe of 256 Sqn whose Mosquito was hit by light flak at Rovigo when he was doing a tight turn to attack a moving train. The hydraulic system was rendered useless and both tyres, it was afterwards discovered, were punctured. When in the circuit, the navigator pumped down the undercarriage after some energetic work, and still without a tailwheel, the pilot made a safe landing. The

shipping season seems to be with us again – a number of sightings were made, and after three attacks on four barges near Venice one of them disappeared and may be presumed sunk.'

DH MOSQUITO NF Mk XII. Two-seat night-fighter. Two 1,460HP Rolls-Royce Merlin 21 or 23 engines. Span 54 feet. Length 40 feet 6 inches. Loaded weight 18,440lb. Cruising speed at 30,000 feet was about 315mph. Service ceiling was 36,000 feet. Armament four 20mm cannon. The maximum possible fuel load was 547 gallons. With maximum useful load it had a range of over 600 miles. The first Mk XIIs entered service with 85 Sqn, commanded by Wing Commander 'Cats-eyes' Cunningham. Immediately after building the Mk XII Marshall converted another 99 Mk IIs to Mk XVII standard by fitting an AI Mk X radar. In 1949-50 Marshall conducted target-towing trials with a B35, VR 793, from Langham airfield in Norfolk. TT35s served with CAACUs until May 1963. There is an example of a TT35 at Duxford.

The war over, 256 Sqn moved to Egypt for six months, the longest stay anywhere to date for Bob. On his return to England a change of career took place. Pilots were ten a penny; engineering officers were not. Transferred to the engineer branch, Bob served at Leeming, Bentwaters and, finally, Farnborough. While at Leeming, the home of 228 OCU, Bob kept his hand in at flying. On 29th May 1947 Bob was airborne on a ferry flight in a Martinet I, PX 188. The Aircraft Safety Branch of HQ Fighter Command released the following statement after the flight:

'After flying for 25 minutes at 2,000 feet on a ferry flight the windscreen started to mist with oil. All pressures and temps were normal. Suddenly the oil leak became excessive, spraying the windscreen and blue smoke became apparent in the cockpit. The engine then commenced to vibrate. The pilot turned towards Worksop calling Sector Control informing them of his condition and intention to force-land. He cut the engine owing to the severe vibration and left the prop windmilling. The aerodrome was reached at 900 feet, the windscreen was then smothered with oil and visibility reduced to nil. In spite of this handicap Flt Lt Smythe made an excellent deadstick landing, wheels down, on the runway into wind and despite the additional hazard of many sheep on this disused airfield. The accident was caused by complete engine failure, which is the subject of a Court of Enquiry. It is considered that the pilot showed skill and coolness in carrying out a successful wheels-down landing under very difficult circumstances. He is awarded a Green Endorsement.'

MILES M-25 MARTINET. Target-tug. Crew of two: pilot & winch operator. One Bristol Mercury XX 870HP air-cooled radial engine. Span 39 feet. Length 31 feet. Loaded weight 6,600lb. Maximum level airspeed 230mph. Cruising speed 225mph at 4,500 feet. It was the first purpose-built target-tug for the RAF. In service from 1942 to 1954.

Bob returned to full-time flying in 1948 and attended 7 Course at the Empire Test Pilots School. After graduation, he stayed at Farnborough, becoming the head of his section in 1949. At Boscombe Down on 6th October 1950 he made the very first flight in the Boulton Paul P111 aircraft, VT 935.

BOULTON PAUL P111. Experimental aircraft built to investigate high-speed characteristics of delta-winged aircraft. One Rolls-Royce 5,100lb Nene jet engine. Span (pointed tips) 33 feet 6 inches. Length 26 feet. Loaded weight 9,600lb. Had detachable wing tips and fin and no tailplane. Maximum level airspeed Mach 0.98.

The following year, in recognition of his test flying activities, Bob was awarded the Air Force Cross. The following is an extract from the *London Gazette* of 7th June 1951:

'Sqn Ldr Smythe recently made the first flight in the Boulton Paul Delta (designated as the E27/46). This is, in fact, the first occasion on which a service pilot has been called upon to make the initial flight in a new aircraft. The Boulton Paul Delta (the P111) is a highly experimental aircraft of a tailless design. There were many uncertainties regarding its longitudinal and lateral control characteristics especially in the approach and landing condition. Sqn Ldr Smythe made the first flight on this aircraft with outstanding skill and courage. Throughout the flight, he kept up a continuous running commentary on the characteristics of the aircraft, giving a complete account of the take-off, climb and general handling qualities and of the approach and landing. In spite of carrying out the first landing of a tailless delta aircraft with unknown characteristics at an approach speed of over 170mph he made a perfect landing. Since then Sqn Ldr Smythe has made twelve more successful flights in this aircraft, maintaining the same high standards in all of them. Sqn Ldr Smythe has also done a considerable amount of high Mach number test flying in Aerodynamics Flight, particularly on advanced prototypes such as the Supermarine Swift and the Hawker 1052. On both these aircraft, he has undertaken a large part of the flying for

the determination of manoeuvre boundaries at high Mach
numbers. This work is both difficult and dangerous because of
the uncontrollable self-stalling characteristics of these aircraft
in turns or pullouts at high Mach numbers. This officer has
also taken a very active part in the investigation of wing
dropping characteristics at high Mach numbers. He has always
shown great determination in diving such aircraft as the Swift
and 1052 to Mach 0.94, at which speed these aircraft become
particularly uncontrollable. Previously he was responsible for
an important part of the high Mach number tests on the
DH108 in which a previous flight commander was killed.'

Soon after flying the P111 Bob was involved in testing such diverse new
types as the Westland Wyvern, the Armstrong Whitworth AW52, the Sea
Balliol, the Percival Prentice and the Scottish Aviation Pioneer. Not content
with powered flying, Bob loved gliding, at which he held the International
Silver C Gliding and Soaring Certificate. In 1950 he represented the RAF
at the UK National Championships.

Bob returned to the night-fighter world in January 1952 when he joined
68 Sqn at Wahn, Germany, as 'A' Flight Commander. Having flown the
Meteor NF 11 at Farnborough, Bob was now to use the aircraft in an
operational role at the height of the cold war. While at Wahn Bob met
Marjorie and they later married. Par for the course, Bob's tour at Wahn
lasted for two years. After a short stay in Trieste, a new direction beckoned
in 1954.

Bob travelled north, to Austria, to command the 2nd Tactical Air Force's
Escape and Evasion School at Ehrwald. He instructed on survival,
international law and skiing. In May of the following year Bob put his
current skills to good use and escaped back to England as OC 2 Meteor
(Night-Fighter) Sqn at North Luffenham. In 1958, thirteen years after he
last flew night-fighters in anger, Bob completed his final RAF flying tour.
A deskjob at the Air Ministry in London must have been anathema to him.
Anyone who knew Bob would have known that he would leap into any
available cockpit as if attached to it by elastic. He did manage to continue
flying and attained, in 1959, an exceptional pilot rating at the Air Ministry
Staff Officers Jet Refresher Course at Manby, Lincolnshire. After twenty
years in the RAF, Bob left to join Marshall of Cambridge at one of its
out-stations.

Located at Shawbury, Bob flew the Vampire and Jet Provost aircraft that
were used as live practice for the RAF's Air Traffic Controller courses. In
1966 he heard a whisper that another test pilot might be needed at
Cambridge. Quick as a flash he took himself southeast to 'Headquarters'
and presented himself to the Chief Pilot, Leslie Worsdell. Leslie told him
that if he acquired the necessary commercial licence he would be in with a
chance. Bob got the licence and the job. Marjorie and he packed their bags

and moved to Cambridge. The move came at about the time of the tragic death of Brian Wass in the MA 4.

His first test flight at Cambridge was in a Canberra PR7, captained by Doug Page, on 21st September 1966. Before long he was assisting with the test flying of Viscounts, Dakotas and the newly arrived Lockheed Hercules, in addition to instructional flying on the Cessna 150s of the Cambridge Aero Club. In due course Bob became the pilot who most often accompanied Sir Arthur Marshall on his flights in his Citation aircraft.

On 24th July 1979, with Bob as co-pilot, I made the last flight in Hercules XV 223 as a C Mk 1 at Cambridge before it left us to be stretched by Lockheed in the USA. The RAF had placed a contract to increase the length of thirty C Mk 1s by fifteen feet, which boosted the cargo compartment volume by 39% and upped the passenger numbers from ninety-two to one hundred and twenty-eight. To achieve the transition from Mk 1 to Mk 3 the fuselage was cut off ahead of and behind the wings. Two new sections were then grafted on, which required the re-making of a myriad of cables, wires and pipes. Marshall stretched the remaining twenty-nine Mk 1s over the next six years. Bob, with Doug Page as co-pilot, gave XV 223 an air test on 10th January 1980 before it was handed to the RAF for operational use. Never one to miss an opportunity to take part in a historical event, Bob captained the very first Company production C Mk 3, XV 197, on 7th August 1980. The aircraft was handed over to the RAF at a formal ceremony at Cambridge on 28th August. So good had the 'stretchers' become at their work that the thirtieth Mk 3, XV 299, needed only one air test before it too was formally handed over on 25th November 1985.

For a while Bob was Chief Test Pilot and he made his last flight as captain in a British military aircraft in Hercules C Mk1, XV211, on 25th January 1982. Before the month was over Bob captained Belfast G52-15 on six flights as part of its civilian certification flight-testing.

On his sixtieth birthday MOD, as standard practice, removed Bob's authority to fly as a captain of RAF aircraft. Being consigned to the right-hand seat was, for Bob, an indignity. As luck would have it an opportunity soon arose for one last Hercules flight as captain. Parked, dumped would have been more a more accurate word, on the far corner of Lagos airport, Nigeria, was a Nigerian Air Force Hercules, NAF 910. It had suffered a heavy landing in the late 1970s. Having won the contract to repair 910 the Company had the task of getting the grubby looking machine to Cambridge. The plan was for a small team of technicians, led by Keith Hogan, to proceed to Lagos and make 910 fit to fly. The Marshall aircrew would then fly down when the Hercules was a few days away from being declared serviceable. Since NAF 910 was not a British military aircraft, Bob declared himself captain for the Nigerian adventure. Mick Milne, the flight engineer, and I accompanied Bob on a Caledonian DC-10 flight from Gatwick to Lagos during the first week of February 1982.

The hotel in Lagos was supposedly top-notch. Heaven alone knows what a bottom-notch hotel would have been like. The electricity supply was unreliable, the water that occasionally dribbled out of the taps looked like Guinness but did not taste like it. The only edible food came from a nearby Chinese restaurant. Service was a word that did not apply to our temporary home. To be truthful, however, we were living in vastly better conditions than most of the indigenous population. The Pope visited Lagos while we were there, not to bless our mission, but to visit a major part of Nigeria. Bob, as always, had his camera at the ready and got very close to His Eminence, setting up some wonderful photographs. Unfortunately he never got to see them. Big enough to make most people think twice was a gun toting 'heavy' who stepped lightly on Bob's right foot. 'Your camera, Sir.' Such a pleasant request even Bob could not refuse. He somehow managed a smile as another man-mountain emptied the undeveloped film onto the tarmac. We sloped off, silently chanting the Lord's Prayer.

Within a few days of our arrival the technicians boldly announced that the first flight was imminent. ATC was, as expected, somewhat more relaxed than we were used to. Importantly though, NAF 910 had few defects but some important items could not be repaired on the spot. For example, the undercarriage had to be locked in the down position, which meant a slow flight home. The oxygen system was unserviceable, which restricted our altitude to 10,000 feet. A number of items of navigation equipment were unfixable. That did not matter too much since we were never going to be far from land. The ground crew had worked wonders in a very unfavourable environment. Completing the crew for the test flight on St Valentine's day were Ken Ashby and Ken Cousens, both of who were members of the servicing party. Soon it was time to set off for the journey home.

Before departure on 16th February 1982, we made a final check with the Nigerian Air Force that our flight up the West Coast of Africa had received diplomatic clearance from all the countries we were scheduled to fly across. We were assured that clearance had been given. Since there was no paperwork to support that statement Bob, no doubt harking back to his night-fighter days in Italy, decided that it would be advisable to route the flight well out to sea. 'Out of range of missiles' he said.

Staying below 10,000 feet we flew westwards. Benin, Nigeria's neighbour, immediately queried our presence when we opened up on their ATC frequency. 'NAF 910, we have no clearance for you. What is your detail?' 'Say again, we are hearing you only intermittently' I lied on VHF. More clues were dropping into place to indicate that the flight would not be plain sailing. Fortunately, we were in each country's airspace for only a short time. We bluffed our way past each of the nine states before heading into Dakar, Senegal, for a night stop and a refuel. It had dawned on us that a crew of civilians in another power's military aircraft might cause us, at best, to be interviewed. At worst, we might be interred in a less welcoming residence than our Lagos hotel. Surprisingly, Dakar ATC did not question our arrival. On leaving 910, however, we were all invited into the office of a senior official of the Interior Ministry. Politely, but firmly, he stated that our presence was unexpected. We were, he said, to leave the next day, advising us not to return.

The hotel at Dakar was wonderful. It was clean, the food was good, service was excellent and there was even a live band in the restaurant. What a shame we could not return for a second night. The next morning we set off northwards, noting that the man from the Ministry had watched our departure. On approaching the border with Morocco unwelcome news came our way. 'NAF 910, you do not have permission to enter our airspace. What are your intentions?' 'We'd like to fly through your airspace, without landing, to Cambridge, please. Marshall of Cambridge services some of your aircraft, including your Air Force.' 'NAF 910, your choices are to return to Dakar or divert to Las Palmas.' Since we would have been unwelcome at Dakar, and we carried insufficient fuel to head out to sea and make for England, Bob elected to fly to Las Palmas. The Spanish ATC raised no objections to our arrival. Ominously, however, several Spanish military vehicles, full of armed personnel, surrounded our Hercules as it came to rest in the parking area.

We were immediately arrested. Bob played a 'blinder' with the Spanish inquisitors. He produced heaps of evidence that we were a civilian crew flying an empty aircraft to England for repair. Sir Arthur Marshall, said Bob, not only serviced and repaired Spanish military aircraft, he was also a personal friend of the King. After more than an hour's grilling we were released. Greatly relieved, we later demolished a huge dish of paella and discussed the next expected hurdle: the French.

To our surprise the French raised not a single objection to our journey. The only hiccup was self-generated. The French kept asking us to report over places that I could not find on my ATC chart. After several such happenings I asked Bob to show me his chart, the one he had used to plan the route and submit the flight plan. The Franc dropped. Bob had used the high-level chart, and I was using the low-level one. The reporting places did not match; the French, however, continued to be amazingly kind and no harm was done. Mightily pleased with ourselves, and after a total transit time of sixteen hours, we delivered 910 to Cambridge on 18th February. Later on that same day, having just made it to my home, I was poleaxed by a late arrival of Lagos tummy. Also rumbling, in the South Atlantic, was another event that was shortly to affect the working routine at Cambridge.

With over 17,000 flying hours and two hundred different aircraft types in his logbooks, Bob retired from Marshall's in 1985 but continued to fly various Citation aircraft as a freelance pilot. He died unexpectedly on 12th December 1994. Sadly, none of the current Marshall test pilots was able to attend his funeral a few days later. However, carrying a crew to Lyneham in Bob's 'delightful honeybun', Citation G-BFRM, we did manage to fly over his funeral ceremony, the nearest we could get to a fitting farewell.

BRIAN OSCAR WASS

Had they been granted the opportunity to meet and talk about their professional lives, Brian Wass and Peter May would have discovered much in common. Brian had been interested in aircraft from an early age. Born in London just before Christmas 1926, he moved to Linton within a couple of years. Brian's father moved to Cambridgeshire to manage the Linton Whiting Works. Later on he became the joint owner and director of the Linton Haulage Company. At the outbreak of war he was employed as a government meat controller in the South Cambs area. He also served in the Royal Observer Corps. Keen on getting it right, he used to involve Brian and Barbara, his daughter, in aircraft spotting practice. Their task was to whip out a spotting-card, hold it for a few seconds and check their father's answer against the description on the reverse of the card. Brian's mother was of Irish descent, also from London. She was very supportive of her husband and her two children.

Brian's education started at the Linton Primary and Junior school. At the age of eleven he moved to Cambridge County High School for boys. In 1942, at the age of sixteen, he started work with Lloyds Bank, Sidney Street, in Cambridge, where he was always called Oscar. However, as a member of the Air Training Corps, Brian's ambition was to fly. After two years with Lloyds, he was called up and joined the Suffolk Regiment. This was not necessarily a good move for a budding aviator, but luck was on his side. Fortune shone and Brian was drafted to the Glider Pilot Regiment (GPR).

The GPR was formed in December 1941, just a few days before the Japanese attacked the American fleet at Pearl Harbor. Gliders for the Regiment, in the shape of the Hotspur and Horsa, had been ordered in 1940 and the Hengist and Hamilcar in the first half of 1941. The routine for GPR recruits was, firstly, basic training as a soldier. Basic flying training then followed. From 1943 onwards this started with eight weeks on the Tiger Moth at a RAF EFTS. After graduation the recruits then moved on to get to grips with their first glider, the General Aircraft Hotspur. Initially ordered as an assault glider, the Hotspur, with a maximum all-up weight of 3,600lb, became the standard Army glider trainer. Towards the end of the war a Miles Master was used to tow it airborne. Eight weeks were allotted for mastering the Hotspur. The next step was a big one for the successful ones: the Airspeed Horsa.

AIRSPEED HORSA. Crew of two pilots. Troop-carrying glider. Span 88 feet. Length 67 feet. Loaded weight 15,250lb. Gliding speed 100mph. The RAF's first operational glider, it first flew in 1941. 3,655 of the all-wooden aircraft were built. It could carry twenty to twenty-five troops. Its first operational use was in November 1942 when two Halifax aircraft towed two Horsas from Scotland to

*Norway for a raid on a German heavy-water plant. The Horsa was next used
operationally in the successful invasion of Sicily in July 1943.*

The conversion course lasted four weeks. Even larger, with a load capacity
up to 19,000lb, was the General Aircraft Hamilcar glider, big enough to
take a seven-ton tank. In late 1944 Marshall was contracted to install two
965HP Bristol Mercury 31 engines in the Hamilcar, turning it into the Mk
X. The first airframe arrived in August 1945. Destined for use in the Far
East, twenty had been produced by VJ day. It was never used operationally.
Before Brian had completed all his training the great airborne assaults of
Arnhem, in September 1944, and the largest air armada ever seen in history,
the crossing of the Rhine, were over.

Brian remained in the army until 1946, during which time the GPR was
virtually axed. By 1948 there were only two squadrons of Horsa gliders
left. One was based at Waterbeach and the other at Netheravon. Just one
squadron of the huge Hamilcar gliders remained, at Fairford. By then Brian
had transferred to the Royal Air Force.

In 1948, with Doug Silk, who also became a Marshall employee, he was
sent to 4 FTS at Heany, Rhodesia. They were both assigned to 8 Course.
Brian went to A Flight, reserved for those with previous flying experience.
The following year, events in the Far East forced a reversal of the rundown
of British and American armed forces. Mao Tse Tung had established a
Communist regime in China and the Soviet Union had exploded its first
A-bomb. The Cold War became increasingly dangerous.

In early 1950, having completed their flying training on Tiger Moths
and Harvards, Brian and Doug returned to England. They were posted to
Feltwell, Norfolk to undergo an acclimatisation course. The purpose of the
course, flying in the Harvard, was to familiarise pilots with the much
cloudier and colder conditions of England. From there Brian and Doug
moved north to 204 Advanced FTS at Driffield, Yorkshire, to fly the Meteor
T7. The training took from May to September. On Sunday 25th June 1950
the North Korean army invaded South Korea. The United Nations voted to
oppose the invasion and sixteen nations, including Great Britain, pledged
troops. As a direct result the RAF entered a period of rapid expansion. Pilot
training was expanded ten-fold and Fighter Command was set to double in
strength. Brian and Doug spent October and November at Stradishall,
Suffolk, flying with 226 OCU, which had an assortment of Spitfires,
Meteors and Vampires on strength.

On completion of the OCU Doug and Brian went their separate ways, to
join operational squadrons. Brian's hop was a short one, just thirty miles
west, to Linton-on-Ouse. There were four squadrons of Meteors at Linton:
64, 65, 66 and 92. Brian joined B flight of 92 (East India) Sqn, whose motto
was 'Fight or Die.' Its aircraft carried the squadron colours, a checkerboard
of yellow and red squares, on the tailplane. During 1951 both 64 and 65

moved to Duxford and 264 moved in from Coltishall. Rivalry between squadrons was intense. They vied with each to be the best gunners, the fastest airborne and the champions at aerobatics. Both 66 and 92 had a formation aerobatics team. Each year there was a formal competition. In 1952 both units were equally confident that they had the best team, with the other outfit being just a bunch of has-beens. From May 1952 the new OC, Sqn Ldr Jagger, led his six-ship team into the competition build up. Brian was a member of his team. In July the adjudicating officers came down on the side of 92 Sqn. There was great jubilation. It was perhaps at such a party that Brian, not particularly musically inclined, learned his party trick of imitating Al Jolson singing 'Mammy, how I love you, how I love you.' Sadly, not long afterwards, Sqn Ldr Jagger was killed in his Meteor 8 when it hit the ground during a solo aerobatics display.

GLOSTER METEOR F Mk 8. Single-seat interceptor fighter. Two Rolls-Royce Avon Derwent Series-8 turbojets of 3,500lb static thrust. Span 37 feet. Length 44 feet 6 inches. Maximum take-off weight, fully loaded with ventral and drop tanks 19,100lb. Maximum airspeed at sea level 590mph. Maximum rate of climb (clean aircraft) from sea level 7,000 fpm. Time to 30,000 feet (clean) 6.5 minutes. Armament four 20mm cannon. Developed from the Mk 4, it was Britain's pre-eminent fighter from 1950 to 1955. No 1 (F) Sqn was the first to be equipped, in December 1949. Served with 77 Sqn Royal Australian Air Force in the Korean War. Nearly 1,100 Mk 8s were built. Many were converted to unmanned target drones, designated U Mk 16. Ten Royal Auxiliary Air Force squadrons, including Pete Else's old unit, 610, were equipped with the Mk 8.

In July 1952 the entire Linton fighter wing was called upon to fly to West Raynham to demonstrate a wing-sized rapid take-off and landing. In front of an eagle-eyed audience all twenty-four Meteors got airborne in fifty-three seconds flat. The whole lot landed in just over three minutes from the first run-in and break. Formation flypasts were also part of a fighter squadron's repertoire. No 92 participated in the September Battle of Britain fly-past over London. During November 1953 the first two North American F-86 Sabre swept-wing fighters arrived at Linton to initiate the changeover from the outdated Meteors. Before the re-equipment was over, Brian had completed his five-year engagement with the RAF.

On leaving the RAF Brian's first objective was to qualify as a civilian pilot. He used his meagre resources to train for, and obtain, his civilian licence. By this time he was married and very hard up. Through sheer necessity he took a six months contract with Pest Control Ltd spraying crops in the Sudan and Kenya and thereabouts from, amongst other aircraft types, an Auster. When he came home at the end of his contract he was easily recognisable; he was bright yellow from the dye in the chemicals. In the spring of 1954 he secured a flying position with Marshall of Cambridge. It was in that year that English Electric gave Marshall's all the modification and development work for Canberra bomber aircraft in service with the RAF.

During 1957 the first of the B8 models were flown in to Waterbeach and then ferried to Cambridge. Marshall's virtually gutted the airframes and then fitted a modified Low Altitude Bombing System (LABS) to permit carrying and dropping a British nuclear weapon. Brian was involved in the Canberra test programme and flew nine different marks of the aircraft. The B16 differed from the B15 in that it was fitted with the Blue Shadow ground terrain following radar. The RAF favoured the use of names for its radar equipment. Some years later, during work on the Buccaneer aircraft, a Design Office 'brain' sent a terse instruction to the technicians in the hangars: 'Remove Blue Parrot.' The technicians were flummoxed. No one could claim knowledge of such a bird. Not to be outsmarted, an ornithologically inclined technician came up with the answer. A couple of days later a well-wrapped parcel winged its way through the post. When the removal 'brain' opened up the package he found inside a paper-mâché model of a parrot, painted blue. Attached to it was a cryptic note: 'Blue Parrot removed.'

Quiet and unassuming, Brian was keen on cricket and soccer, was good-natured and very easy to get on with. This would have made him an ideal personality for instructing, at first on the Tiger Moth and then later on the Cessna 150. He frequently flew with Arthur Marshall as his personal pilot. At Cambridge he also flew the Vampire T11, Valetta, Valiant and Varsity plus a wide assortment of single and multi-engined civilian aircraft. Brian made his first flight in the orange painted MA 4 on 1st February 1966.

Brian's second, and fatal, flight was on Tuesday, 8th March 1966. The MA 4 departed from runway 24, as it was then, at about mid-day and headed out to the southeast. Several witnesses observed the MA 4's final descent into a field close to the village of West Wratting. Flying with Brian as a flight test observer was Mr Ramaswamiah Krishnamurthy. Both occupants died in the crash. Investigations into the accident failed to reveal the cause.

Father Nightingale celebrated Requiem Mass at the Church of Our Lady and the English Martyrs, Cambridge, on Saturday 12th March, before interment at Linton Cemetery. Further tragedy was to afflict the Wass family six years later. Ann Wass, Brian's widow, was driving along the A604 near the Gog Magog Hills when the car, with John, her youngest son, aboard, skidded. Ann died in the resulting crash. Barbara Birch, Brian's sister, and her husband Derek brought up the four Wass youngsters in addition to their own two children.

PART TWO

Post-World War Two Pilots and Activities

Top left: Sir Arthur Marshall, 1991.
(Marshall Aerospace (MA))

Top right: Leslie Worsdell, 1990. *(L Worsdell)*

Above left: Tap Tappin in Tiger Moth, Cambridge, circa 1950. *(HE Tappin)*

Above right: Peter Else, 1990.
(Cambridge Evening News)

Top left: Leslie Scatchard
in Whitley bomber at
Cambridge, circa 1943.
(Mrs Jean Scatchard)

Top right: Brian Wass,
1945.   *(Mrs Barbara Birch)*

Above: Doug Page at
Cambridge with ATC
cadets & Tiger Moth, 1963.
          *(*Cambridge Evening News*)*

Right: Ron Frost at
Dalcross, 1952. Airspeed
Oxford.   *(Ron Frost)*

Top left: Marshall pilots early 1987.
Left to right – John Blake, John
Preece, Tim Mason, Dennis Pasco,
Rob Butterworth, Colin Rudder.
(Author)

Top right: Presentation of 10,000
flying hours award to Colin Rudder
in July 1991. Left to right – Michael
J Marshall, Daz James, Colin, John
Blake, John Brownlow.   *(MA)*

Above: David Bywater at
ETPS, 1984.   *(David Bywater)*

Left: Marshall pilots, May 1999.
Left to right – Mark Pickavance,
Iain Young, John Blake, David
Healy, Daz James.   *(Author)*

Top left: Sir Arthur's Gipsy Moth, 1929.
(Sir Arthur Marshall)

Top right: Avro Cadet.
(Bruce Robertson, via Michael J F Bowyer (MJFB))

Middle: Hawker Hind at Oxford, 1939, with Tap Tappin in rear cockpit.
(HE Tappin)

Bottom: Avro Tutor, Old Warden, 1998.
(Author)

Top: Wellington III, X3763 of 425 (Alouette) Sqn Royal Canadian Air Force. *(MJFB)*

Middle left: Cambridge Aerodrome in World War 2, looking south. *(AM)*

Middle right: Spitfire Mk I, P9496, of Peter Else, 610 Sqn Biggin Hill, 1940.

(Peter Else via Alan Milne)

Bottom: Albemarle P 1514. *(MJFB)*

Top: Hurricane Mk IIC. Tap Tappin landing
at Hunsdon, 1941/42.   *(HE Tappin)*

Middle: Whitley Mk V, EB 302 at Cambridge.
                                      (MA)

Bottom: Bristol Beaufort Mk II torpedo-
bombers.   *(MJF*

Top left: Bristol Blenheim, 40 Sqn, Wyton.
(MJFB)

Top right: Avro Lancaster PP 687. *(MJFB)*

Middle: Short Stirling III of 90 Sqn. *(MJFB)*

Bottom: Hawker Typhoon IB, probably JP132. *(MJFB)*

Top left: Douglas Dakotas at Croydon. Nearest is KG783. *(MJFB)*

Top right: DH Chipmunk UM072 at Centralia, Canada. *(John Blake)*

Middle: Miles Martinet LR224. *(MJFB)*

Bottom: Percival Proctor II, Z7197. *(Malcolm Gault)*

Top left: Hawker Hunter F6 of 14 Sqn over Germany, flown by John Preece, 1962.

(John Preece)

Top right: Boulton Paul P111. *(Boulton Paul via Mrs Marjorie Smythe)*

Above: Gloster Meteor Mk 8. Nearest is VT150.

(MJFB)

Left: Canadair CL-41G Tebuan FM 1137 over Malaysia, 1969.

(John Preece)

Top: SEPECAT Jaguar. John Preece delivering the first one to Lossiemouth, May 1973.

(BAC, via John Preece)

Above left: Harvard Trainer FT375, 1976. *(Tim Mason)*

Above right: Avro Anson trainer VM393.

(Malcolm Gault)

Right: Piston Provost T1, WV564, at Lindholme. Flown by author at Tern Hill, 1959/60. *(Malcolm Gault)*

Top left: Vickers Varsity
WF410, 1966.
(Malcolm Gault)

Top right: Vampire T11
WZ419. *(MJFB)*

Above: T-33 T-Bird,
21032. *(John Blake)*

Left: Jet Provost Mk 4
XP662. *(John Blake)*

Top left: Venom fighter-bombers.   *(MJFB)*

Top right: MA 4 at the stall. Taken from Tiger Moth.   *(Doug Page)*

Middle: Mosquito TT35, VR793, of No.2 CAACU.   *(John Kellock)*

Bottom: Vickers Valiant B (K) 1, XD814.   *(Malcolm Gault)*

Top left: Canberra B (I) 68 of Peruvian Air Force at Cambridge. Doug Page on left, Dave Ryding on right.   *(MA)*

Top right: Avro Vulcan B Mk 2, XH539 personalised for Tim Mason.   *(Tim Mason)*

Middle: Vickers Valetta of 84 Sqn at Beihan, Aden 1957. Aden Airways DC-3 in background.   *(Author)*

Bottom: Hastings Met Mk 1 TG623 of 202 Sqn at Ballykelly, Northern Ireland.

(RCB Ashworth)

Top left: Vickers Viscount at Bournemouth/ Hurn.   *(Malcolm Gault)*

Top right: Andover C Mk 1 XS 608 of 52 Sqn Seletar, Singapore 1967.   *(Author)*

Middle: Lockheed Hercules W Mk 2, XV208, over Cambridge airport.   *(MA*

Bottom: Short Belfast G-BFYU (G52-15) at Cambridge.   *(MA*

Top: Hercules C Mk 1 XV 206 with
MAROC modification, April 1984.   *(MA)*

Middle: Hercules G52-17 at Cambridge,
1986.   *(Tim Mason)*

Bottom: Meteor U16 WK800, flown by
Tim Mason.   *(MA)*

Top: Lockheed SR-71. Bill Weaver about to fly. *(Lockheed Martin)*

Above left: RAF TriStar tanker with Tim

Gooch at flight engineer's panel. *(Author*

Above right: Bulldog trainer of CUAS, Cambridge airport. *(Tug Wilson*

Chapter 6

A 'Fat Albert' Flight Test

BY DENNIS PASCO

The flight test of this particular 'Fat Albert' from Cambridge today, in March 1980, will be different. We are going to drop a 'body' from it over the North Sea. In the RAF I had dropped umpteen hundred live paratroopers, or moving freight, from the Hercules, but this drop would be unique. We had rehearsed it a couple of weeks before and it had worked without a hitch. As a civilian pilot, with Colin Rudder as co-pilot, I am now waiting to airtest Hercules C Mk1 XV 303 after the Marshall technicians have completed a major service on the teenaged aircraft.

The aircraft is, unusually, ready by mid-morning. A flight of about two hours and forty-five minutes lies ahead. The weather looks good, except that an anti-cyclone to the north of the British Isles is pushing an easterly wind across southern England. In East Anglia, only Mildenhall has an Instrument Landing System (ILS) on an easterly runway. Since it is a Saturday the USAF noise-abatement policy prohibits approaches and go-arounds. As we need to carry out at least one ILS approach we must look further afield. Brize Norton, west of Oxford, accepts us for the ILS and also acts as our weather diversion. Good. Most importantly, Colin gets lunch organised. Pauline swiftly fills the cardboard box with bread rolls, Kit Kats, crisps, tea, coffee, milk and cups. Tim Gooch is the flight engineer today, so in goes an extra Cornish pasty. ATC confirms that Brize will accept us for the ILS between 1130 and 1230, gives us our likely departure route, and states that the air temperature is +15°C (for take-off speed calculations) and the sea level air pressure, or QNH, is 1,008 millibars. We pass our callsign, endurance seven hours, flight time, number on board, our initial altitude requirements, and state that we wish to cross the UK central airways system via the Daventry VOR beacon. I sign the authorisation book, and leave a copy of the Flight Test Briefing form and load sheet in it. A trip to the 'loo', flying suit and boots on, a final word with Neville Rose in the front office about the afternoon training programme, and we are ready to go.

Colin and I climb on board the Hercules (known as Fat Albert to many servicemen) as it pauses behind the tractor in front of No 1 hangar. Still visible along parts of the cargo compartment floor are two parallel scars, which run for half the length of the cargo compartment floor. The scars were the consequence of damage caused in 1976. That same year I had headed a RAF Board of Inquiry to discover how and who had caused the damage. We failed in both respects. As XV 303 squeaks and clanks the two hundred yards to the engine running bay I check the RAF Form 700 (technical log) for any 'red' or 'green' entries (restrictions that might affect the flight) and I confirm that the fuel state is as requested. Satisfied, I sign the Form 1090 – the authorisation to proceed with the air test – and the technical log. When the aircraft is in position, I carry out my walk-around check of the outside (once, at Lyneham, I heard a fuel pump still running. It was defective, in that it would not switch off when selected off). Sitting in the right-hand seat, Colin checks out the VHF and UHF radios and gets an update of the air temperature and altimeter pressure setting from ATC. A word with flight engineer Dave Ryding, acting as the fourth crew member today, to inform him of our taxi-out route. Next, because Dave is also the navigator today, we review the required tracks and distances for the Doppler and Decca navigation systems. Slipping into the left-hand seat is like pulling on my favourite suit. I feel at one with the aeroplane. Rather than strapping-in the seat, it is more a question of strapping the aircraft onto myself. Rudder pedals and seat height adjusted, oxygen and intercom checked, it is time to go. Pre-flight checks complete, we crosscheck the data for the take-off and run through the procedure to follow if an emergency requires us to return for an immediate landing. We start No 3 engine first and then 4, 2 and 1. After a final look around, Dave climbs aboard and shuts out the deafening engine noise by closing the crew entry door. ATC gives us the word and we taxi off quite slowly in case the steering is awry. On one trip the Captain found that turning the nosewheel tiller to the left caused a turn to the right! I check the brakes using the emergency system and then Colin checks them using the normal system. As we backtrack runway 06 (060 degrees), as it was then, towards Coldham's Lane we carry out a check of flight instruments, fuel and electrical systems, and set the flaps to 50%. In 1985 the main runway direction changed from 06/24 to 05/23 as a consequence of the ever-dropping magnetic variation. In the early 1930s magnetic variation was about 12 degrees West in East Anglia. By the late 1990s, due to the earth's changing magnetic field, it is down to just 3.5 degrees.

Lining up on the runway we carry out the power checks on all four engines. Everything is in order. We run through the take-off checks and await ATC clearance to go. 'Liquor 14, with the Tiger Moth on crosswind in sight, clear take-off.' We spot the yellow puddle-jumper. 'Tiger Moth in sight, clear take-off, Liquor 14.' The radio callsign used by Company pilots when on airtest changed in 1982 from Liquor to Marshall. The head of flying, Leslie Worsdell for example, is always allocated the number 10, and other pilots choose their own number from 11 to 20.

Monitored by the flight engineer, I push all four throttles forward until 18,000-inch/lb torque is set and then ease my feet off the brake pedals. With a reassuring push up the rear XV 303 at first trundles, then accelerates swiftly, along the runway. Initially keeping straight with the nosewheel tiller, I switch to the rudder for directional control as we pass sixty knots. A few seconds later, at 106 knots, Colin calls 'Rotate.' I heave the nosewheel off the ground, keep the wings level and aim for a pitch attitude of about seven degrees. Glancing at the gauges to check that each engine torque is still below the maximum permitted, I call 'Gear up.' As soon as the gear (American for undercarriage) lights are out I ask for 'Flaps zero'; Colin acknowledges and raises the flaps. We swing left onto a heading of 300 degrees (Northwest) and then work through the after take-off checks. Levelling at 5,000 feet I let XV 303 increase airspeed to about 270 knots, reduce power to maintain it, and then trim the aircraft in pitch, roll and yaw. Satisfied that it looks and feels right, I ease the throttles back and head for 200 knots. Tim, taking notes the whole time, performs engine checks and I reduce power yet again to check for satisfactory flight control behaviour at low speed and carry out some of the auto pilot checks. Cambridge ATC hands us over to London, who, on the UHF radio, clear us to climb to 10,000 feet for the airways crossing overhead the Daventry VOR beacon.

We carry out as many checks as we can for the next ten minutes, keeping a good eye outside in this busy part of the sky. Passing Daventry London steers us towards Brize and gives us descent clearance. Thinking ahead, Colin passes 'Souls on board four', hoping to pre-empt Brize's question. Over to Brize radar, who ask 'Liquor14, souls on board?' Failed! Brize ATC clears us for two ILS approaches. The first one is carried out on the autopilot as part of the test schedule. Checking that it performs within specification, and that the two ILS lights and aural beacons work as advertised, I deselect 'George' (the autopilot) at two hundred feet above the runway and carry out a 'roller' landing. Colin flies the second ILS, also for a roller, and then we climb up for the return to East Anglia. Dave is working away at the navigation equipment, and starts the Doppler on track A as we leave Brize. Passing 12,000 feet in the climb, I ensure that XV 303 is spot on 180 knots and trimmed out to fly hands and feet off the controls. Tim records the three trim settings. Colin and I check the elevator trimming system works correctly in normal and emergency modes. So far, so good. Time for a drink. Dave knows our needs; he hands me the white coffee and the black one to Colin. Tim has already demolished his first Cornish pasty. Passing through 15,000 feet we burst out of the anti-cyclonic haze into a clear, endlessly blue sky. At 24,500 feet London puts us under radar control. We shall now need their consent for any heading and altitude changes. Our climb takes us to 30,000 feet. We all check that our oxygen masks are available for immediate use; at that altitude a sudden loss of pressurisation would give us about thirty seconds of consciousness without oxygen. Through the haze below we can just make out Bedford airfield. How co-operative Bedford ATC is whenever we use their aerodrome; sadly they are closed on Saturdays and Sundays. We await London's word that we are clear of the airways.

An altitude of 30,000 feet is well below the maximum achievable in a Hercules. A requirement for the air test, it is also well below the record for Marshall test flights. Venoms in the 1950s, with an initial climb rate of

9,000 feet per minute, were routinely whisked up to 40,000 feet. Easily exceeding those, however, was one particular Canberra. A B2 model, WK 164 had developed a LOX (liquid oxygen) system leak. In 1959, Gordon Hubbard, Tap Tappin and Leslie Worsdell had all had a hand in taking WK164 ever higher. Its quoted service ceiling of 48,000 feet was reached on 18th April. The LOX system promptly failed. The next day, repairs hopefully complete, Ron Frost and Doug Page coaxed the erstwhile leaky lady above its best so far and reached a figure of 50,000 feet. Landing back at Cambridge at 1335, they were able to report 'LOX system satisfactory.'

While Tim and Dave get involved in a multitude of engine checks, Colin and I check all five radios and top and bottom aerials. The Burndept emergency homer, the IFF on normal, height and emergency 'squawks', the radio compass, TACAN and VOR navigation aids all work as advertised. London radar pops up with an alteration of heading to avoid a gaggle of USAF F-111s inbound to Upper Heyford. We are now heading towards Blakeney Point. Glancing down, I recognise Fakenham. Next to it I can just make out the now disused aerodrome of Little Snoring. Horsa gliders of the GPR were stored there in 1944. The Korean War expansion pulled in Spitfires of No 2 CAACU. The runways, however, had deteriorated rapidly since 1945. With an army dispatch rider astride a BSA motorcycle at the end of each runway, to warn off stray vehicles, the Spitfires would roar off to do their 'co-operation' duties with the gunners. The slipstream of the mighty Merlin's propeller lifted lumps of tarmac from the runway surface, shooting them back like bits of shrapnel. The shrapnel bounced off the runway on to the fuselage underside, and damaged the 'Spits' almost as much as an over-enthusiastic gunner. CAACU operations were subsequently transferred to Langham, just a few miles south of Blakeney. Langham was another aerodrome to benefit from the Korean War. The main runway was resurfaced and supported the CAACU sorties for several years. Temporarily based at Cambridge, target towing Beaufighters were once more reunited with their CAACU colleagues. Later on, Mosquito TT-35s joined the unit, the whole shebang being run by Marshall on behalf of the RAF.

The TACAN dials start to wander and oscillate. Looking down, five miles below us, I spy Coltishall. No 66, John Preece's old squadron, operated from there in 1940. So, too, did 242 Sqn, led by Douglas Bader. The aerodrome looks too serene and orderly to have supported so many illustrious RAF fighter units. 'Captain, are you with us?' 'Uh, yes, just thinking. It's about time to turn and then have another drink, isn't it?' The autopilot, when connected to the Doppler equipment, is not working too well today. On both leg A and leg B, from Coltishall to Wattisham, it wants to turn the aircraft away from track instead of towards it. Tim logs the defect. We eat our way through the rations, keeping a close eye on the door warning light and the cabin air pressure gauge, in case we have to drop everything, don oxygen masks and rush into a descent. When Dave and Tim have finished their engineering wizardry, Tim records all the flight instrument readings to assess them later for accuracy. Only the standby magnetic compass is awry; it is out of limits on one heading. With a few minor engine snags logged, XV 303 is in good shape. Updating the aircraft weight Tim, Colin and I compare speeds for the descent and stalls. We try to avoid errors by not relying on just one person's calculations. The aircraft weight is easy to assess, in that the Hercules uses about 4,500 lb. of fuel each hour when on a standard air test. Satisfied that the speeds look safe I push the nose down for a descent under control of London radar. Leaving the power alone, XV 303 increases airspeed rapidly towards 260 knots, the maximum airspeed permitted at this altitude. Approaching Vne (the 'never exceed' speed) as we pass 26,000 feet, I reduce power and gently manoeuvre the Hercules in pitch, roll and yaw. No unusual noises or responses occur, no bits fall off so we carry on down to 20,000 feet, losing speed the whole time. London clears us 'in to the block' – an altitude band between 20,000 and 15,000 feet – for stalling. Slowing right down, we are ready for the two stalls.

The stalls are conducted with power at zero torque. Colin flies the first one, trimming out the stick forces at a speed of 40% above the expected stall speed. Heading towards the stall, aiming to decelerate at one knot per second, we are looking and listening for any unusual behaviour. A moderate amount of buffeting occurs as we approach the 'clean' stall speed, as expected. At the stall, the right wing drops slightly, the nose pitches down gently, and Colin initiates the recovery drill, being careful not to apply power too soon or too swiftly. Tim asks for the minimum speeds seen on the pilots' airspeed indicators; Colin hauls the Hercules into a gentle climb before handing over to me for the second stall. Back up at 20,000 feet, we turn back towards Coltishall and reduce power for the 'dirty' stall (gear and flaps down). Speed below 180 knots, flap to 50%, down with the gear, a final look around and I call for flaps to 100% (the landing configuration). With a hefty rise in drag, our airspeed drops rapidly; I trim swiftly so that we are 'trimmed' as we pass 109 knots. Heading in to the stall the flight controls feel less assertive and buffeting is heavier this time, again as expected. A slightly quicker wing drop occurs as we reach the stall speed: 78 knots. Nose down, a little left rudder, pause, gently on with the power, flaps to 50%, then gear up. Staying at 16,000 feet, I call for flaps to zero. Next on the agenda is a descent to 10,000 feet in preparation for the safety valve check. Tim logs the airspeed readings and Colin advises London of our need for further descent. Down we go as Dave takes up his position at the rear of the cargo compartment to watch for the safety valve to open at the correct moment during the soon-to-come rush down to 5,000 feet. A good look around and we are ready. Up spouts London, to hand us over to Wattisham radar. Delaying the 'dirty dart' (a rapid descent) we establish communications with Wattisham Approach. Now we are ready.

Airspeed back to just above 100 knots, I push the nose down to about a thirty degree pitch angle, not too quickly or Dave will fly weightless into the roof, and we can say cheerio to any more drinks. Speed rises rapidly as Fat Albert plummets down, doing its best to copy a dive-bomber's act. 'Open' calls Dave. With the airspeed rushing up past 250 knots, the nose is already pushing up, so I let it continue up in to a climb. Power on, we climb back to 7,000 feet to complete the air test schedule. With flaps at 50%, speed at 150 knots, we continue.

Dave now works flat out as he winds the gear down manually and operates all the different ways of lowering the gear and the flaps. He relaxes for a while as we time the gear through a normal down and up sequence. Airspeed below 140 knots, Colin opens the air deflectors and Dave then opens and closes the two parachute doors, rear doors and the ramp. Not unusually, the ramp is reluctant to go down without some assistance from Dave, who jumps up and down on it. We try it again, and then enter another snag in the log. In the meantime I head out just a few miles over the North Sea. 'Exit tube is in position, ready for the drop' calls Dave. Speed is just right, 125 knots, and we can make out the coast to our left. 'Count us down, then do the drop' I inform Dave. 'Three, two one, now.' The suction through the tube extracts every last speck of ash from the container. 'Load gone.' I log the time and our position. One of the longer-serving employees of the Company had recently gone to the big hangar in the sky. His widow asked if we could carry out her late husband's wish to have his ashes dropped over the North Sea. It was an unusual request, but I agreed to do it. Mission complete, and now 'cleaned up' (gear and flap in), we turn inland and accelerate to 180 knots for the final few checks.

In turn, we shall 'feather' (shut down) and restart each engine. With everyone in position to watch for normal behaviour and to time the feathering, we work through all four engines. After each engine shutdown, we wait a while for the Turbine Inlet Temperature to cool down to 200 degrees C before we 'relight.'

Nearing Cambridge, I set up an east-west racetrack, so that we are ready to drop into the circuit without wasting fuel. All four engines checked out, final engineering check complete, we head in for a downwind join for Runway 06. ATC give us the necessary clearance. We drop down to the circuit height of 1,500 feet, head towards Shelford, then descend further as we pass Addenbrooke's hospital and turn on to the final approach. A final check that the runway is clear of obstructions, gear is down and locked, flaps to 100%, we need only to make the 'Final' call to obtain landing clearance. In days gone by such calls were often non-standard, not like the expected conformity of today's generation. 'Topsy' Turner, when flying in Marshall's Rapide G-AGZO, would light up the ether with his biblical 'Zachariah Obediah turning the corner.' To the textbook call from Colin ATC gives the reply 'Liquor 14 clear land.' Aiming for the displaced threshold of the runway, it is time to correct for crosswind. It is pushing us left, so in goes a bit of aileron to turn Albert to the right. To straighten up the fuselage so that it points along the runway I feed in a bit of left rudder.

Over the hedge, on to the runway at just over 100 knots, I place the Hercules firmly on the concrete. A satisfying crunch announces the end of flight time. Safely down, I give a good firm press on the brake pedals to bed-in the new set of brakes. The excellent 'anchors' and reverse thrust soon slow XV 303 to a fast walking pace. We start on the 'after landing' checks. Turning off the runway at taxiway three, we spot the marshaller and head towards him. All four engines can now go to low-speed ground idle. They each drop down with a gentle sigh, and the noise outside subsides to a more acceptable level. Happy that all is well we come to rest, wait for chocks-in and run through our shutdown checks. Three hours after taxiing out we are home. We debrief with the assembled ground party and hand over a near perfect XV 303. Of the original sixty-six RAF Hercules, six have been lost in accidents at Colerne, Fairford, Tromso in Norway, off the coast of Italy at Livorno, one on a hilltop in Scotland, flown by a good friend, Sqn Ldr Graham Young. The most recent loss was in Kosovo. After many years in service, and much modified, no two Hercules are now exactly alike.

Out of flying kit, another coffee, Colin and I head for the front office to get on with the afternoon's training programme with Cessna 150s of the Cambridge Aero Club. Dave and Tim disappear towards the bowels of the hangars. Back in my office I give Mrs X a call. She is very pleased to hear that her beloved's wish was carried out. Later on, one of the flight engineers will give us a call as to the necessary short re-test, 'What are your plans for Sunday morning?'

Chapter 7

Ron Frost

Just to the west of Sheringham on the north Norfolk coast lay the Weybourne gunnery range. It was here, just a few miles from Langham aerodrome, that we carried out target towing in the Mosquito TT 35. The target drogue, at which the Army gunners fired their guns, was trailed at the end of 5,000 feet of cable extending from the aircraft's winch. In theory, only aircraft specifically engaged on range work should have flown within the range airspace. On one occasion I spotted a Meteor 8 enter the range just prior to the guns opening up. The pilot was obviously intent on having a close look at my Mosquito. Suddenly a burst of flak appeared in front of him. His about turn was the fastest I had ever seen a Meteor execute. He no doubt thought that Norfolk had declared independence! Seeing that Meteor's volte-face reminded me of how I had first decided to join the RAF.

Whilst awaiting call-up for National Service I went to Shoreham Airport to see a Battle of Britain display. During the afternoon I was spellbound by an electrifying display of one of the early Meteor 3s. I decided there and then that flying was what I wanted to do for my National Service. After several discouraging visits to the RAF recruiting office in Brighton I finally convinced them that there was a scheme for National Service aircrew. I was eventually sent to Hornchurch for selection procedures. The end result was that I was selected for navigation training – a disappointment but nevertheless I still felt I had an interesting and productive National Service ahead.

I was born in Brighton on 13th March 1933. At the age of three my parents separated and my mother brought me up. The Second World War started when I was six and a half, and it was probably from that time that my interest in aviation started. During the war one of the activities that my peer group and I engaged in enthusiastically was aircraft spotting and recognition, both Allied and German. In 1944 I passed the early 11-plus exam and won a scholarship to Varndean Grammar School for Boys in Brighton. There, in 1949, I passed the General School Certificate with exemption from matriculation. Family finances did not permit me to continue my education beyond the age of sixteen so I got a job as a clerk in an insurance office for the next two years whilst awaiting call-up.

My military career began on 28th May 1951 at Padgate, a reception unit well known, I am sure, to thousands of RAF National Service recruits. From there, with a few other hopefuls, I moved to No 2 Air Grading School at Digby, Lincolnshire, for a five-week course. We were given twelve hours flying on Tiger Moths as grading to see whether selection had put round pegs in round holes. I was lucky, with one other student, to be re-graded for pilot training. I do not know whether an experience on one flight may have influenced the decision. On that flight, in very hazy conditions, my flying instructor became uncertain of his position. He decided to land alongside the main runway of a large bomber airfield and taxi back to the runway caravan to ask where he was. On the way back to Digby he said 'Not a word about this Frost.' 'Of course not', I replied, 'I am going to be a pilot, aren't I Sir?'

Our Initial Training was then completed at Kirton-in-Lindsey, also in Lincolnshire. At the end of September 1951 we became Acting Pilot Officers to start basic flying training. This was carried out at 2 FTS, Ansty, near Coventry. First solo was carried out in the average time of seven hours. The course lasted three months and included sixty hours of Chipmunk flying. On completion half the intake was posted to Canada for advanced flying training on Harvards. The rest of us went to 8 AFTS at Dalcross, Inverness, to train on the Airspeed Oxford.

We started the course in early February 1952. Dalcross was an excellent place for flying training with a surprisingly good weather factor and the most superb scenery. Many of the instructors were reservists recalled due to the Korean War. Approximately one hundred and thirty flying hours later I got my 'Wings' and was commissioned as a Pilot Officer on 25th June 1952. I was also awarded the prize as best all-round student.

Following instruction on the static ejection-seat rig at Driffield I then commenced my jet training on Meteors with 206 AFTS at Oakington at the beginning of July. After five hours dual in a Meteor 7 I went first solo; subsequent solos were then flown in either a Meteor 3 or 4. My ambitions to fly a Meteor after the air show at Shoreham two or three years earlier were thus achieved. The Mk 3, with an early Derwent engine, was unpressurised and lacked the performance of the 4s and 7s but was fun to fly. With its non-clipped wings it produced superb wing-tip vortices in the right atmospheric conditions. We completed the course in three and a half months and seventy flying hours before being posted to an Operational Conversion Unit (OCU).

In my case it was to 231 OCU at Bassingbourn, Cambridgeshire, on the seventh course to convert to the Canberra bomber. After three weeks of ground school we flew two dual flights on a Meteor 7 and then one solo. We were then introduced to the Canberra B2. The trainer version of the Canberra – the T4 – was not yet in service. Dual instruction consisted of two flights sitting on the 'rumble' seat of the B2, watching an instructor demonstrate the capabilities of the aircraft. The instructor then jumped out, leaving me and my brand new navigator to head off for the first solo on type. It was this flight in the superbly agile Canberra that made me feel very grateful for my re-grading to pilot training at Digby. At this time I also decided to take a new four-year commission that was being offered and which included the National Service time to date. My OCU training was completed after fifty hours flying in two months. With a grand total of 325 hours in my logbook I was now ready for a squadron posting.

On 11th February 1953 I joined 109 Sqn at Hemswell, Lincolnshire. The squadron had recently converted from Mosquitoes to Canberra B2s, and I was one of the first 'new boys' to join the experienced crews. Both 109 and 139 were pathfinder squadrons and continued in this role with the Canberra for about a further year. The Canberra was a superb aircraft both in its low-level role as a pathfinder and as a high altitude main-force bomber. Its low wing loading gave it an excellent turning capability at altitude. On some exercises we were restricted to 30,000 feet rather than a more usual cruise at 48,000 feet in order to give the Meteors, Hunters and Swifts a more 'sporting chance.'

Apart from normal operational flying the squadron was involved in some trial work. One was to see what life expectancy the Avon engine could achieve. An aircraft was flown virtually twenty-four hours a day until the engineers decided the engine had reached its limit. From memory, I believe one engine achieved two hundred hours and the other four hundred hours. What a change from today, where engines are lifed in thousands, not hundreds. Another trial was with a radar system known as 'Blue Shadow.' This was a sideways looking radar that produced ground returns, not on a screen, but 'burnt' returns on special paper that rolled out like a toilet roll. The theory was that it could not be jammed or detected. Because there was always a record of where the aircraft had been, our navigators got very good at using the system. As far as I know it did not see widespread service in the Canberra fleet.

In October 1954 the Canberra B6 started to replace the B2. The engines on the B2 had two-stage bleed valves and swirls but those on the B6, the Avon 109, were variable. With the B2's engines one had to be fairly careful with the rate of throttle opening to prevent engine stall or surge. In theory the more advanced engines in the B6 eliminated this problem. On some occasions, however, surging was experienced during climbs at high altitude. Rolls-Royce found the cause to be a consequence of very low temperatures at high altitudes. The solution was to restrict climb RPM in accordance with a formula dependent on the Outside Air Temperature.

At the beginning of 1955 I had to start to think about whether to continue in the RAF or not. My time was up in June. After my squadron tour was finished the RAF options appeared to be either a ground tour or to go to CFS to become a flying instructor. Neither option appealed to me. My ambition was to become a production test pilot, so I left the RAF on 6th June 1955 with a grand total of 920 flying hours. I had written to most of the aircraft manufacturers, but no positions were available. However, about a year later, I did get as far as an interview with English Electric.

For three months after leaving the RAF I was unemployed whilst actively looking for flying jobs that looked interesting. Then, in August 1955, I spotted an advert in *Flight* magazine. Marshall's Flying School Ltd was looking for pilots at 2 CAACU, Langham, to fly Vampire 5s and Mosquito TT35s. It sounded very interesting. I duly applied, was accepted and commenced work there on 1st October 1955.

Langham is in Norfolk, just south of Blakeney. We used Vampires for two roles, and the flying was varied and enjoyable. One was army co-operation work carrying out low-level beat-ups of army gun positions. These were normally sited on disused airfields in Norfolk. The other was in training RAF radar controllers in GCI. For this a pair of Vampires was used, one as target and the other as interceptor, with the flying carried out over the North Sea at average altitudes of 30,000 feet. My conversion to the Vampire consisted of a study of the Pilot's Notes and a look round the cockpit with the Chief Pilot, before being told to take it up and enjoy myself. It really was a delightful aircraft, light, manoeuvrable and a pleasure to fly. The Vampire flying task was also great fun. Lots of authorised low flying – any young pilot's dream – was balanced with high-level GCI work.

We used Mosquitoes mainly for target towing to give live gunnery practice to Regular and Territorial Army gunners at the Weybourne range. We also used them occasionally for GCI work. The Mosquito TT35 was a converted B35. It carried a winch, four drogues and a crewman to operate the winch. The Mosquito was an aircraft I had always wanted to fly. An instructor from the RAF Standardisation Flight based at White Waltham carried out my conversion to it. The Mosquito T3 was a super aircraft to fly and the instructor took great delight in demonstrating its performance by carrying out rolls with one engine live and the other one shut down. After three dual flights on the T3 I went solo in it. A few days later I carried out a solo familiarisation on the much heavier TT35. It obviously lacked the performance of the T3 due to higher weight and drag from the winch mounted underneath it. Nevertheless it was equally satisfying to fly. An Anson C21 was also based at Langham. It was occasionally used for naval radar training and calibration over the Thames estuary at Chatham.

Target towing was carried out at the Weybourne range. The winch operator deployed a 5000-feet length of cable, at the end of which was a drogue. Both crossing and head-on runs were made. When the Range Safety Officer gave clearance, the anti-aircraft guns fired mica shells at the drogue. Once a drogue was hit it meant a quick fly-over at Langham to drop the damaged one before deploying another. I was very impressed with the accuracy of the gunners, especially those of the Territorial Army on their fortnight's annual camp. They were as keen as mustard to match up to their regular counterparts. I remember on one occasion that a new radar-controlled gun was being tested. For this we deployed a radar drogue, similar to normal but with wire mesh inside. The new gun started firing, but quite quickly one could see the computer thinking 'There is a much bigger, more appetising, target up there.' The gunfire started to track up the cable towards the aircraft. Luckily the Range Safety Officer was very quick to cease the firing, much to the relief of the winch operator and myself.

Jeff Barclay, the manager of Langham, knew of my interest in test flying. He had allowed me to attend an interview at English Electric earlier in the year. Later in 1956 he called me in to say that there was a possibility of a vacancy at Marshall's main base at Cambridge. It would involve test, charter and instructional flying; if I were interested I would need to get a Commercial Pilot Licence by the New Year. This I duly did and after an interview with Leslie Worsdell, the Chief Test Pilot at Cambridge, I started work there on 1st February 1957. The move to Cambridge was a good one. The flying was very professionally run with a happy atmosphere and a variety of flying that was probably unique. Colleagues were very friendly and helpful, and Mr Marshall, now Sir Arthur, was very much in evidence with an obvious and welcome interest in all his employees.

My Ministry of Supply approval gave me authorisation to fly the Vampire and Canberra plus co-pilot duties on Valiants, Valettas and Varsities. It also approved me for Venoms, Brigands and Beaufighters but I flew none of them as the contracts had finished by then. My first flight at Cambridge was on 1st February, the day after I had finished at Langham. It was with Leslie Worsdell in a Vampire T11, to initiate me into the test programme required for that aeroplane. A further flight a few days later with Gordon Hubbard cleared me for the T11 test programme. During my first month I also flew the Vampire FB9, Canberra B8 and the Valetta T4 as co-pilot. In addition I was re-united with the Tiger Moth, in which I started my flying instructor's course.

Marshall, over a four-year period, fitted 240 Vampire T11s with ejection seats. After the modification virtually a full production test was required, with particular emphasis on satisfactory stall and spin characteristics. We flew the majority of the flight tests from Waterbeach. Any unsatisfactory wing drop at the stall required the engineers to adjust the offending wing by means of filler to the leading edge, and I was always impressed by the accuracy of the adjustment they made following the debriefing given to them. The T11 spin characteristics were very interesting. Entry into the spin invariably produced about two horizontal flick rolls before the aircraft sharply tucked its nose down. It then developed into a steep spin with quite a fast rate of rotation but with some erratic yawing and pitching movements. From memory, I believe students under training were liable to become disorientated during a spin, and it was recommended that the turn part of the turn-and-balance indicator should be checked to ensure correct recovery rudder was applied.

During that first month I also flew the Canberra again – a delivery from Hatfield to Cambridge of a B8, a mark I had not flown before. The main differences from the B6 were the tandem offset cockpit and associated canopy, toe brakes instead of differential braking via the rudder and the handbrake on the control column. The Canberra testing programme continued throughout my time at Cambridge. There were various types of tests but I remember two particular trial series that were both absorbing and challenging.

Firstly, there was a series involving Tail Plane Incidence (TPI) tests. During the early days of the Canberra there were several accidents thought to be caused by a runaway TPI. My roommate at OCU was one of the statistics. Shortly after take-off his aircraft appeared out of cloud in a steep dive, straight into the ground. The tests involved flying the Canberra level at 5,000 feet at speeds up to 450 knots. If full nose-down incidence were reached before that figure we would record the speed at which it occurred. However, if the target speed was reached with further nose down trim available, the trim was left at the 450 knots position and not touched again. After landing, the engineers would readjust the TPI down-limit to this point. This ensured that in the event of a runaway in the worst case the aircraft would be in trim at high speed. Leaving the trim set at that point obviously caused increasingly strong downloads as speed was reduced. It needed great strength of will not to touch the trim switch when returning for landing. As far as I know everybody managed to resist the temptation.

The other trial was in 1959 for the British Oxygen Corporation (BOC), carrying out liquid oxygen tests on a Canberra B2, WK 164. This involved a trial engineer from BOC, our own flight test observer – Dave Nightingale – and myself. Over a series of four flights the test schedule included a cruise at 50,000 feet, various yawing and pitching manoeuvres and sustained positive and negative-g (+4g to -2g). The Avon engines had fuel recuperators, which gave up to fifteen seconds fuel flow in negative-g conditions before a flameout would occur. Dave was very aware of this and had the stopwatch running with great alacrity during the negative-G phase. By the time I left Marshall's in 1961, except for the PR9, I had flown all series of Canberra up to and including the B15.

My other main test duties were as co-pilot on the Valiant, Valetta and Varsity on the military side and as co-pilot on civilian Viscounts and Ambassadors. We carried out charter flying mainly on the four Rapides that Marshall's owned, although an Auster was used occasionally. The Rapides were surprisingly well equipped for that time, having a 12-volt Decca navigation system operated by a wind driven generator on the upper mainplane. There was no flight log fitted but use of the three Deccometers made navigation easy. It was in fact possible to do a form of Decca approach at Cambridge. A position-line from one chain ran down the runway and other lines from another chain conveniently crossed the runway-line at approximately one-mile intervals.

The bulk of the work was racing charters taking jockeys, trainers and owners to various horse race meetings around the country. Certain courses, Haydock Park and Newbury for example, had their own landing strips. A pleasant afternoon could be spent watching the racing before returning to Cambridge. There was also a fair amount of interesting ad hoc charter work. I remember one contract that involved taking technicians regularly to the various Thor missile sites that had been set up in the depths of the Cold War. My old RAF station, Hemswell, was one that had 'phallic symbols' in place. It had ceased to be a flying station in 1956 and later became a main base and launch site for a squadron of three of Bomber Command's sixty Douglas Thor intermediate range ballistic missiles. Landing at Hemswell in the Rapide always brought feelings of nostalgia.

Another interesting contract was the use by Dr St Joseph of Cambridge University of an Auster for aerial photography. His objective was to find sites of Roman settlements by means of crop markings. Underlying foundations in fields can cause the crops above to be darker than their surroundings. They then show up quite clearly from the air. Sometimes quite large settlements can be seen. I remember once he got very excited when over the Peterborough area. A new road being built was heading towards some promising looking crop markings, and I believe the road was delayed whilst excavations were made.

We carried out flying instruction on Tiger Moths and an Auster. Having obtained my assistant instructor's rating, later upgraded to a full rating, I was used in this capacity by the Cambridge Aero Club. I also carried out glider towing and joy rides. I found instructing to be very gratifying and one of the interesting contracts was to train Air Training Corps cadets to PPL standard. One of my students by the name of Robertson possessed very much above average flying abilities. I asked him if he intended to continue in aviation. 'Unfortunately no', he said, 'I'm destined for the family business.' He then mentioned the well-known Golly symbol and the penny then dropped that jam making was his future.

Towards the end of 1960 the CAA issued new regulations for the conduct of charter flying. The demise of the Rapides for economic charter work was clearly imminent. My first wife, who I had married shortly after moving to Cambridge, was six months pregnant with our daughter at this time. I felt I needed to consider what the future held. The C of AT at Hamble had just been established to provide new pilots for BEA and BOAC. It was offering what seemed to be a very rewarding and secure career in flying instruction. I applied, was accepted in spite of not being CFS trained, and started work on 1st March 1961. Tap Tappin from Marshall's had, incidentally, started at the C of AT three months earlier. I had been very happy at Marshall's and had very mixed feelings about leaving. I shall always be grateful for the start they gave me in civil aviation.

To be in at the start of a new venture is always exciting, and the calibre of students at the C of AT was high. To be acceptable, they had to have good academic qualifications and had to undergo selection procedures similar to the RAF's, including the flying grading procedure that I had experienced. The course took two years and consisted of a high standard of ground school, liberal studies and a flying course of 225 hours of which sixty were spent on twin-engined aircraft. The students also had training on a flight procedure trainer whose performance was based on the Comet. Initially the DH Chipmunk was used for the single engine flying and the Piper Apache for twin flying. In 1968 the Piper Cherokee and Beech Baron 95 replaced them. The Chipmunk was, however, retained for spinning and aerobatics training.

During my time at Hamble I became a Type Rating Examiner (TRE) and a Deputy Flight Manager. In 1965 I was given the special task of taking charge of an experimental course of twelve university graduates. Together with two other instructors, the task was to see whether the course could be completed in half the normal time. BEA and BOAC wanted to attract students of university calibre but felt a further two years of study would be unattractive to them. In fact the course took about thirteen months and was considered a success. Further graduate courses then went to the Oxford Air Training School.

Whilst at Hamble I obtained my ATPL. During 1970 I felt I wanted a break from instructing and that, at the age of thirty-seven, my jet experience was beginning to diminish in value. I have always maintained that regular breaks from instructing are essential to prevent one from becoming stale. I applied to Dan Air for a position as a first officer on Comets at Gatwick. Dan Air accepted me and I joined them on 1st January 1971. Having successfully completed the Comet course as a first officer, I got my command in just over a year. We flew all three varieties of the Comet: the 4, 4B and 4C. It was a great aircraft to fly; we used it mainly for the inclusive tour market. One of the perks was to be based in Berlin to fly for the German tour operators. The fuel crisis in 1974 meant that the Comet's future as an economic aircraft was limited. In early 1975 I transferred to the BAC 1-11. The Company operated all series of the 1-11: the 200, 300, 400 and 500. The 500 series carried one hundred and nineteen passengers, the same as the Comet 4B and 4C. Obviously, with only two Spey engines as opposed to the Comet's four Avon engines, it was much more economical. Initially the majority of the work was charter but over the next few years an increasing proportion of scheduled operation was introduced. One was the Heathrow to Inverness/Dalcross route where we would stay for a few days operating this schedule. Fond memories of my RAF time there were always rekindled.

My instructional background led to me being asked to join the training team. I became a TRE and Instrument Rating Examiner and later Deputy Chief Training Captain of the 1-11 fleet and spent a considerable amount of time in Dublin using the Aer Lingus 1-11 simulator for conversion and continuation training as well as carrying out competency checks. Further conversion training was carried out on the aircraft at various airfields, such as Shannon, Teeside and Stansted.

During 1987 I resigned my training post for basically the same reason as I left Hamble. My training commitment had become more and more intense and I felt I needed a break from it. This gave me the opportunity to transfer to the Airbus A300-B4, of which the Company had recently acquired two. It was a superb aircraft and my first taste of a wide-body jet, complete with inertial navigation and automatic landing systems. The Dan Air configuration was for 336 passengers, three flight deck and nine cabin staff. The B4 was cleared for Category 3 operations, which meant we could start an approach to land with a cloud base of only fifteen feet and a touch-down runway visibility of just two hundred metres. This capability was a great benefit during foggy autumn and winter nights at Gatwick. Regrettably, I had less than two years on the aircraft before Dan Air decided to phase them out for financial reasons.

My final move was in 1990 onto the Boeing 737. I had not flown a Boeing type before and I was impressed by a lot of Boeing's technology: simple but functional. My initial conversion was on the 200 series before later moving on to the more advanced 300 and 400 series. Like the Airbus, the 300 and 400 models had inertial navigation, flight management systems and automatic landing, which gave them a CAT 3 capability down to fifty feet. Additionally, the 400 model had the Electronic Flight Instrument System that enabled me to experience 'glass cockpit' technology towards the end of my aviation career. Modern technology has certainly relieved a lot of the workload on short sector day-to-day operation. The work was a mix of charter and schedule. On 22nd October 1992 I flew a schedule from Oslo to Gatwick in a 400 series aircraft. At the time I was unaware that this was to be my last flight for Dan Air. Sadly, very shortly afterwards, the Company ceased to exist and was sold to British Airways for the grand sum of £1.00. British Airways continued some of the Boeing 737 operation and I was offered the chance to stay with them until my retirement in March 1993. However, it seemed pointless to take the offer up for such a short length of time. Furthermore I was heavily involved with the Dan Air pension scheme as a trustee.

My final logbook summary shows a total of just under 17,000 hours flying and about 2,000 hours of simulator time. I consider myself lucky that aviation has given me such a happy and rewarding career. Since our time together at Marshall's, Tap Tappin and I have been friends and we both now live in Brighton. He has always kept me up to date with any news from Cambridge and, in 1998, invited me to a lecture in London given by the Guild of Air Pilots and Navigators. It was a very great surprise, privilege and pleasure to meet Sir Arthur Marshall once again after more than thirty-five years and to see how very active he was approaching his ninety-fifth birthday.

Chapter 8

John Preece

The Percival Provost T1 was very manoeuvrable, with a big, exciting radial engine – it pulled well – but it was smelly. Near the end of our course, at 3 FTS, Feltwell, we had to do a navigation flight to Tern Hill and back. Bad weather had delayed the event, we were now behind time, and none of us had done it. Normally, a couple of us would go each day, but with just five days left, all twelve of us were launched at five-minute intervals. At Tern Hill we met up with a few mates from Kirton, had lunch and exchanged 'war stories.' For the flight back we just happened to board our Provosts at the same time. We took off one after the other and formed up in a giant 'Vic.' I had no idea who the leader was, nor whether he knew what he was doing, but we were heading roughly in the right direction. Now and again people would peel off to do a barrel roll around the outside of the formation and then rejoin. It was all most jolly. Nearing Feltwell a great dogfight developed. In the midst of all this I heard the voice of the OC Flying Wing, 'Sugar Charlie', who was obviously about to intercept us. I remember hearing him say, 'This is Sugar Charlie. I've got one and I'm going after another.' After landing we were herded into the squadron commander's office, to be told that our futures would be decided the next morning. There was an air of gloom and doom for some time while the staff discussed our future. They would either kick us all out or put it down to high spirits and let us go. They decided to give us all a great 'stiffening' and send us on to advanced training. Of the original twenty trainee pilots about twelve of us moved up to 8 FTS, at Swinderby, Lincolnshire. I was relieved to be one of them, since I was now hooked on flying, having been very undecided just a year before.

HUNTING PERCIVAL PROVOST T1. Two-seat trainer. One 550HP Alvis Leonides 126 engine. Span 35 feet 3 inches. Length 28 feet 9 inches. Loaded weight 4,400lb. Maximum airspeed 200mph at sea level. Cruising speed 160mph at 5,000 feet. In RAF service from 1953 to 1969.

My first memory of aviation was a joy ride in a little aircraft, probably a Miles Magister, in about 1938. The flight lasted about fifteen minutes, and I recall being not very thrilled by the aircraft, but I was impressed by the view.

Exeter, where I was born in 1936, suffered a couple of serious 'Blitzes.' My father, a First World War pilot, was frequently on duty as an Air Raid Warden, so it was usually my mother who hurried her two boys and very young daughter into the Anderson shelter. Once, I came out from the shelter and saw a red glow over the city, probably from the widespread fires. I saw a Spitfire shoot down a Messerschmitt that had flown past our house, and, on another occasion my brother and I were cycling along when somebody yelled 'Get into the hedge.' A German aircraft was hurtling up the road, firing its guns.

I went to a private school called Bramdean, then on to Exeter public school, and I recall that I preferred rugby to the academic subjects. I joined the Army element of the Combined Cadet Force. I had no particular desire to join the RAF; the Army side was more fun. After a few extra tries I finished up with a basic six 'O' level subjects. With absolutely no idea of what I wanted to do as a career, National Service caught up with me. At the initial selection process I tried to get out of military service by playing on the fact that I had just had a rugby injury. It was not to be, so, at the end of 1954, I volunteered for aircrew. The recruiting officer laughed 'Nobody ever gets that for National Service.' I replied 'Well, put it down anyway, you never know.' Much to my surprise, with about fifty others, I was called to Hornchurch, at that time the aircrew selection centre.

After the selection process we were all sent to Cardington, the reception centre, for kitting out and so on. To my delight three of us were selected for officer training at Kirton-in-Lindsey, Lincolnshire. The course lasted three months and we graduated in spring 1955 as Acting Pilot Officers. We moved to Feltwell for our basic flying training and then to 8 FTS at Swinderby to fly Vampire T11s and 5s.

My first Vampire flying instructor was obviously a very frustrated fighter pilot. For the first ten or twelve hours I did not get much handling of the flying controls. For example, on one flight, he spied a Boeing B47 bomber coming overhead, took control and chased after it for the next fifteen to twenty minutes. After an hour's flying, I had probably done a few things, and he had flown at least half of it. When the squadron commander flew with me on a check ride, to see what progress I was making, I was not. I was put on 'review' and decided that I had better fight for my future and ask for a change of instructor. I was unpopular, but a Navy instructor, 'Mitch' Mitchell, took me on. He was great, he gave me back my self-confidence and in no time at all I was making good progress and flying solo in the Vampire 5.

I saw my first Hawker Hunter at Swinderby when Flt Lt Bairsto, 43 Sqn's formation team leader, flew it in from Scotland. On departure he stayed low, did a tight circle and roared across the tower at about one hundred feet. I thought 'Umm, yes, that's for me.' It inspired me to move from National Service, which would have finished at the end of the advanced training, to a short-service commission. That meant I could go on to 229 OCU, Chivenor, to fly the Hunter Mk 1.

At Chivenor there was no simulator or dual-seat Hunter, but there was a cockpit procedure trainer, to familiarise us with the cockpit layout. An instructor said, 'That's the way it goes boy', patted us on the head and sent us off. On 6th February 1957, I strapped myself into a Hunter, taxied out and, at the holding point, noticed that the ejector seat pin was still in. I had to taxi back in, a bit of an anti-climax. Out I went again, lined up for take-off, when I looked out and thought 'Where have the wings gone?' Every aircraft up to now had had straight wings, and you could see them. In the Hunter you sat ahead of the wings and you could not see where the lift was coming from. I think the Hunter was one of those aircraft in which you immediately felt at home; it was certainly exhilarating, with a tremendous sense of power.

At the end of the OCU we all expected to go off to Germany. However, because of the Suez crisis, there was petrol rationing and we were all sent on leave without a posting. Soon I was notified that I was to join 66 Sqn Acklington, Northumberland. Even though I was told that it was a good squadron I recall being upset because my heart was set on going to Germany. With petrol coupons and joining instructions, I drove my 1936 Riley Falcon saloon to Acklington. I found that 66 was away in Cyprus. With me was another new pilot, John Walker. Known as 'Whisky', he went on to become an air marshal. There was just one 66 Sqn pilot left at base, and he gave us details of the squadron and who the various characters were. He also checked us out on a Hunter Mk 6.

HAWKER HUNTER Mk 6. Single-seat fighter. One Rolls-Royce 10,000lb thrust Avon Mk 203 axial-flow jet engine. Span 33 feet 9 inches. Length 46 feet. Loaded weight 17,750lb. Maximum airspeed 715mph at sea level & Mach 0.95 at 36,000 feet. Time to 45,000 feet 7.5 minutes. Served with the RAF from 1956 to 1962.

Eventually Whisky and I joined the rest of the squadron in Cyprus. After arrival we were obviously a bit cocky in the bar because the next morning we were herded in to 'Sammy' Osborne's office, the OC and a former Battle of Britain pilot. He gave us a tremendous dressing down. We had not made a good impression, we were to sit in the crew room, read our pilot's notes, speak when spoken to, call the flight commanders 'Sir', and he would tell us when we could fly. So we sat, read our pilot's notes and Flying Order Books and waited. Most of the squadron set off to do some air-to-ground gunnery.

Told that we were too inexperienced to do that, John and I were sent to a radar station at Cape Greco, on the far southeast corner of Cyprus. We were royally entertained, very often we went to bed with a hangover, only to be woken at the crack of dawn by fighters coming across the top at about fifty feet. The guys at Cape Greco said 'Don't forget, whenever you've got time give us a beat up, it really brightens our day.' Eventually we got flying again. One day I had a solo flight to practice some aerobatics. I sneaked down to Cape Greco to show them my skills as a display pilot, with all of my fifty Hunter hours. I did a couple of low passes and wingovers. Then, to my surprise, the low-fuel warning lights came on. Quick calculations caused me to reckon that I had insufficient fuel to reach Akrotiri, and there was nothing closer. I set a low power setting, crept up to 10,000 feet and edged my way home, praying that the fuel would last. Fortunately there was just enough fuel to give me a chance of a straight-in approach. I landed, taxied in and shut down, hoping that the refuellers would not notice how little fuel was in the tanks. It certainly taught me a lesson.

By now the squadron had a new OC – the previously mentioned Bairsto, now a squadron leader. His task was to clean up 66, which was not doing very well. We were in the doldrums with few serviceable aircraft and our weaponeering results were poor. Bairsto came to ring the changes, and he certainly did that. In just over a year we changed from being the Cinderella of Fighter Command to winning the renowned Dacre trophy, which meant that we were top of weapons scores, aircraft serviceability and all sorts of other efficiency criteria. During Bairsto's time in charge we revisited Cyprus, due to a scare in Lebanon, I think. The Americans were landing there and the British were going in to Jordan. We provided an armed air escort for transport aircraft. It was just incredible. We were based at Nicosia, where the airfield was crammed with aircraft. The hangars were full and two of our airmen were working on the ejection seat of a Hunter parked in the open. Somehow they managed to release the firing mechanism. The airman kneeling on the seat inside, because he realised the seat was going to activate in no time at all, pushed the other guy off the ladder. He then forced himself back against the instrument panel. With a huge bang the seat went off, missing this cowering wreck inside the cockpit. The seat dropped harmlessly about fifty yards away, just missing a number of parked aircraft. We then tried to work out how the man in the cockpit could possibly have stayed there without being hit. A crane moved the seat up and down the rails with him in the cockpit. There was no way that he could find a space for that seat to miss him, but in the heat of the moment he had somehow done it.

Soon it was time to go back to Acklington, and I was allowed to fly back instead of travelling in a Beverley. The Hunter formation headed out, to stage through El Adem, in North Africa, then to Malta, where I noticed a brake hydraulic leak. One of the locally based technicians serviced the undercarriage, and said that we really ought to do a retraction test after all the work that had been done, but the necessary equipment was not available. 'You'll probably be alright' he said. We flew next day to the south of France, where I noticed that the undercarriage was slow to come down, but I thought no more of it. However, when we joined the circuit at Acklington, the starboard undercarriage refused to come down. I tried the emergency system, negative and positive g and I bounced it on the runway, but nothing would shift it. I was committed to a two-wheel landing.

After discussing the problem with the 'boss', who had raced to air traffic control, we decided to leave the underwing drop-tanks attached. The tanks were made of synthetic material, not metal, so we felt there was not much chance of a tank exploding. I touched down and held one wing up as long as possible. Eventually it hit the ground, the aircraft slewed off the runway and stopped. The Customs officer, there to welcome us in, said 'Were you in that aeroplane that did the forced landing?' I said, 'Yes, it was me.' 'Wow, it was worth coming out just to see that. Don't worry about declaring anything, I'm happy to let you through with anything.' I had nothing to declare, but I did not know that some of the groundcrew had stuffed cameras and other things in the back end of the drop-tanks. They watched with horror as my aircraft landed with the drop-tanks taking the force of the landing. I never did find out if the cameras were damaged.

In mid-1959 I was short-toured slightly and posted to Gütersloh, Germany, to join 14 Sqn, also on Hunters.

Gütersloh was a great fighter station, and had once been a Luftwaffe base. In the Officers' Mess there was a tower, half way up which was a special room that was supposed to have been where Goering used to entertain his young fighter pilots. He would sit at one end of the table and any junior pilot, or somebody with whom he just wanted to have some fun, would sit at the other end. There was a panel in the floor by Goering's seat. He would raise the panel and pull a handle that released a beam in the ceiling. The beam then fell on to the 'swede' of the other guy. He obviously saw this as a great joke; we carried on that custom, and I recall that I went through the 'Goering' ceremony.

From dawn to dusk there were aircraft on two minutes standby, ready to protect the Air Defence Identification Zone, a 'buffer' zone between the NATO and Eastern Bloc countries, from incursions by Russian aircraft. By now I seemed to be developing some skill at weaponeering and I really enjoyed the gunnery camps on the island of Sylt, just off the German coast near the Danish border. In winter the island was a miserable spot, but in summer it was a holiday place where very few people wore any clothes on the beach. The mixture of nudist colony and Air Force station was a bit explosive. After a couple of camps I was selected for the RAF gunnery team for the RAF Germany/NATO 'meet' so I spent a lot of time at Sylt in about 1960. Unfortunately the social life was compelling, and although I probably had the ability to make the first team, I probably also had too many hangovers so I finished up with the reserve group and, sadly, never made it to a NATO shoot.

In 1961 I met Audrey. She had come out with the British Forces Education System to teach Service children at the Sundern Primary School, close to Gütersloh. A friend brought her over to the mess one day, and, in 1962, we married.

Soon afterwards I had another fun trip to Cyprus, where 14 Sqn took on the resident squadron: 208. We had a gunnery competition, with each squadron able to put up four pilots, of which I was one. There was one flag for each squadron, and if you shot the flag off that was your bad luck. At the end of the day the holes in each flag were counted up, and the flag with most holes was the winner. We upstaged 208 in just about every part of the competition, including taking our four Hunters in line abreast on the runway and doing a beat up on the way back. We also got more holes through the flag so we were delighted and went home happy.

My squadron disbanded at the beginning of 1963. By that time I had been back to the UK a couple of times, had done an Instrument Rating Examiner's course and then later the Day Fighter Combat School (DFCS) course to become a fighter leader and weapons' instructor. I was delighted to get posted to Binbrook, Lincolnshire, as an instructor on the RAF Central Fighter Establishment – the DFCS and the RAF equivalent of 'Top Gun.' We arrived in Lincolnshire in the January of 1963, which was the time of 'the big freeze.' Eventually we bought a bungalow in Tetney, near Grimsby.

We had courses coming through from all the Hunter squadrons around the world. It was an excellent job with lots of exciting flying, low-level air combat, rocketing, bombing, fighter tactics and gunnery – air-to-air and air-to-ground. We did most of the instruction during the spring to autumn time, and in winter we would visit sunnier parts to evaluate squadrons in their own environment.

I managed to get on two Far East visits, where we flew with the RAF in Singapore, with Australians at Butterworth, Malaya, and with the little RAF squadron at Hong Kong. There were only five aircraft based there, but it was one of the most sought after postings at that time. The four of us from DFCS had a gunnery competition with the Hong Kong unit, using an air-to-ground gunnery range on the other side of the harbour from Kai Tak airport. I was the last one to fly in our team, with the event evenly poised, so my efforts would decide the outcome. On my final pass, as I was pulling out, a spare round ricocheted off the ground, hit my windscreen and grazed it. The local OC was livid that I had damaged his Hunter. He was also 'gunning' for me because he thought that I must have come too close to the target. We waited with bated breath for the film to be developed. Fortunately it showed that I had come to the minimum range but not a yard closer. Not only that, my score was good enough to give us the edge, so we won the shoot-out. Another great event was the birth of our first son, Roger, in 1964.

One of the little highlights at Binbrook was that during one of the fighter leader courses we used to fly low-level air combat at much lower heights than the squadrons were allowed to. The station put out a warning in the local paper, asking the local population to bear with us for a limited period. A resident wrote in to say that 'In recent weeks the amount of local flying activity has been quite incredible. I have had my apple trees pruned and my rose bushes trimmed. This latest announcement of intense low flying means that I can dispense with my lawnmower.' We invited him to the Officers' Mess for a drink.

While at Binbrook I had another landing incident, this time in a Meteor 7. I had been tugging a target off the Lincolnshire coast, and after I had dropped the flag, a main wheel would not come down. I was not too familiar with the aircraft. However, an experienced Meteor pilot, helped by another one flying a Hunter, gave me advice. Because the external fuel tanks were metal we decided that it would be safer to jettison them rather than land with them attached. With their help I got rid of the drop- and ventral tanks. The Meteor swung off the runway further than the Hunter had a few years earlier, but I climbed out unscathed.

GLOSTER METEOR Mk T7. Two-seat trainer and target tug. Two 3,600lb Rolls-Royce Derwent 5 or 8 jet engines. Span 37 feet 3 inches. Length 43 feet 6 inches. Loaded weight 17,600lb. Maximum airspeed 590mph. Climb to 30,000 feet 5.5 minutes. Entered service in 1948 as the RAF's first jet trainer.

After eight years of continuous flying on Hunters, I was posted to Chivenor as OC the General Duties (OC GD) Flight for some serious work as the station commander's right-hand man. Fortunately I was able to keep flying. I kept current on the Hunter, and used my lunch break to fly a Meteor 7 off Lundy Island, where people fired at my flag while I chewed sandwiches. The job was quite pleasant. In 1966 our second son, Clive, was born. He later followed the family footsteps and is now a pilot with United Airlines in America. Half way through my tour I had a change of station commander and OC Administrative Wing (OC Admin). Two very pleasant gentlemen were replaced by rather more difficult officers. I started to find the job less than enjoyable. The OC Admin, a secretarial officer, made life extremely miserable for those of us in the admin department, so I thought that I would apply to become a flying instructor. 'Yes, you can be accepted, but you will have to wait until the end of your tour.' That was distressing, since I did not want to go to CFS that much anyway, particularly when volunteers were sought to go to America to fly Phantoms. The TSR 2 had just been cancelled and the Labour government had just bought American Phantoms that were to be built with Rolls-Royce engines. As a weapons instructor and all the rest of it, I thought I was a natural. I put my name forward, only to be told that I was reserved for CFS and I could not go to America. In 1967 my tour ended and I went to CFS, at Little Rissington.

CFS had the Jet Provost Mk 3, known as the 'constant thrust and variable noise' machine. On my first take-off in one, I thought the brakes had stuck on, we hardly moved. Advanced training was done at Valley on Gnats or, for multi-engines, on the Varsity, which I had never flown before. The natural thing for me to do was to go to the Gnat squadron, but I felt that a change would be pleasant. An old rugby mate, now a Varsity flight commander, said he would do everything he could to get me to Oakington. With no large aircraft experience, I obviously had an awful lot to learn.

Things came to a head when we flew to Berlin. The staff pilot said to me 'Well look, you can be the co-pilot on the way out and I'll be the captain. However, I am only a student captain, so you have got to do your normal job as a co-pilot and instruct me on how to be a good captain at the same time.' I had no idea how to be a 'route' co-pilot. My normal Fighter Command-type radio calls made him wring his hands in horror. At the post-flight de-brief he took me aside and said that my standard was totally unacceptable. He would let me fly back as the student captain, with him as co-pilot. If there were not a dramatic change in performance I would be off the course. I must have improved slightly because I was given an extra navigation exercise. I was to go to with the CFS Commandant on a really nice 'jolly' to a helicopter school, used by the French for mountain-flying techniques. After this extra tuition I was let loose on the advanced, multi-engined RAF students at Oakington.

VICKERS VARSITY T1. Advanced trainer for pilots and other aircrew. Two 1,950HP Bristol Hercules 264 engines. Span 95 feet 9 inches. Length 67 feet 6 inches. Maximum loaded weight 37,500lb. Maximum airspeed 288mph at 10,000 feet. The Varsity entered RAF service in 1951 as a replacement for the Wellington T10 crew trainer and remained in service at Oakington until 1974. Similar to the Valetta, but with greater span, length and wing area, the Varsity had a tricycle undercarriage. Marshall carried out auto-landing trials in one at Bedford and Marham from 1952 to 1966, and also modified one to carry nuclear materials. Leslie Worsdell captained the last five Marshall flight tests, in Varsity WL 691, on 3rd and 4th July 1969. The schedule included contamination tests.

We bought a house in Bluntisham village, near St Ives. Soon after arriving at Oakington a signal arrived, which called for volunteer pilots to take part in a film of the Battle of Britain. Pilots needed to have significant fighter experience, be a flying instructor and have piston-engine experience, preferably on tailwheel aircraft. I qualified in all aspects and was selected for the filming unit, which was to be based at Duxford. There were no longer any squadrons at Duxford, which was probably under Care and Maintenance.

We duly assembled at the beginning of 1968 and waited to be converted to Spitfires. I had previously met the OC of the little unit, Wg Cdr George Elliot, when he was OC a Venom squadron in the Middle East. His Spitfire experience was way back in the past, but at least he had flown it. He managed to get hold of a couple of two-seaters, from Ireland, I think, and then checked us out. It was a matter of two circuits as far as I was concerned. Each time we came round on finals, the controls got heavier and heavier as George was helping me to round out and get the thing back on the ground. After two circuits he obviously felt that he had had enough. He leaped out, saying 'Off you go then laddie.'

The Spitfire was great, a bit like a vintage Bentley. It felt superb once in the air, with a lot of noise and power. As far as landing and take-off were concerned, particularly on a tarmac runway, it was a real handful. The brakes were woefully inadequate. Probably, the ones we were flying had not been kept all that serviceable because the aircraft had been on camp gates, museums and all sorts of places. However, about a dozen had been made 'serviceable.' There was one glorious occasion when all twelve flew at the same time, but even on that flight one had an engine failure and force landed. A bunch of RAF technicians worked really hard to keep the Spitfires serviceable and in good condition. There was a production line over at Henlow where a company was preparing all these old aircraft, and a former RAF Group Captain, Hamish Mahaddie, was scouring the world to find the aircraft. He would get them to Henlow, where they were put in to flying condition. I was sent there one day to pick one up, registration G-AIST, that had been prepared off the production line. When I arrived at Henlow everyone had gone to lunch and the Spitfire was sitting on the apron. Some guy chewing sandwiches said 'Yeah, help yourself, it's ready, take it away.' I went out to it and I noticed that the pneumatic pressure, which worked the brakes, was low. I managed to get this guy to come out and charge up the pressure, thinking that if the pneumatic pump did not work at least a full reservoir would last until I got to Duxford, half an hour away. After starting the engine I called Henlow ATC, but there was no reply. I presumed that they were having lunch as well, took off and headed for Duxford.

Things started to go wrong fairly quickly. The cylinder head temperature went up, the pneumatic pressure dropped to zero, the generator warning light came on and all the electric services faded rapidly. I thought 'The sooner I get this heap on the ground the better.' I knew that Duxford had a grass runway, so with no brakes I could land on the grass and at least I could keep it somewhere under control. Arriving at Duxford with no radio I could not tell anybody that I was coming. I looked down and there was a tractor, with a lawn mower on the back, going up and down the grass runway. Despite waggling the wings, the tractor driver obviously thought I was having a bit of fun and did not get off the runway so I was now obliged to land on the tarmac. I noticed that there was quite a significant crosswind, and I dare not stay airborne any longer because the cylinder head temperature was now firmly in the red. I did not want the engine to seize, so I had to make the best of it. The runway at Duxford was nice and long, about 2,000 yards. Touching down at the beginning of the runway I just managed to stop by the end, turn off and shut down. The ground crew came out to meet me as I was climbing out. One of them climbed up and looked in the cockpit. He called out 'Excuse me, sir, come back and have a look at this.' I had a look. The airman gave a couple of pulls on the seat harness, an old Sutton model with a pin through the middle. The webbing was so rotten that it just snapped. I was really glad that the Air Force guys were there to make safe the job that the commercial people had not done over at Henlow. That was a lucky escape.

The filming was fascinating; there were all sorts of things going on. One pilot took off, and was supposed to go through smoke and appear out the far side of it, to be filmed as he emerged. Going through the smoke he lost his sense of direction and finished up heading straight for the camera crew, poised on the far side to film it. We saw the 'rushes' the next day. The last thing was this aeroplane heading straight towards us and the world turning upside down as the camera man flattened himself on the floor to avoid the whirling four-bladed propeller. On another occasion we were trying to film a pilot taxiing in, having made an appalling landing. I had to taxi the aircraft in. The 'marshaller' was a film extra that had been taught to do the job. I had to taxi in a fairly confined space, spin round, and he was supposed to be out front directing me round. Because he was not experienced enough in the role he kept getting lost underneath the propeller. I was terrified that I was going to chew him up, but he survived. When I stopped the engine, I had to get out, and give my white sweater to, I think, Michael Caine. He would then wear the sweater, and climb out of the cockpit looking exhausted from the tricky mission he had just 'flown.' The producer did not want RAF pilots to be seen in the film. We were to be in the aeroplane, but we were not to be recognisable. Every time the camera did a close up an actor had to be there, not the pilot.

Some of the flying was at the Battle of Britain airfield of Hawkinge, on the cliffs of Dover. We had to do a series of low passes coming over the cliffs. We were running in fast over the coast, in Vic formation, banging around as we hung in there in close formation. It was a very bumpy day, and I remember thinking 'Boy, I hope these wings are stuck on properly.' I was quite glad when that was over. At one stage the weather was so poor that we were not getting enough filming in. The film company decided to move the whole show to the south of France. We then had an exciting trip down to Montpellier, being given a hero's welcome everywhere we went. An armada of Spitfires and Messerschmitts all going along together attracted a fair amount of attention. We got rather spoiled.

I did have a try in a Spanish-built, Merlin-engined Messerschmitt 109 and Heinkel 111, a Hurricane and a B-25 – the filming aircraft. The Hurricane seemed terribly slow compared to the Spitfire. It had a big fat wing and although it turned remarkably well it seemed to have a natural cruising speed of about 185 knots. It was a solid old thing. The one that I flew had been rebuilt by a Canadian and had not got genuine Hawker parts in it. It used to run out of elevator control at low speed on finals, so the chances of doing a decent landing were fairly remote.

As for the Messerschmitt 109, I did only one flight in it. It had a lockable tailwheel. You had to get yourself lined up on the runway, lock the tailwheel, hit the power and try to get the tail up as quickly as possible before the aircraft became uncontrollable. A fast and rugged aeroplane, it struck me as being a pretty brisk aeroplane in a straight line, but it did not seem to turn or handle as well as the Spitfire and it was also a brute of a thing to land. The Me 109s used in the film were mainly flown by Spanish pilots that had been flying them in the Spanish Air Force up to about five years before the film was made. A lot of the pilots had got quite considerable experience on the aircraft. Even so, a number of them had landing accidents, and it was not an uncommon sight to find a 109 in the hangar with some significant damage to the landing gear.

One of the big film shots that we had to get was a mass dogfight. The plan was to have all the fighter aircraft behind the B-25, stepped up either side, with one Spitfire and one Messerschmitt sitting right underneath the B-25. In the astrodome halfway down the back of the B-25 the director was keeping an eye on things. When he saw all the aircraft in position he was going to call 'Background action.' The aircraft stacked up either side would, alternately, in fours, come across the back of the B-25. When a lot of aircraft were 'in camera', located in the rear gun turret, he would call 'Foreground action.' The two aircraft sitting underneath would then pop up, with the Spitfire trailing smoke and the Messerschmitt firing at it. We tried this several times, getting very mediocre results. All the aircraft were just like little dots in the background, looking a bit pathetic. We kept trying to get closer and closer. The poor old producer was getting mad with the expense of putting all these aircraft up over a period of three days, trying to get a decent shot, but failing to get it. The position I had was the lead Spitfire in the first four that had to come across the back of the B-25. We were edging further and further forward. I thought 'If I don't get my four *really* close behind the B-25, nobody else is going to do it.' I just aimed to fly past at about fifty feet away. As we closed in on the camera I would call 'Break' and my echelon of three would go all over the place. Following behind would be four Messerschmitts that would all follow us and try and get on to somebody's tail and we would all stay in camera view as long as we could. Eventually I got it close enough. The foreground aircraft then had to squeeze in to the gap between. The next morning, when we saw the 'rushes', it was brilliant. It was the best mass combat shot of the whole film.

The film slowed down in the autumn of 1968, and I was due to go back to Oakington. Another signal came along, asking for volunteers to fly with the Royal Malaysian Air Force (RMAF) at Kuantan on the east coast of the Malay peninsular. The RMAF was forming fighter squadrons because the British were pulling out of Singapore and would no longer be responsible for air defence within the South East Asia Treaty Organisation. I had the right fighter and instructional qualifications so I put my name forward for the two-year posting. The next thing we knew we were heading for the Far East.

The journey out, in September 1968, was through Lyneham. At Singapore we boarded a Twin Pioneer that flew us up to our new home. At Kuantan I was to fly the CL-41, which in Canadian terms was a Tutor, made by Canadair. The RMAF called it the Tebuan (Wasp). It was the only model sold for ground-attack and fighter work. When I arrived, there was a pile of drop tanks, rockets and gun pods in a corner of the hangar. They had been bought with the aircraft but nobody had got round to putting them on and doing any flight trials. Initially, my job was to work with two or three other RAF instructors to train up the Malaysian pilots to be fighter pilots. Then, because nobody else had had any experience in that area, I did the weapon aiming, carriage and release trials for all these various bits and pieces. It was a lot of hard work, but also fun. The CL-41 was a good little aeroplane, two seats side-by-side, with a single jet engine. It performed very well, a bit like a Strikemaster.

CANADAIR CL-41G TEBUAN. Two-seat attack/trainer. One General Electric J85-J4 jet engine. Span 36 feet 6 inches. Length 32 feet. Loaded weight 11,300lb. Maximum airspeed 480mph at 28,500 feet.

An air test in a CL-41 provided me with some excitement. It had been in for a repair and had been cleared back for service. I climbed to 30,000 feet over the South China Sea, and was just going through a layer of cloud when there was a huge bang. The engine ran down to zero, and seized. There was no chance of a restart, so I had to do a deadstick landing. Fortunately, I was only thirty miles from base, and I had plenty of height to glide back home. I can remember looking down at this airfield and thinking 'Well, I have practised this on many, many occasions, so now I have got to do it for real.' The glide approach worked out okay. Probably hoping to see me slide off the end of the runway, the firemen in their 'crash' trucks came rushing out, but I landed successfully. It was the only engine failure or serious incident during my time at Kuantan.

By the time I left Kuantan the Tebuan was quite an effective little fighter, and we had also trained up weapons instructors on it. I got a Queen's Commendation there, which I understand was for that work, although nobody says what you get it for. My posting came through, to join 229 OCU. I was back in the fighter instruction role, flying Hunters again.

The fighter weapons school at Binbrook had closed, and this was the remnant of it. At this time we were experiencing some family problems; we prayed about what to do. Out of the blue came the most extraordinary posting. In 1971 I was sent to the British Aircraft Corporation (BAC) – later to become British Aerospace – factory at Warton, Lancashire. I was to be the RAF liaison officer, with the new rank of squadron leader, helping with the development of the Jaguar fighter. The aircraft was flying in prototype form, but was not yet in RAF service.

SEPECAT JAGUAR GR Mk1. Single-seat fighter-bomber. Two 7,140lb Rolls-Royce Turbomeca RT 172 Adour 104 turbofan jet engines. Span 28 feet 6 inches. Length 51 feet. Loaded weight 32,600lb. Maximum airspeed 1,055mph (Mach1.6)

at 33,000 feet. Climb to 30,000 feet 1.5 minutes. Ceiling 46,000 feet. Ferry range
2,270 miles. Two 30mm Aden cannons. A Franco/British development of the
Breguet BR 121 project, it entered RAF service in 1972 and, in 1999, is still in
service.

I settled in to my new job, which was fascinating because it was very much
a development and testing role. The RAF liked to put a typical ground
attack pilot in the factory, to fly with the Company test pilots. Although
they had the expertise with the slide rule stuff, the performance and so on,
it really needed somebody to say 'Well, it might be alright in theory, but
does it work in practice?' That was my job, to take part in the development
of the weapons-aiming and navigation system. The Jaguar was a very
sophisticated aeroplane for its time. Until then, in the Hunter certainly, you
flew around with a map and a stopwatch and hoped that you found the
target at the end. This aircraft had an onboard weapon-aiming and
navigation computer, with a moving map and a head-up display.

The Harrier was moving along a similar, albeit a little more primitive
road and I was able to visit Wittering to fly one for comparison. We were
really breaking new ground and learned a lot about using head-up displays.
We discovered that although all the information was presented on the
windscreen, it was not quite as easy to interpret it as we had first thought.
You are looking through the information and are not necessarily conscious
that some of the digits are changing. With an instrument, if you see a needle
move, you get an analogue presentation of the change. If it is digits just
ticking over, you do not see that. There is no demand on your eyes to see
the change; you need to focus on each little presentation in turn. As time
went on we realised that we needed to get more of a trend indication on the
head-up display, particularly with heights and speeds. As a weapons
platform the Jaguar was very stable, it had a lot more fuel than any previous
aircraft I had flown, and it went a long way at low level. A two-seat version
was used for engine development work, but was not normally available for
dual checks. I was put in the back seat for a flight to Boscombe Down. The
chief test pilot, Paul Millett, flew the aircraft, gave an air display for,
I think, the Shah of Iran, and then went to a meeting, saying 'You fly it back
to Warton.' That was my check out. I got it back in one piece.

Shortly after that I got a flight in a prototype. I had to go at maximum
power at low level with a device on board which upset the rudder with a
series of deflections. The objective was to see how stable the aircraft fin
was. I had to do a run out, turn and come back the other way. The boffins
had worked out that there was just sufficient fuel to do this. When I started
to prepare for the flight the weather was quite good. By the time I launched,
the weather was deteriorating, but I felt that I could not give up. Off I went
in to the murk over the Irish Sea, turned at the end of the outbound leg and
set off back, hoping that I could find Warton again.

This Jaguar did not have the navigation system so I was completely dependent on visual landmarks to get back to the starting area. Using absolutely full power, steaming along at about 600 knots, with things vibrating progressively more and more, then dying down again, the fuel was going down very rapidly. I thought that I could not stop the trial, as it would make the whole thing null and void. Fortunately Blackpool Tower emerged from the murk at just the right moment and I picked up Warton just beyond. Trying to get down quickly before I ran out of fuel, I made a rather poor approach and decided to overshoot. While I was going round the next circuit the low-fuel lights came on. I mentioned during the de-briefing that the fuel lights had illuminated. There was a deathly hush, apparently no one had ever got down to that level of fuel before. I said 'Well, at least I have proved that the lights worked.' I was forgiven and was allowed to continue flying.

While at Warton I had to make a decision whether to stay in the RAF or to leave. It was difficult, but with Audrey's mother living with us, and not wishing to send the boys to boarding school, we felt that it was right for me to leave. I started to look for a job and prepared for my Airline Transport Pilot's Licence during my last year at Warton. I had thought that I might perhaps be offered a job at Warton, but I was really the wrong age and was not ETPS qualified. One day I went into the pilot's restaurant. There was a stranger there, older than the average pilot was. He had whitish hair, a dapper grey moustache and he was on his own. I went over to chat to him. He was from Marshall of Cambridge, and he told me about the Hercules test flying, the flying school, and the other activities. At the end of our discussion I said 'By the way, do you happen to need any pilots?' He replied that they were looking for one right now, someone who would also be interested in airport management as well as flying. 'Would I do, and who would I approach?' I said. 'Well, me' he replied, 'because I am the airport director and chief pilot.' His name was Leslie Worsdell. I was invited down to Cambridge for an interview. Funnily enough, I still had my house near Cambridge, which I was trying to sell because I thought that Cambridge would not be a good area for finding a job.

The interview, in early 1974, was unusual. Like a number of other people, my first contact with Sir Arthur was in the ground floor corridor of the Control building. 'Who are you?' he asked. I said 'I'm John Preece.' 'Oh yes, you've come for an interview Preece.' He then proceeded to do most of his interview on the spot. Later, with Leslie, I was taken up to Sir Arthur's office for the rest of the interview. It seemed that the decision had already been made, and I was promptly offered a job. At that time, assuming that I came with the correct licences, my salary was to be £4,300 a year. I then had the panic of getting my licences and the Instrument Rating in time, and I had to take one exam twice before I passed it, which nearly caused me heart failure.

At Cambridge the first thing I was asked to do was to go to Wichita, in Kansas, USA, to collect the new Citation aircraft that the Company had just purchased. Bob Smythe had already gone out there. As I already had a lot of jet experience, which some of the other pilots lacked, I was chosen to be the second pilot on the new Citation. It was a lengthy ferry flight back. Although the course qualified both of us as captains, Bob made it quite clear that he was in charge and he was going to fly it all the way home. I would be co-piloting the whole way; I had to live with that. At Fort Chimo, in North Canada, we had a snag with the undercarriage. This caused us to stay overnight, where we lived in a wooden cabin with guys who did helicopter patrols in that region. By chance the only engineer in the north of Canada just happened to be visiting Chimo to do a repair on a Boeing 737. He managed to fix our problem. We continued to Søndre Strømfjord, in Greenland, and then over to Iceland for a night stop.

Back at Cambridge I got a welcome from Marshall's and a flavour of how things worked there. I said to Leslie Worsdell 'Now we are back from this rather arduous ferry flight, when do you want us to come in to work?' thinking that I might get a few days off to get over the fatigue. 'What's wrong with tomorrow morning?' he said. I got the feeling that there was a fairly high pressure of work. So it proved to be, with the Aero Club, the business flying with the Citation and the Aztec, and the test flying. After a couple of years I became qualified as a Hercules captain.

A typical month at Marshall's would be perhaps ten flying hours on the Citation, five or six on the Aztec, maybe two or three Hercules air tests, and forty to fifty hours of Cessna 150 instruction. Often we would pick up some other aircraft types, like Michael Marshall's Rallye Minerva and Hercules aircraft of the Royal Jordanian and Swedish Air Forces.

The RAF decided to fit its only Beagle Husky, a tailwheel aircraft, with new radios. The aircraft, XW 635, had been given to the RAF for Air Training Corps cadet flying by Billy Butlin, Hughie Green, and Fred and Bobby Pontin. It would take three cadets in one go, against a single cadet in the Chipmunk. Ironically, after the expensive radio refit the aircraft did not remain in service for very long.

At one stage I had quite a number of VIPs to instruct. I taught Earl Mountbatten's grandson to fly, and Lady Adeane, who had a farm to the southeast of Cambridge. There was also the Marquess of Bristol: John Jermyn. I took him right up to revision for the final handling test, but he was not the easiest of people to teach to fly. Unfortunately, he never did that test so he did not complete his course. Later he bought a helicopter and passed his flying test on that. Aged just forty-four, he died in January 1999.

I became a CAA check pilot on the Citation and the Aztec. This involved some fairly demanding work with other Citation owners. One businessman had bought a Citation and then leased it out to an air operator. I became the check pilot for this operation and went on a flight to Italy. The idea was to do route checks and training with two of the company pilots. We were then to pick up the owner from Cannes and fly back. The owner wanted to fly the aircraft home, saying that he wished to pick up some tips

from me. He held an American CPL and Instrument Rating. The trip back
to South Wales convinced me that he was not very competent. When I got
out of the aircraft I advised him to do some more training. As a
businessman, and not flying the aircraft that often, I suggested that he
needed to be very careful and not take undue risks. Perhaps he ought also
to consider having a professional pilot with him. A few months later he was
flying from South Wales to Jersey where he had a tax-free home. When he
arrived at Jersey the weather was very poor. He made an ILS approach,
from which he tried to overshoot because he could not see the runway,
somehow lost control of the aircraft and collided with a house. Sadly, both
he – the sole occupant of the aircraft – and somebody in the house, died.
This event convinced me that businessmen and business jets should not
really go together. The professional pilot should really be flying that sort of
aircraft, with the businessman in the back, or at least sitting beside the pilot.

When the Falklands war was declared in 1982, there was soon an
immense amount of activity. That couple of months gave me more flying
than at any other time in my flying career. In one of the early trials I was
flying a Hercules tanker giving fuel away to another Hercules. The
refuelling route was over the west of England, running down to the Scilly
Isles and back again. There was a lot of cloud about and, on this particular
run, with the other Hercules linked to us, we did not know exactly where
we were. Because of the ease of formation flying while in straight and level
flight, I tried to keep going in a straight line for as long as possible.
Eventually Dave Ryding, the flight engineer, cut off the fuel going to the
receiving Hercules. We then realised that because we had gone so far south-
west and had given away so much fuel we were in danger of running out of
fuel ourselves. We certainly had insufficient fuel to reach Cambridge with
an acceptable reserve. Consequently we diverted to Lyneham to pick up
some more fuel. How embarrassing.

During trials with Hercules tankers and receivers I had my first attempt
at coupling to a tanker from the receiving end. I had done a number of
flights with Boscombe Down pilots who were assessing the Hercules for
suitability as a receiver behind a Hercules tanker. It looked fairly
straightforward so I was somewhat embarrassed to find just how difficult it
was to put the probe into this wretched 'shuttlecock' bouncing round in
front of me. It took me four or five goes before I made the first contact. The
thought of heading off down over the South Atlantic, knowing that a
successful flight depended on getting the probe successfully into the bucket
without bending or breaking anything, was quite daunting. I took my hat
off to those Air Force pilots that did that very much as a matter of routine.

We then had a trial with a Citation of the Spanish Armada (Navy). The
Spanish bought Citations as coastal reconnaissance aircraft, to look for
smugglers and drug runners. Marshall fitted an infrared pod underneath the
fuselage and then we did the flight trials to see how effective the infrared
filming was. We flew with the Spanish pilots on board, either to the Thames

estuary or down to the Avon where we knew that a lot of ships would be around. Flying at low level we could pick up a blip on the aircraft radar and home in on it using the infrared TV screen. By the time we got within half a mile we had a very clear picture of the ship. We could recognise what sort of ship it was and identify the vessel without making visual contact with it. After several trial flights we were satisfied that it was working properly.

In 1984 I became chief pilot and chief flying instructor when Doug Page retired. I was slightly surprised at this, expecting that Leslie would be retiring at some stage and that I would just stay on the airport management side. Nevertheless, I had two or three enjoyable years in those roles, and Dennis Pasco became chief test pilot.

I was still understudying Leslie as airport manager, however. One of the jobs he used to give me was to be in charge of the snow plan. There was one day when I got it totally wrong. We were expecting a Queen's Flight Andover aircraft to come in to drop off Princess Margaret. It had been snowing wet snow most of the day; some of the snow, not a huge amount, lay on the runway. We decided not to clear it, but let the aircraft land on top of the slush. If we had started to sweep the snow off, we would have had to delay the Royal Flight. The aircraft, after one missed approach, landed, dropped off the Princess and headed off again. We decided not to start sweeping, as the forecast was for the temperature to stay just above freezing. We thought a lot of it could melt off overnight; we would then clear off what was left the next day. On coming in early the next morning I found that the forecast had been totally wrong. During the night the sky had cleared, the temperature had dropped, and the slush had frozen solid. It was not level at all; it was rutted ice, just like the North Pole. There was nothing we could do to shift it. The airport was closed for about three days. Sir Arthur was not impressed. 'The runway is our lifeline and the gateway to the hangars' he used to say. 'If the airfield is not open no work can be done.' Eventually we managed to persuade Stansted to send us a special chemical sprayer to help clear the runway. We waited until midday, when the temperature was at its highest. The machine got to work, spraying pellets out of the back. The pellets started to melt the ice and snow, which we managed to clear off before it froze again. Generally the snow plan worked well. We had some good equipment organised and driven by the fire crews. I had to work closely with them, and found them to be cheerful and hard working, often in miserable conditions.

In 1986 Leslie had to go to hospital to have an operation. He left me in charge of the airfield, during which time we had to resurface the main runway. Up to that time the runway had been concrete, but it was showing signs of deterioration. It was decided to coat the runway with a slurry seal. I was responsible for trying to keep the airfield open for most of the time and to allow the work to progress. Just after we got it finished we had the chance to witness the first wide-bodied departure from the new runway surface: a Royal Jordanian TriStar. The aircraft taxied out for departure, and I went out in one of the fire vehicles to see it off. I was horrified to see that when the TriStar turned, with the inner bogie virtually stationary, all the slurry seal came off onto the tyres. The aircraft finished up ready for departure with the left-hand set of wheels coated with muck. We had to hold him there while the crash crew and I got under the aircraft and, with crowbars and various other implements, got all this stuff peeled off the tyres. If the slurry had flown off during the take-off it would have severely damaged the flaps. It seemed like an hour, although it was probably only twenty minutes. Generally the resurfacing was successful and I quite enjoyed my time of running the airport. It was about this time, however, that I was beginning to feel I should make a move.

I had been working voluntarily with an organisation called Missionary Aviation Fellowship (MAF), a Christian charity that provides flying services in third world countries. I had been helping to fundraise for them for some time. In the latter half of 1986 I felt it was something I could do full time. MAF was very keen to have me come and work in Nairobi for them, mainly flying a Beech 99, but also to get involved in some of the management work later. After a lot of heart searching, I gave in my notice in November 1986, aiming to finish in January 1987. It was a big wrench and I did not do it light heartedly, particularly as it meant Leslie would have to find a new deputy. But I felt that it was the right time to mix my Christian faith with my professional skills, and this was one way I could do it. At the end of January 1987 I got a very warm send-off from my friends at Marshall's, and headed off to the USA to get my American licences. I then started my career as a mission pilot in Africa.

Flying in Africa was very different, but maybe that is another story. During my twelve years at Marshall's I flew around 6,000 hours. About 3,500 were on Cessna 150/152s, about 1,000 on the Hercules, another 1,000 on the Citation and about 500 on the Aztec. The job was always varied and challenging. Changing from four turbo-props to twin-jets to twin-piston, right down to the little trainers always kept you on your toes. There was probably a little too much flying instruction, but on the other hand I met some interesting people and I was never bored. In my time with the Company aircrew status changed significantly, with our salaries and conditions of service improving considerably. We also had to introduce some of the CAA rules for flight and working hours. But moving on, leaving Dennis, Colin, John Blake and Tim to carry on, it seemed that the place was in good hands. It was a most enjoyable twelve years, and I would not have missed it for anything.

[John continues to fly part time as an instructor with the Cambridge Aero Club].

Chapter 9

Colin Rudder

My employment as a pilot was probably the most unlikely thing ever to have happened to me. In my early days I had never had the slightest interest in flying other than buzzing around holding a Dinky toy or trying largely unsuccessfully to build a glider out of scraps of fragile balsa wood, glue and tissue paper.

Having been born at Wylde Green, Sutton Field, on 24th March 1937, I was educated at Wylde Green College and Smallwood Manor, in Staffordshire. After five years at Denstone College, also in Staffordshire, I served my National Service in 1956 and '57 with the Royal Artillery at Gravesend, Wales and Cyprus. My first real flight was from Nicosia to Beirut in what was probably a Viking of Air Liban. This and the return flight were impressive and marked the first time I saw a Lockheed Constellation, bringing in refugees from the Dutch East Indies. At this time I was on a short skiing holiday from Cyprus where I was stationed with an Artillery Regiment on ground security duties during the 'troubles.'

In 1958 I ambled through the entry requirements, which did not seem very great in those days, for the Faculty of Law at Birmingham University. I was soon exploring the campus with a few hundred other hopefuls and not really sure what it was all about. While discussing which pubs would be fun to visit that evening fate grabbed me by the scruff of the neck and drew my attention to one or two figures in blue uniform standing beside the recruiting stand urging all and sundry to 'Learn to Fly' with the UAS. Later I discovered that learning to fly was not particularly pushed and any comparison with flying clubs was strongly disapproved of, the emphasis being more to encourage officer material for the RAF. Calling it 'Raff' was even more strongly disapproved. Had I not set eyes on this stand I would never have pursued aviation again and almost certainly would never have learnt to fly as a private pilot. I had no personal or family reason to have interest in flying and the nearest connection was an uncle who had told me he had once been launched off an aircraft carrier in the back of a Fairey Swordfish. He was a Paymaster Lieutenant at the time! After five years in the Combined Cadet Force and two years National Service the idea of being a part time serviceman again appealed to me and the idea of flying intrigued me in the same way as being an astronaut might in later years. Not the sort of thing ordinary mortals would do and a leap into the unknown.

I was invited to a preliminary interview in the spacious late Victorian house that served as HQ and then to an intelligence test. This confused me because there was then an element of doubt as to how to tackle these IQ tests. I thought a carelessly answered paper would be unsuitable for those wishing to learn to fly but then again, were they looking for 'chancers' to go boldly into action and to hell with the consequences? I was a ditherer and did not complete the questions nor did I get them all right. I think it was all a formality as much later I sneaked a look at my records. I discovered that they had high hopes that with my National Service background (I was the only one) and being in the Faculty of Law (most were engineers) I would have a mature and steadying influence on my fellows. These hopes were not fulfilled.

Later still I was called back for another interview just when I thought they had rejected me. The adjutant, Bill Loverseed, interviewed me and informed me that they flew Chipmunks. At first I took that as a joke. I spoke to Bill twice in later years. The last time I saw him was not face to face but from a distant grandstand as he flew the aircraft he was demonstrating into the main runway at an early 1990s Farnborough Air Show in the most spectacular arrival I have ever seen. Nobody was hurt but the aircraft disappeared in a cloud of sparks, smoke, wheels and bits of flying metal. Aged sixty-six Bill died in a Dash-7 accident in November 1998.

Three years after joining the UAS only four of the original seventeen recruits were still left. Most went in the first few hours of flying, and I nearly did too. I had reached fourteen hours flying without going solo, but we did do an unreasonable amount of pre-solo stalling and spinning, which built up the hours. On 10th April 1959 'Mac' McLauchlan, an ex-Dakota pilot, walked into the crew-room and said 'Get your flying kit on Rudder. Solo today or you are chopped.' Needless to say, after a few passable landings at the grass airfield of Chetwynd, I was sent off on my first solo in Chipmunk WP 900. I sang to myself as I approached the field for the one landing I was authorised to do and laughed as I saw Mac's lonely little figure standing by his parachute beside the landing strip. I was still laughing as I bounced down the runway and took off for a second try. You can do just a few too many circuits and bumps with somebody in the back watching you and it usually comes as a relief to set off by oneself although some people think it is worse for the instructor watching you stagger off all alone. I have never found this to be so even after authorising over two hundred first solos. They are either good enough to justify relaxing as they go or so bad that you almost do not care any more. You cannot bring them back once you have got out of the aeroplane and only fate and their skill determine the rest.

My time in the UAS was very happy with good friends and great fun. I flew the best part of two hundred hours, mostly from Shawbury but also during camps at Martlesham Heath and Tangmere. We lived in the Officers' Mess and, being nominally AC 2s, full board cost about fifteen pence a day. So good was the service that I spent most of one summer vacation there even though there was no flying to be had except at weekends. In addition there was often the chance of a free flight with someone and I flew in a Piston Provost, Vampire, Hunter and a Comet.

DH CHIPMUNK T10. Two-seat primary trainer. One DH Gipsy Major 8 engine of 145HP. Span 34 feet 3 inches. Length 25 feet 9 inches. Loaded weight 2,000lb. Maximum speed at sea level 138mph. The first design of DH Canada, it first flew in May 1946, entered RAF service in 1950, and was finally retired from the AEFs in 1996.

Tangmere was, like Martlesham, an old fashioned place where for some extraordinary reason ATC maintained the wartime custom of clearing us to 'pancake' instead of land. The Mess was museum stuff with score boards for Spitfires airborne and 'kills.' It was a wonderful experience as it was still a living Mess while feeling like a film setting. The station commander was a young-looking man who had flown from Tangmere during the war and could not wait to tell us about it. 'The weather factor is excellent here and during the war we always knew we could get into 'Tangers' however low the cloud. Just drop down, low over the sea and slide over the coast to Tangers.'

I recall three incidents from that summer camp. My first real navigation flight was to the Long Man of Wilmington cut into the hillside, during which I asked for a time check to ATC while flying upside down as my contribution to the great outlandish time check competition. Taxiing slowly along in my Chipmunk and suddenly seeing the reflection of an enormous shape in my windscreen I turned round to discover a Hastings was closely following me. David Legg, a fellow student, who could land perfectly but was not allowed to go solo because he was unable to take off in a straight line. Eventually he joined the Fleet Air Arm with his bow tie and all and was last heard of by me as a picture in one of the tabloids after crash-landing his Scimitar in Aden harbour.

I was usually the standby for the Hack Trophy heats. These were spot glides for first year, 2,000 feet spot landings for second years and formation team or aerobatics for third. My favourite was the formation. Being number three and seeing the first two coming back down in the opposite direction whilst I was still going up in a stall turn or wing-over manoeuvre was very exciting and the first time so unexpected that I broke free and lost the formation. 'You got me' I transmitted and the poor leader thought it was my stiff upper lip saying goodbye as I crashed. I was always getting too close in formation and the leader was constantly instructing me over the radio to move off or move down or something. One day after a session of this calling 'Red Three move out,' or whatever, another instructor with a raised eyebrow greeted me on return with 'Red Three?'

I flew with twelve instructors in all but one or two of them only flew with me once. Sam Newington, being fresh out of CFS after a tour on Hunters, was eager to get to grips with a real student. One day he took me up for spinning and I was so laid back about it that I could not seem to recover and he had to take over. I was always nervous and unhappy about spinning ever after whereas before I had spun happily both deliberately solo and once accidentally.

Having to ask for a 'Steer,' a heading to fly to reach base, was considered infra dig and to be avoided at all costs. One day I was messing about with another student in conditions of deep haze. Later he told me that he thought I was keeping a check on position when in fact I was convinced that he was. On completion of our allotted time I tucked alongside him and followed him home. After a while I began to get suspicious and moved away in a different direction. He followed me. The next decision to be made was who was to suffer the humiliation of asking for a steer. After much gesticulation between us I gave up and transmitted to Shawbury for a steer. An urgent voice requested another transmission and then snappily issued climbs, turns, descents and God knows what to somebody and then returned to me with 'Steer 270 degrees; what is your altitude?' It turned out that we were both in thick haze, lost in the middle of the instrument letdown lane. Oh dear. For some time I was known as '270 Rudder.' Similarly, Mike Bishop became known as 'Ten seconds Bishop,' a reference to the time taken to down a pint of a particularly strong and potent cider that for a while became the subject of a timed drinking game. No one beat Mike's record and it took him almost two days to recover from the inevitable results of his achievement.

Evenings in the HQ house involved a lot of hard work and bar sports, the traditional way of letting off steam and showing the competitive spirit. One officer's wife, a formidable lady, was fond of picking up young men and carrying them around the room, a fate I avoided by constant vigilance. Once I was threatened with disciplinary proceedings for defending a girl friend that was drunk and asleep in the OC's office and whom an officer was trying to kiss. I fought him off her manfully.

My happy days with the UAS ended on completion of my third year, somewhat under a cloud after yet another failure to pass ground exams, which confirmed my dislike of the theory of flying. I maintained my PPL and spent the next few years in idleness frittering my inheritance mostly on cars and girl friends. The time for leaving the Midlands was fast approaching.

I moved to Saffron Walden and took a brief job with an estate agent. Later I used what remained of my money to buy a cottage, in which I still live thirty-three years later. With money requirements now looming I had to look to anything I had done or qualified for that could present me with a career of sorts. Previously I had rejected trying for a career in the RAF because the time coincided with a period of cuts in aircraft numbers and rumours that military flying would be phased out and replaced by missiles. Any flying requirement would probably be for helicopters a fate that made me shudder at that time. Later I applied for the Fleet Air Arm but after some consideration was told that I was one year too old, a decision that probably saved my life as it appeared that the attrition rate was extremely high with tragic accidents happening almost daily. This was, of course, at Wardroom parties and although flying accidents were more rare they did tend to be rather spectacular. A life of sea-borne Buccaneers or Sea Vixens is something I would have liked to have looked back on rather than lived. All that was left to me was the long and at times seemingly endless route of flying instruction.

I went to Bedfordshire for a residential course in flying instruction. I still had a few hours to make up to the minimum requirements and these I used to get familiar with the Cessna 150 and 172. I had done a few hours at Cambridge on the 150 to renew my PPL but my recent experience was not very extensive. I was a bit nervous at times, particularly in gusty turbulent conditions when the 172 felt like an out of control canoe. On one occasion I started a trend where everyone flying jacked it in and landed, but we were all turned round and sent off again as fast as we taxied in. The instructor's course was very good but in my opinion suffered from the pre-war RAF syndrome. Far too much time was spent stalling and spinning. At the completion of the course I was turned out as a fully qualified assistant flying instructor (AFI) but with only the vaguest notion of how to deal with someone having difficulty with landing. This I had to learn for myself with no course memories to fall back on. At stalls in turns with and without flap and power – yes, I was an expert. But telling a novice how to approach and land – not a clue. My instructor was an excellent pilot and instructor but with all his experience I felt he was a bit of a show off at times. Like many a good man before him he had become supremely confident in his own undoubted abilities. Once, when returning to base low level at five hundred feet above the ground I was flying with him and two passengers. 'How long will the engine run with the fuel off?' said one of the passengers. 'Let's see' said the instructor as he turned the fuel off. So we were soon gliding over hedges and woods at just two to three hundred feet. What a foolish trick, I thought. He also insisted on demonstrating and making me demonstrate flicks off turns and incipient spins at five hundred feet. This made me even more nervous. He often did barrel rolls in an aircraft able, but not cleared for such manoeuvres and once demonstrated slow flight at one hundred feet over the runway going backwards in the strong wind. He was an excellent instructor particularly in the classroom where he would pick a subject and dissect it to bits before us. It was not so much the subject matter that was useful to us as the enthusiastic manner of his delivery and his encouragement to us to think things out for ourselves. One of the course members later met his end, I was told, when he flew off in weather conditions beyond his ability somewhere in East Africa.

I first began instructing with the Cambridge Aero Club (CAC) in April 1967, two weeks after my thirtieth birthday and thirty years before my retirement from the same club. I had previously flown ten hours there in Tiger Moths in 1964 and more recently in Cessna 150s. The CAC took me on board expressly to help out with a series of courses of air traffic control cadets (to PPL standard) and annual refresher flying for past courses. We also had Air Training Corps cadets at this time but, not having been checked out by CFS, I was not allowed to fly with them. My second instructional flight was with Keith Rosson, whom I still meet occasionally.

After five months I had passed my upgrade to full instructor and could now send students on their first solo, their first cross-country flight and instruct without supervision. I was also eligible to be checked out by CFS and instruct ATC cadets on scholarship courses. For my upgrade I had to hire a Chipmunk as in those days it was a compulsory requirement that one demonstrated aerobatics. I had not seen a Chipmunk to fly for four years and had never operated one from the rear seat. I took off in a daze. After flying at 2,000 feet for some time I realised that, instead, I was looking at the rev counter and 2,000RPM. I had drifted up to 3,000 feet. The aerobatics were 'dodgy' to say the least but I think it was generally accepted that this section of the test was not too important. Unfortunately my demonstration forced-landing was poor and we returned to the departure airfield in silence. The examiner sat me down in his office and went through the test point by point. 'Well we can pass the aerobatics and most of the general handling exercise but the forced landing was not good. There again, it was a strange aircraft that you had not practised on. I am almost inclined to pass you but really I ought to do the forced landing again. I just don't know.' 'Well, are you going to pass me or not,' I demanded. 'No' he said. So I was back for a rerun in a Cessna 150 four weeks later. When he passed me I was overjoyed, until he asked when I could return for the ground examination. For this we went to Newton where I was given a royal welcome and introduced all round as a UAS member and ate lunch and drank beer in the Mess bar. Later, in a classroom to which a few instructors and club members had been invited, I answered a few questions on technical subjects. All went well until the examiner asked me to draw a Lift/Drag curve or something. I confused this with a drawing of range or endurance and, realising my own confusion floundered on talking absolute nonsense. 'All understand?' I chirped hopefully. One hand went up and, to my consternation, the owner said 'No.' 'Well I do' said my examiner and proceeded to ask me a question on Air Law. Ten days later I was proud to send the first student I had instructed from the beginning on his first solo. Thank you, Hector Taylor, for your generous handling of all my early instructor tests and upgrades that set me off on my instructing career with such confidence.

A job that was largely left to me during the air cadet season was the checking out of 'refreshers.' These were members of previous courses of air traffic students who now held a PPL and needed at least four hours solo flying to renew their licence. It was while dealing with these pilots that I learned how to assess someone's flying ability very quickly and positively so that I had no cause for doubt when I launched them on their four hours solo. Present day pilots might bite their lips if they knew what I had to make the poor fellows, and girls, do before they were passed. I strictly followed the brief I had been given, which covered all the items for a PPL test. Take-off, engine failure after take-off, full-flap power-on stalls, steep turns, full spin and recovery, forced landing and enough landings to show me they were safe, and all in one hour.

The qualifying cross-country route was then to Sywell and Oxford. I always had qualms about reaching Sywell, as it was all-grass and set in the middle of the countryside. One of the Sywell controllers claimed that he could give a 'radar' service by rushing outside and listening for engine noise. On the return to Cambridge we routed near to Bedford's air traffic zone. We rarely called them, preferring instead to dogleg around.

CESSNA 150/152. Two-seat trainer. One Continental O-200 100HP engine. Span 32 feet 9 inches. Length 24 feet. Maximum weight 1,670lb. Maximum speed 125mph at sea level. Entered service in late 1958.

It is customary in light aircraft to practice engine failure after take-off by pulling the power back at a reasonable height and then watching what the student does about it. Firstly he should maintain airspeed by lowering the nose. Next he must indicate a suitable field within about fifteen degrees either side of the nose. Then, if he wants to make top marks, indicate that in reality he would turn off the ignition and fuel cock to minimise fire risk and prevent the engine from suddenly bursting into life after touchdown. On one occasion the pilot was slow to react at all and I had to bully him into some sort of action. He eventually flew the aircraft, put down full flap – a formidable degree of drag in the Cessna 150 – and then dithered. 'What else,' I coaxed, 'Switches off, isn't it?' And, of course, that is what he did, leaving us at two hundred feet above the ground over the Wandlebury hills with a gently turning propeller (thank God), full flap and a rapidly reducing airspeed. The ignition key was hanging out of its slot by a thin strand of plastic thread, again thank God because the plastic thread was not always intact. I did restart the engine but I still have a small scar on my left forefinger where I cut it trying to insert that wretched key. It was my entire fault and I agreed after a long silence to forget the incident if he would.

In my last few months at Cambridge I had been instructing Jeremy Pemberton – about the last real gentleman I have met – firstly in the 150 and latterly in his private Piper Tripacer. He later bought a new Beagle Pup and hearing of this I rang him up one day to ask if I could hire it to do some flying. 'Well, not at present' he replied, 'but in a few days I am going to fly to Italy and would be glad of some help with the flying and navigation. Would you be interested, all expense paid of course?' He was as good as his word and off we went on what for me was the greatest flying adventure yet. Our route out was through Gatwick, Clermont Ferrand and Genoa. We came back through Clermont, Bourges, Le Touquet and Stansted. This was my first experience of long distance flying in a light aircraft and I learnt a great deal from it. I shall always be grateful to Jeremy for this knowledge as well as a delightful holiday. Jeremy was the last man I saw raising his hat when greeting some hangar staff – a true gentleman of the old school.

My first tour with Marshall's came to an end just before Christmas 1968. The contract for the air traffic control courses had not been renewed and Henri Frans, a fellow instructor, and I were both surplus to requirements. And so I left and once again was subject to the whims of fate to determine my future. Much of my time was spent loafing around but I did two short flying jobs before finally settling down again.

The first job lasted four weeks, which I was later told was twice as long as anyone else had stuck at it. The outfit ran two or three Cessna training aircraft and an Apache for charter work. A strange man supervised it. Firstly I was not permitted to view any of the personal flying records of students, but had to rely on a short briefing from him before each flight. He told me to check out and send a customer on his second solo. In the absence of any record I asked what the student was like. 'What do you mean' said the boss. 'Well, is he good, bad or indifferent?' I replied. He then informed me that any student he sent on his first solo had to be of a very high standard indeed, and so the stage was set for my first big incident.

The quite likeable middle-aged man taxied rather unsteadily along the spare runway and seemed to have a little trouble stopping gently but otherwise his circuit and landing went well and after another wobbly taxi ride I left him. The boss told me I could go home early. Shortly after I reached home he was on the telephone. 'Mr X has had an accident' he said with some relish. After a pause he informed me that although the aircraft was damaged, no one was hurt and I did not need to come in until the next day. The following day I winkled out what had happened. The Cessna 150 wing tip had hit a parked Sea Devon. 'What were you thinking of?' I screeched. 'Well, I thought I was in my car and forgot I had a wing sticking out' was the innocent reply. 'You see, although I have about fifteen hours of instruction time I have never taxied much before. My instructor always taxied to save time. He used to fly it a foot or two off the ground along the straight bits and gave it to me for take off.' I was not invited to the local court of enquiry but I bet that somewhere in the records is my name with an account of how this inexperienced instructor let an incompetent student loose solo.

Next day as I sat in the damaged Cessna carefully going through my take-off checks a Piper Apache roared overhead. 'What is that 150 doing still on the ground' said the voice of my boss through the loudspeaker. 'I am doing my take-off checks' I replied. 'Never mind about that, get airborne' came the stern and unexpected reply. I stuck it out for two days short of a month and had had enough at £15 per week and after a few pleasantries I left. I did not instruct again for two years but resumed flying again for a while with the Ipswich School of Flying, owned by two amiable schoolteachers, both called John, and run by Peter Collier as Chief Flying Instructor.

An occasional purchase of *Flight* magazine saved me. Standing out boldly was the Marshall of Cambridge advert asking for a pilot with instructing ability. On 7th December 1971 I started my second tour with the CAC and within four days had flown seventeen hours and sent two students on their first solos. So began the long slog up to the commercial licence and what followed. Having eventually passed all the papers I was in possession of a nice pastel blue coloured licence but the difficult bit still lay ahead. I had an instrument rating to collect before I would be of any use.

I flew around a few times as safety pilot, occasional instructor with J J Astor in his Cessna 182. He had learnt to fly with the CAC and he now had his licence. He liked to get around, mostly to race meetings. As we flew back one day to his landing strip he called up to announce his imminent arrival. 'Good evening, Sir. This is Hatley Park. The wind is a light breeze from a direction of west and the pressure reads 1003 millibars. Please inform me after landing. Out.' It was his butler speaking. He had been given a short course in air traffic control, a subject he would otherwise have known nothing about.

One day 'J J' announced that he wished to pay for his chauffeur, 'Mac' Macleod, to learn to fly so that he could ferry his aircraft and act as safety pilot. I was agreeably surprised when Mac later converted to the larger four-seater, constant-speed propeller version of the Cessna 182. He had no trouble at all as I remember and I had every confidence in his ability to operate the aircraft safely.

Having obtained my instrument rating I embarked my first passengers, Joe Gates, the Marshall Personnel Manager, and two ladies from Accounts, on board Aztec G-AREF for a journey to Shawbury on 24th June 1974. We arrived uneventfully on a hot summer's day, and landing a bit long on the North runway I had to taxi for a long way to reach the parking area. The generators on the Aztec were not sufficient to power the radios unless about 1,500 RPM were maintained, which in turn necessitated frequent use of the brakes. I parked and the passengers disembarked. Joe walked a little way then turned and said, as I sat in the pilot's seat, 'Did you know that your wheel is on fire?' Panic set in as I ran around the aircraft like a headless chicken. I compounded the emergency by firing off a long shot of CO_2 gas at the wheel, which should then have exploded as the cold gas hit the red hot metal and then possibly killed me. It did not. After it had cooled down the fire section examined it and declared it was safe enough for me to fly home. So ended my first commercial flight.

PIPER PA-23 AZTEC E. Six-seat commuter. Two Lycoming IO-540 engines each of 250HP. Span 37 feet 3 inches. Length 31 feet 3 inches. Maximum weight 5,200lb. Maximum speed 215mph. Normal cruising speed 185mph. Maximum range 1,200 miles. Developed from the Apache, it entered service in 1970.

G-AREF was not really well equipped for flying in cloud for long periods, particularly in winter, as it had no de-icing of any kind aside from pitot heaters and its instruments and autopilot were very basic. My worst moment came after a flight to Liège on a cold cloudy day. I sat all afternoon gazing despondently at the low dark cloud racing overhead until the darkness of night concealed it. I took off with four aboard and before very long realised that we were in trouble as ice began to form on the protruding bits of the aircraft. I also discovered for the first time that in this model of Aztec the fuel vents would freeze up and for some technical reason this would cause the fuel to vent over the upper wing in large quantities. So much so that by the time we arrived home over ¾ of the fuel had gone when in fact less than ½ should have been used. I asked Brussels for a lower, warmer level. They were very good and co-operated with all my attempts to leave the icing zone, with the cloud now down to below 1,000 feet. Eventually I found myself in and out of light cloud with the ground in sight and heaved a sigh of relief. Too soon. Gradually the horizon became lit up by flashes of lightning and I went into cloud again, but more turbulent this time. More ice built up and Brussels could no longer help me as I was getting below their radar coverage. They suggested I call Ostend radar for assistance, which I did. By now I was in and out of heavy wet, icy cloud with sudden flashes of lightning and alarming turbulence and little idea of what to do next. Ostend came up trumps. They consulted another pilot, giving my position, and he told me that I was almost through a gap in the worst of it and would soon be clear. And so I was. To my immense relief I broke out into clear, starry skies with the lights of Clacton and England on the far horizon.

Out of the blue I found myself packing my bags for a flight to Wichita, USA to accompany Leslie Worsdell home in the Company's new Kingair G-BAAM. The aircraft developed some engine faults and other snags, or squawks in American, and we ended up on Thanksgiving Day flying down to Miami via Jackson as a shakedown cruise. All this was wonderful to me as mass tourism had not begun and such destinations were not as commonplace as they are today. The Americans of course drive everywhere and I boasted that I was the first person in recent years to walk from Miami Beach to Miami City. We were in fact told that passing motorists would jeer us if we tried to walk anywhere. In Wichita at least, some cars slowed down for the drivers to gaze at such weird behaviour. On the way home we refuelled at Bangor, Maine and continued at night in worsening weather towards St Johns, Newfoundland. We never made it and after a hair-raising VOR approach in a howling crosswind and snow between two mountain ranges, which blessedly we could not see, we landed on an icy runway at Stephenville. For the first and last time we were directed to taxi inside a large hangar, a procedure usually frowned upon elsewhere.

Our hotel was all exposed wood construction, very fuggy and inhabited by moose hunters. Next day Leslie sent me to locate an engineer to cure a fuel system snag. The problem turned out to be caused by a small piece of swarf blocking a valve in the fuel system and the tanks on one side had to be drained into drums. The temperature was so low that some of the fuel solidified into a soft substance like candle grease. We got so tired of Stephenville that we took off without a word into a howling snow storm and crossed the short distance to St Johns. The next day we took off for Santa Maria, in the Azores. The weather ships were then still in existence and it was encouraging picking up the VOR signals and having our position confirmed by radar. We returned to Cambridge via Lands End.

One of my frequent Aztec trips was to Warton and I discovered not to completely trust anyone on the ground or in the air. Always try to keep a mental picture of what is going on and it will often get you out of trouble. On one trip up I was handed from one radar unit to another that had a similar aircraft under their control, supposedly about three miles on my right-hand side and at the same altitude. Somewhere in the proceedings it became clear to me that I was the right-hand aircraft. There was no apology from ATC.

As time passed I travelled to more and more interesting and often very busy airfields in Aztec G-BATN. Destinations included Paris, Brussels, and Linköping in Sweden, Stavanger in Norway, Cologne and Frankfurt. The last named was undoubtedly the busiest I have ever visited. One evening, at the time of an ATC go-slow, there were dozens of airliners and lighter aircraft waiting for departure. There were so many that all the taxiways were blocked and some unfortunate pilots were being told to return to parking and renegotiate 'slots' if they were unable to reach the take-off point imme-diately. In the middle of all this ATC asked me if I could reach the runway. I was not even on the taxiway full of aircraft but I took a swift look and said 'Affirmative.' Getting to the runway involved overtaking a few light aircraft and with a daring flourish taxiing under the wing of a large airliner and weaving between several Kingairs and Lear-jets before streaking off down the runway. How this favour came about I shall never know.

When the Cessna Citation appeared it was, and still is, a revolutionary concept in passenger-jet flying. It has a very basic, virtually foolproof fuel system for the pilot to manage, it has a fine logical cockpit layout, good all-round visibility, flies higher than most airliners and, apart from a little heaviness in the controls, is very easy to fly. My flights in the left and right-hand seats of the Citations were what kept me going over the years as much of the remainder of my flying was relatively tame.

CESSNA CITATION II – MODEL 550. Commuter or business jet. Crew – normally two pilots. Two Pratt and Whitney, Canada, JT15D-4 turbofans each of 2,500lb static thrust. Span 51 feet 9 inches. Length 47 feet 3 inches. Maximum take-off weight 13,300lb. Speed limit: .705Mach above 28,000 feet and 277 knots between 14,000 and 28,000 feet. Climb to 30,000 feet uses 320lb fuel and takes twelve minutes. Maximum altitude 43,000 feet. Six to eight passengers. Range, with fuel reserve: 1,750 miles.

I travelled to Wichita to join Bob Smythe to collect the Company's second Citation, G-BEIZ. After completing abridged ground school and simulator sessions all that was required was a twenty-minute flight, which was to include an ILS approach at the famous Love Field, on a bright and sunny day without a cloud in sight. Having recently completed an instrument rating course and all its stupidities in the UK and being exceedingly nervous I astounded the instructor by demanding an icing check. 'What the heck are you talking about, the temperature is 75 degrees' he almost yelled. Later I learned that I had become quite famous at American Airlines as the pilot who had asked for an icing check at 2,000 feet above Dallas when there was no cloud. 'Flew the simulator brilliantly but the aircraft – jeez.' People from the UK that had been on the course later and who met me said 'It was you! They still talk about you there.' The Yanks just did not understand the UK instrument rating where you failed if you did not constantly ask for icing inspections, whatever the weather. I do not think the people who started this nonsense understood pilots either, because the one thing I learned when flying for real was that you quickly started to notice icing when it appeared regardless of whether you were told or not.

On our route home we called at Toronto, Sept Isles and Fort Chimo where I first discovered what real cold was like. I had taken a glove off to fiddle with the fuel caps and, feeling no pain, but with the job finished, I tried to put the glove back on. I discovered that I could hardly move my fingers. From Chimo we flew to Søndre Strømfjord, which was a wonderful experience. As we entered the mouth of the fjord in brilliant clear air we could see the tiny dot of the airport perhaps fifty miles away. As we descended at closer range the hills rose either side of us until we were in a narrow corridor with the black runway on our nose getting closer and closer. Greenland is a large ice plateau with most of its flat top over a mile above sea level. The airport is well below the level of the surrounding terrain, which makes the after take-off climb-out interesting. Next day we flew to Reykjavik, in Iceland, had lunch, then took off into horrendous turbulent gale-force winds and an uneventful return home.

On most flights in the Citation we did turn and turn about with one pilot flying the outbound leg and the other flying the return. We never followed the usual practice of having the co-pilot flying one leg and/or approach and for this I am grateful because it enabled the captain to fly the route in its entirety and in a theoretically one-pilot aircraft this suited me.

In the fullness of time I was appointed the TRE on the Citation and Aztec, which added to my position as a PPL examiner. Being TRE meant that I flew with all of the Marshall pilots at least twice a year for their licence validity renewals. For myself I enlisted the help of David Simmonds who kindly came up to Cambridge once a year to check me out on all our aircraft, while I in turn signed him up. The system sounds a little corrupt but that is the way it is usually done, because otherwise there would not be enough examiners to keep everyone going. In David's case it was more for his practice than any kind of test as he was always perfect. A keen and natural pilot he had paid his own way up the ladder from being a junior instructor at the CAC to being one of the more experienced inspector/examiners for the CAA. David is the perfect example of how an examiner should be. He puts the candidate at ease, gives praise where it is due or might give the sitter confidence and points out errors in an almost apologetic manner. All the time he does not miss a trick and would never dream of letting anyone get away with a serious error.

Marshall's had converted an Airspeed Ambassador for Jordanian's Royal Squadron in the 1950s and later maintained the Royal Jordanian TriStar. Combined with co-operation on such matters as the Fairford International Air Tattoo, this meant that Sir Arthur had become one of King Hussein's many friends. Back in the 1930s Sir Arthur had taught Sabah El Said, the son of the Prime Minister of Iraq, to fly. Before attaining his licence Sabah gave a flight to King Hussein's father. This, besides being a topic of conversation between them was another good reason why the King, in September 1987, had invited Sir Arthur and Lady Marshall to visit him in Jordan. Because of Lady Marshall's ill health they had been unable to go. In 1989 the King invited Sir Arthur, his daughter Judy and her husband, Simon Boscawen. They flew to Jordan the following year, with John Blake and I as pilots.

After a prodigious amount of planning and re-planning we set off on the first leg of a most enjoyable trip. First stop was Brindisi. I endeavoured to get a weather forecast for Cairo, where sandstorms were not unknown and the nearest diversion was three hundred miles further on, at Luxor, and at the limit of our range. 'Have you got a forecast for Cairo please?' 'Nah, is not possible today.' 'Why?' 'Telephone line to Roma not working. Weather at Cairo is okay.' 'Please, I need a proper forecast and weather report.' 'Cairo is okay.' And so on until I had to give up. We arrived at Cairo with no problem, and after a hair-raising taxi ride through the city arrived at the Mena Palace Hotel. A little sightseeing gave me my first view of the magnificent pyramids. The next day, after distributing dozens of dollars to all the hangers-on, we were ready to go. Just as the first engine came to life Sir Arthur called out that being early was just as bad as being late, and so the fun began. Our Israel-dodging route involved flying round the Sinai Peninsula and up in a straight line through Aquaba to Amman where we were to land at the old City airport, Marka, now used by the Royal Jordanian Air Force and the King's Flight. It soon became clear that an enormous tailwind was pushing us; if it continued we would arrive thirty minutes early. We radioed the new ETA ahead. Unfortunately the wind got stronger and stronger and ATC gave us more and more advantageous flight levels and short cuts so that it became clear that we would arrive even earlier. The Citation's Global Navigation System that worked off a long-range radio system was a godsend on this occasion. Once we were on the straight leg to Amman I selected the ETA facility and slowed the aircraft down as much as

I could. In the end we cruised along with the nose in the air and reduced power until we were not that far off the stall. We cruised in, landed and taxied with one eye on the clock and, to my lasting pride, stopped in front of the reception building, flung open the door and tumbled out with my uniform cap on within a few seconds of the promised time. I am sure that the King, an expert pilot himself, would have approved the performance.

Then began a week of pure pleasure for me as we were taken around the tourist sights of Jordan, including Petra, by private car with an Army Sergeant driver. On our first night we found our rooms at the end of a corridor on the top floor. Overjoyed by the novelty of it all I flung my belongings down on the bed and walked out on the balcony that stood at the top of the emergency staircase and gazed at the view over Amman. With an uncompromising click the door closed behind me revealing a surface devoid of any kind of handle or other means of opening it. I realised too late that this was an emergency-only staircase with entrances designed to bar access by intruders. There was only one possible move and that was downwards. Night comes quickly behind sunset in the East and as I passed floor after floor of locked doors the darkness moved in. Finally I reached a closed door in front of me that led into a darkened room without windows. I saw a chink of light ahead and pushing forward, terrified of snakes, found myself in a back yard behind the clatter of kitchens. I had to pass a security box with two guards inside. They found the whole thing hilariously funny and after an excursion through the busy kitchen complex I found myself in the hotel lobby. Only about ten minutes had passed since I first entered my bedroom and I thankfully pushed the still-ajar door and began to enter. I will never forget the scene before me.

A young man stood bent over the bed. Before him lay my travel bag, open with my passport, documents and about one thousand dollars in cash plus traveller's cheques. In his hand, held up as though in witness to the occasion lay a twenty-dollar note. It became clear later that he had just taken a smallish sum so as not to arouse my suspicions and it is true that after the largesse I had been distributing in Cairo twenty dollars would not be missed. Perhaps I was over-tired or anaesthetised by the trauma of the last ten minutes but I then did something unwise. I strode into the room occupied by an unknown thief in an unfamiliar Middle East country after dark in a lonely hotel room and with uncharacteristic confidence shut the door behind me and demanded to know what he thought he was doing. I gave him a severe and pompous telling-off, saying that I was a guest in his country, the money was not mine to lose and how could I believe his protestations that he had taken only twenty dollars? I listened to his tearful pleas that he would lose his job and his wife and children would starve. At last we both quietened down and became bored by it all. 'Well, are you going to report me' he said. 'Not this time' I replied and precipitated one of the most embarrassing scenes of my life. He fell upon his knees and kissed my hand causing me to snatch it away and mutter 'Oh for God's sake.'

I heard nothing more of this incident but was lucky not to have felt a knife in my ribs.

During the visit King Hussein conferred on Sir Arthur the Order of the Istiqlal First Class, the highest award that can be made to a non-Jordanian other than a Head of State. John Blake and I were honoured by the presentation of gold watches, a complete surprise to us.

Our return flight was via Aquaba to pick up Sir Arthur, Judy and Simon, on to Iraklion to refuel, then to Nice for a night stop. After a few setbacks we reached Cambridge; so ended the best series of flights I had with Marshall's.

Bob Smythe and I flew the Citation with a team of accident assessors to El Ayoune, in what was then known as Spanish Sahara, to view a damaged Hercules. Not too far from the coast, but deep into the bleak desert-type country the town itself was quite basic although our hotel was built in the classic Arab style with cool corridors laid with colourful rugs and plenty of tinkling fountains.

The Hercules had had its nosewheel fold after an aborted take-off and the front of the aircraft was extensively damaged on its underside. It now lay deep in sand with all its instrumentation and other kit removed and there was no sign of any engines. To my astonishment the team confidently proclaimed that they could have it flying back to Cambridge in a few days for full repair, but unfortunately we did not get the contract.

My civil flights enabled me to see a little more of the world than I would otherwise have done. From time to time they gave me the satisfaction of planning and conducting flights, sometimes in difficult conditions and seeing a bunch of passengers safely off at their destination. Much of the time I was at the sidelines looking on. I saw some of the first RAF Hercules arrive at Cambridge on delivery from the States and much later took part in the conversion of some into refuelling tankers with many minor modifications besides. I was flying from the airport when the film 'Battle of Britain' was being made at Duxford and once had the pleasure of being in the circuit when all the Spitfires, Hurricanes and Messerschmitts came in to refuel.

In a Cessna I flew alongside the Concorde when it came in to Duxford. Unfortunately the pilot decided to make a go-around and I was left at 1,500 feet with a Concorde turning towards me at an unknown height. Once I saw a Comanche land with its undercarriage up and if I had not been trying to explain some difficult point to a student as we taxied along I would have seen the situation earlier and been able to warn the pilot. I watched the white Vulcan that was used to test Concorde engines take off after many lost days waiting for ideal weather, and soar into the air after using only a small portion of the runway.

In 1979 the Company decided that it needed another second pilot in the Hercules test programme. I was given a few rides on the back seat of the Hercules cockpit for several hours and in November was sent to Lyneham to attend No 69 Course of 242 OCU for ground and simulator training only. I would do the flying back at Cambridge. The course was not difficult and everybody was expected to get about 100% in the final exams, but it was very lengthy due to the RAF insistence on long weekends, many coffee breaks and early knock-off times. The day began intensely at about 0800 but petered out towards mid-afternoon and great concentration was given to ending on mid-day Friday for an early getaway. Lengthy problems of angle of climb, drift-down parameters and worst of all V1/VR ratios did little for my confidence. I would have been far happier spending more time on engines and propellers. To emphasise my feelings we were given only forty-five minutes instruction on Hercules pressurisation, a subject that was introduced as being particularly hard for pilots to understand!

I did about thirty-five hours in the simulator and quickly learned that it was not much like a real aircraft in its handling qualities. All of this flying I did as aircraft captain in the left-hand seat as there were two RAF co-pilots under training. The main simulator instructor was excellent and made me enjoy the task better than otherwise I might have. On 16th January 1980 I received official approval from MOD to act as second pilot on Hercules. I was from then on in a position to have my days off mucked about by air tests but this time in a green 'gro-bag' suit instead of just standing by to work in the flying club.

After a while the air tests became quite monotonous but just occasionally there was something different to do and even more rarely something went seriously wrong enough to make the flight more memorable. From my point of view as the so-called expendable co-pilot I just had to do the few jobs that were my responsibilities, keep a good lookout and operate the radios. Every major air test and some follow-up tests required each of the four engines to be shut down and restarted in turn. On restart the flight engineer had to have about four eyes in his head, each swivelling remotely and checking up that the sequence of engine items was following the plan. One of these jobs involved looking for and calling as seen the green light that briefly illuminates and shows the propeller system is unfeathering correctly. From the time that the RPM gauge starts to move until in has passed 10% is only a few seconds but this light must be seen and called during that period. My job was to pull the engine condition lever back to feather if I did not hear that call and I took a sadistic pleasure in doing so although in 99 times out of a hundred it was just a slow call from the engineer. A more exciting call was if a device pushing extra fuel into the engine for start failed to cut off. This caused a huge surge of fuel and a rocketing needle on the gauge and needed a quick feather to prevent overheat damage. Twice this happened to me in the air and I think I reacted well to the occasion. In the simulator such things were always happening and do not really count. Having been a second pilot on air tests and simulator sessions two or three times a year I must have shut down more engines on the Hercules than anyone else in the world. The total must run into the late hundreds. On every major air test and some follow-ons I usually had the opportunity to fly an ILS approach somewhere or other.

Although it was satisfying to handle the aircraft in the air or land back at base I never really felt it was for real as it was not my flight. It is the difference between being the captain and just the spare. Special station-keeping equipment gave us interesting flights in loose formation and towards the end of my time Daz James and myself flew up to the Orkneys checking out a new fitment of GPS equipment. All this may sound boring but was at times great fun for me to make approaches at strange airfields and see parts of the country I had previously only read about.

The Company's contract for maintenance of the Swedish Air Force C-130s included a full air test and my contacts with the Swedes were always a great pleasure due to their friendly demeanour and kind hospitality. I made several visits to their base at Såtenas and once attended a competition arranged to celebrate the twenty-fifth anniversary of the C-130 with the Swedish Air Force. Aircrews from Norway, Denmark and the RAF took part and after the navigation and precision landings had finished a Swedish pilot gave a display of what the C-130 could really do. He forced it into incredible manoeuvres not usually associated with a transport aircraft.

Test flights in the Hercules were not the only test flights I took part in. I took a few trips in the newly fitted out Dominies. If ever I felt a distinct lack of confidence in an aircraft it was the Dominie. Aged, noisy and under-powered, to my mind it had all the hallmarks of a forgotten age of flying and bore no comparison to my jet experience in the Citation. The cockpit, engine and pressurisation controls were a nightmare of unnecessary complication, particularly during the start sequence. I always had the uneasy feeling that if either of the engines failed just after take-off the whole aircraft would instantly slow down to a stop and fall vertically to the ground without any attempt at gliding.

Air tests in several singles and Citations and Aztecs were the sum total of my test flying except for the Bulldog and the Chipmunk, both single-engined aircraft owned and flown by the RAF. The Bulldog had been chosen some years previously as a replacement for the Chipmunks of the basic flying training units and the UASs (but Chipmunks remained in service with the AEFs) and by 1988 it had been recommended for a navigation refit and radio replacement. I was given the job of converting officially to the Bulldog and pass on the knowledge to other Marshall pilots. This I did. But I had also been given the honour of doing the first few flights with the new equipment and checking everything out for range and so on. Before this happened an ugly rumour was started that because a new aerial had sprung up on the tail, part of the test would be to spin the aircraft to see if it made any difference. Anybody who knows me or has read into my flying recollections will know that I have a deep aversion to putting aircraft out of control and then trying to regain control. I had also fortified these opinions by spinning the Bulldog on my checkouts and not enjoying it at all. If very prompt action is taken at the incipient stage of the spin by more or less centralising the controls, the Bulldog will drop out and not spin. Accidental full spins I cannot speak for. But if deliberate pro-spin controls are initiated, namely full rudder and stick hard back, the aircraft will enter a spin from which recovery is standard full opposite rudder, pause, stick fully forward (so crucial is this that some aircraft have the forward and central spots marked on the panel). If any deviation is made from this recovery action then a high rotation spin occurs. The high rotation spin is quite unpleasant as the earth goes by in a blur. How somebody like me would determine any unusual characteristics and then sort out some new recovery technique was beyond my imagination.

I spoke to a friendly UAS instructor and asked his opinion. 'Don't touch it, I wouldn't. Give the job to the test flight at Boscombe. They are trained for the job, are paid for it and strangely enough actually seem to enjoy it.' I returned to the office even more depressed for the showdown to come and was given a test document of spinning the Bulldog made after some fatal accidents. This made my hair stand on end but I knew that now I had read this I was convinced that I would resign rather than try. Fortunately the plan to spin our Bulldogs died as it had already been checked out elsewhere. The flying was fun and we had to transit to other airfields for the ILS, which I used to check out at high speed to save time and not block the approach. This flying made a welcome change from the usual round of instructing and a little aerobatics were allowed at the end of the test. Most of my attempts at anything but a loop ended up facing the ground and having to recover as rapidly as possible.

BAe BULLDOG T Mk1. Two-seat primary trainer. One Lycoming IO-360 engine of 200HP. Span 33 feet. Length 23 feet 3 inches. Maximum weight 2,350lb. Originally designed by Beagle Aviation, the Bulldog entered RAF service in 1973. Maximum level speed 150mph at sea level.

The Chipmunk refurbishment programme involved a complete dismantling and repaint job, always a sure sign that military equipment is about to be abandoned, which indeed the Chipmunk was, by the Bulldog, a couple of years later. After re-assembly we had to run each aircraft through a short test schedule and then deliver it back to the home base. Once again the dreaded spectre of spinning came up and some sadist had decided that nothing less than an eight-turn spin in each direction would suffice. The Chipmunk, now that it had tail fuselage-strakes fitted, came very readily out of a spin although what we were supposed to do if it did not I never learned – except that baling out was in order. It took me about two minutes to climb out of the cockpit on the ground so how I would have fared in the air I do not know. I found the spin reasonably easy to take but the abruptness with which it stopped turning left my brain still going in one direction while the rest of my body was going in another. Consequently after sixteen turns and two recoveries I was not feeling on top of the world and the second flight of this nature sent me back home feeling so awful that I had to take to my bed for forty minutes before I could begin a normal life again. Who says that test pilots lead a glamorous life!

On the test flying side I believe that good pilot records of every flight would have been of help for future contracts with each aircraft. Some parts of the airframe and systems remain with the aircraft for life, and some of these parts may be introducing faults elsewhere. I recall spending the day at Salmesbury, Preston, at a period where we were having constant problems and re-flights with a Canberra that showed a trim inconsistency. I mentioned this to a man who happened to work in records and he looked up that aircraft's record from its first construction. The same problem had occurred on its maiden flight and throughout the test programme but the information had been lost over its service record. That kind of information could have jumped a few steps in its new test flight schedule had it been passed on.

I have had some very narrow squeaks in my time and the fact that I am here writing this is due, in my opinion, to a number of factors, of which I think sheer luck or Fate is the most important. On a few occasions I have been shocked by the sudden appearance of an unexpected intruder and none of them was likely to have been avoided by strenuous lookout. My rules are: look out as much as you can, listen out and make use of the information you may glean and have lots and lots of luck.

At the end of my career I have several flying logbooks prettily bound in half leather which record memories that are as clear to me as a written history would be. They contain hundreds, maybe thousands, of names of people I have flown with or tried to teach. A logbook can be a wonderful record of a career and it is fortunate that the law requires one to be kept, probably unique in business life. Instruction amounted to over 8,500 flying hours, 740 hours are logged as sitting in the right-hand seat of Hercules – I flew in all the RAF fleet except the early crashed ones. I sent two hundred and twenty six students on their first solos, the first being Mr Taylor, an air traffic cadet, in Cessna 150 G-ATHF on 18th October 1967. The last was Mr Freeman in Cessna 152 G-BMJC on 27th November 1996. Of the rest of my 12,000 hours maybe 1,500 were in the Citation. Never one to collect aircraft types I concentrated on destinations and at the end of my career had visited about two hundred airports and landing grounds in about twenty-five different countries including of course my United Kingdom home.

I have not missed flying since my retirement but I do miss one thing that nearly all people seem to regret after leaving a long-standing employment. It is missing the company and feeling part of a team through all the gripes and pleasures of the job. Not the least is the awareness of all one's skills and expertise no longer needed and slowly being forgotten. This fate belongs to most of us and I suppose I am fortunate in not desperately wanting to get back to work. I am idle by nature and retirement suits me. Good luck to anyone else that joins the Marshall pilot team. I certainly had it.

Chapter 10

Dennis Pasco

The Vampire T11 was a delightful and responsive aircraft to fly. The ability of its pilots, however, did not always match the quality of the aircraft. I still wince when I think of one particular flight. Of all days, it was on my 23rd birthday, in XK 637 – the very last T11 built for the RAF. Flt Lt Ron Williamson, my instructor, carefully briefed me on what to do in the event of an engine failure after take-off. The procedure depended on how much height and speed had been achieved after lift off. With sufficient of both, it was possible to execute a 'turn back.' This involved an immediate decision to lower the nose to conserve airspeed and avoid a stall, roll on the bank, and head back to the runway. Various technical drills would follow, including checking levers and switches, with an attempt at a hot relight to bring the engine back to life. The briefing also included a reminder: 'Remember, we are simulating an engine failure; we never switch anything off, unless the emergency is a real one.' The flight went pretty much as briefed. Ron managed to fit in a turn back, not that easy in a busy circuit. Heading back to the runway, he ran quickly through the drills. A very insistent voice in my head said, 'Turn it off.' 'It' was the HP cock that controlled the fuel flow to the engine. Switch it off, and the Goblin would run down. The voice said, 'Switch off the HP cock.' I did. The engine immediately ran down. Ron worked flat out with one hand on the relight button and the other aiming the Vampire at the best place to land in the event that the engine did not come back to life. Up to twenty seconds could be required for the engine to relight successfully. With just a couple of seconds remaining before the final 'Eject, eject' decision had to be made, the Goblin began a steady wind up. Not saying a word, we climbed away. Needless to say, the post flight de-brief was pretty explicit. Ten years previously, watching Vampires flying out of West Malling, I was certain that none of my heroes would be as dumb as that. Two days later Ron got me up to scratch for my first solo flight in a jet aircraft. My childhood ambition was achieved.

Nell Pasco gave birth to three girls and two boys. I was the middle child, born in September 1937 at Crayford, Kent. Our home was on a large council estate built in the mid-1930s. Flanking the back door was an unlit, unheated toilet and a cellar. Coal, coke and logs were stored in the cellar. The small internal door from it led in to the front, sitting room. In the early part of World War Two we used the cellar as the air-raid shelter. With a single candle in the corner, our mother comforted us whilst air raids were in progress. When the nearby 3.7 inch AA guns opened up against the Jerry bombers the black dust would float down from the uneven walls.

Before long an Anderson shelter was dug into the back garden. It competed for space with ducks and the chicken coop with its egg-providing occupants. Rabbits, bred for food, lived out their brief lives in a hutch alongside the chickens.

The house opposite ours, a mere thirty yards away, was destroyed by a direct hit from a high explosive bomb. Two incendiaries hit our house. My father, an air raid warden, extinguished the bombs by dropping them smartly into a bucket of water. I recall seeing German bombers trapped by clusters of searchlights while flying along the river Thames to raid London. Later in the war I saw some RAF fighters chasing Focke-Wulf 190s. Primary education for the Pasco youngsters took place at St Paulinus Church of England School, at the top of the High Street. With its hypnotic pulsating noise the Doodlebug was a common sight and sound throughout 1944. One demolished a crowded shop up the High Street, killing a great number of bargain hunters in a sale. All the aerial activity above this corner of Kent shaped my ambition to join the RAF and become a pilot.

At the age of eleven I moved to Dartford Grammar School. Harry, my father, was a keen angler and he took Ron, my brother, and I on many trips to venues close to RAF aerodromes at Manston and West Malling. One bright, clear spring day I sat on the bank of the River Medway watching the float gently bob along. Looking up, I saw a string of aircraft tail chasing each other: rolling, diving and climbing. Within a few minutes the aircraft disappeared from sight and sound. My attention returned to the float, willing it to bob under. Suddenly, along the river, below treetop height roared a Mosquito. Close behind it, a Meteor and, even closer, a Vampire. Then, in a crescendo of noise, all three arced up towards the cloud-spattered sky in a vertical climb. Wow! I was really thrilled by that. I would love to have my hands on the controls of one of those, I thought.

In April 1952, I joined the Air Training Corps. Four months later, at Thorney Island, Hampshire, I made my first flight. It was in an Avro Anson navigation trainer. During the nearly three-hour flight I fell asleep. In December 1954, by courtesy of 30 Sqn, I left England for the first time. The Valetta, an ice bucket of a 'plane, flew first to RAF Wildenrath, Germany, and then on to Gatow, Berlin. While I stayed at Gatow, slowly thawing out, the Valetta flew on to Prague and Warsaw, then back to Berlin the following day. Did it have on board, I wonder now, any whisky for the Air Attaché?

In early 1955 I applied to join the RAF and went to Hornchurch for aircrew assessment. I was offered an air signaller engagement; I accepted and signed on for eight years. My expectation was that I would be able to re-muster to pilot after completing one tour on a squadron.

Having spent one week at Cardington, being bellowed at, processed and kitted out I arrived at Swanton Morley, the home of No 1 Air Signaller School. Every two weeks, a new course started. The regime was tough, but not brutal. Most of the time we had great fun, and were paid 7/– (35p) a day for it. Wireless telegraphy (W/T, or Morse code) was still the primary method for RAF aircraft to communicate over long range. For most cadets the biggest, seemingly never-ending, set of hurdles was Morse code training. Every two to three weeks a practical test was set. To fail the test and the subsequent retest meant either slip back to the next course, or the 'chop.' Numbers on most courses steadily decreased as training progressed. From nine at the start, my course soon dwindled to four. We all eagerly awaited our first flight.

Mine came along in January 1956, seven months into the year-long course. The weather, as so often in winter, caused a delay. Our air signaller training was held up and Fighter Command routine training, which included working up on the Hawker Hunter, fizzled out in the dismal weather. Suddenly, approaching mid-February, the fog cleared. Most of RAF East Anglia headed skywards. My Anson was just one of the many. Half way through the flight, relayed by the staff signaller, came the message 'Diverting to Waddington, ETA 1205 Zulu (GMT). Signal to base.' Translating that swiftly into the 'Q' code, I sent off the Morse code message '...QRE EGXW 1205.' 'Roger', came the reply. All part of the training, I thought. What next, I wondered? A night at Waddington, which had recently reopened after a major rebuild for V-bombers? With no night-stopping kit, we would have to tramp around in our World War Two-issue flying kit, trying not to look like complete sprogs.

AVRO 652A ANSON T21/T22. Navigator and air signaller trainer. Crew of four to six, as required for the role. Two Armstrong Siddeley 420HP Cheetah 15 or 17s. Span 56 feet 6 inches. Length 42 feet 3 inches. Loaded weight 8,000lb. Maximum airspeed 170mph at 5,000 feet. The RAF's first retractable undercarriage aircraft, 'Faithful Annie' entered service in 1936. It was the first British aircraft to attack a German U-boat in World War Two. Over 11,000 were built in Great Britain and Canada before production ended in 1952. It served in a wide range of roles until 1968.

'Put on parachutes' someone shouted. The four student signallers obeyed. All part of the training, I supposed. In addition to the task of sending and receiving messages, the workload was being increased to see how we coped. Parachute on, I recorded the fact in my signaller's log. Working away like a beaver in the bowels of the Anson, I had not looked out for some time. When I did, all I saw was fog. It then dawned on me that perhaps this was for real. Unbeknown to me, hosts of aircraft were diverting because of the unexpected early return of the fog. Many of them were short of fuel. Four or five Hunters from West Raynham, I think, failed to reach a suitable airfield in time. Their pilots ejected when the fuel ran out. Luckier than many, the Anson had a good reserve of fuel. Consequently, we were well down the landing queue. There was a real concern that we would be joining the Hunter pilots in baling out. As mere cadet signallers, however, we were spared all those details. Keep the log going, keep pounding the Morse key; no need to lose marks unnecessarily. Finally, we landed at Waddington. A post-flight fry up, then off we went to prepare for the flight back to Swanton. Next morning, the fog was gone. The remainder of the course, totalling seventy-three flying hours mostly in a Percival Prentice, went by without incident. After a month at Thorney Island on the advanced air signaller course I arrived at No 1 Parachute Training School, Abingdon.

I was destined for Transport Command, to fly in the Vickers Valetta. As air signaller on board the Valetta, one of my duties would be to act as air dispatcher. At that time the powers that be had decided that to be properly qualified to dispatch the paratroopers, the air dispatcher had first to complete a parachute course. The course was hard work; the jumps truly exhilarating. Feeling considerably fitter, and with one jump from a tethered balloon under my belt, I headed north to Dishforth, the home of 242 OCU.

VICKERS VALETTA C1. Short to medium-range transport aircraft. Normal crew: three. Two 1,975HP Bristol Hercules 230 engines. Span 89 feet 3 inches. Length 63 feet. Loaded weight 36,500lb. Could carry up to 34 troops or 20 paratroops. Maximum airspeed 258mph at 10,000 feet. Maximum cruising speed at 6,000 feet 210mph. Maximum range 1,400 miles. Entered RAF service in 1948 as a replacement for the Dakota and served until 1966. Marshall's converted 18 Valetta T3s to T4 standard – used as radar trainers for 'rear-seat' aircrew. First T3 converted was WJ 465; its first flight was on 15th March 1956. Last recorded Valetta airtest at Cambridge was WJ 487, on 6th June 1963, with Gordon Hubbard at the controls.

Apart from a few weeks' delay caused by fog and the Suez crisis, the conversion course went smoothly. Unlucky for some, 13th February 1957 stays clear in my mind. The finale of the conversion course was an overseas flight. Ours was to Malta, via Lyneham. Lyneham had little room for transit crews, so we were billeted out to Clyffe Pypard, a few miles away. Operated by Marshall as 29 EFTS during World War Two, it was a desolate place. Colder than a 'fridge, each Nissen hut boasted just one tiny stove to help overcome the icy temperature. Pyjamas, uniform, greatcoat and gloves helped not at all to keep the cold at bay. An early call at 0400 was a blessing; shaving in freezing water was not. Roll on Malta; warmer weather was virtually guaranteed. We spent only one night in Malta, however. Up with the sun for a departure at 0630, we landed at Istres, near Nice, after a five-hour flight. Thanks to an engine problem, we stayed in France for four days. Merveilleux, I thought. Wrong! Many of the natives were unfriendly. As we, ten RAF aircrew, walked into one bar, the French all stormed out. A taxi driver, risking the obvious wrath of his fellow countrymen, explained the reason. The locals, he said, judged the allied invasion of southern France in 1944 to have been unnecessary. They took their anger out on the British and Americans by vacating the bar. The same exodus occurred when we entered a restaurant for an evening meal.

To balance those unfortunate experiences was the amusing event of the missing RAF raincoat. Almost ready to leave, on 19th February, a halt was called; one of the officers had misplaced his raincoat, and he wished to locate it before our flight to Lyneham. In no time flat, having remembered where it most likely was he raced off in a Citroen to retrieve it – from the local brothel.

With the conversion course over, we air signallers returned to Abingdon to complete the parachute course. By March 1957 I was ready for my first squadron – 84, based in Aden, on the southern end of the Arabian Peninsula. My father, a Royal Fusilier on the way to India, had passed through Aden in the 1920s. His voyage on a troopship would have taken longer than the five days of my flight through Malta, Nigeria, French West Africa, Uganda and the Sudan.

The Colony of Aden was a free port and trading centre. Until Colonel Nasser closed the Suez Canal in 1956, Aden was strategically important to the British, who had an airfield on Khormaksar isthmus. To avoid the searing afternoon heat, Khormaksar burst into life at 0700 each day. Flying, however, could not be confined to mornings only, so work often continued well into the afternoon. In the Valetta the navigator sat on the port side behind the pilot and the signaller beavered away at his station behind the co-pilot's seat. After a few flights I soon felt at home in my very own suite of World War Two technology. The main radio, the T1154 transmitter and the R1155 receiver, was the same as that fitted to the Whitley and Lancaster bombers. The 1154 had groups of coloured knobs on its front face. Yellow knobs controlled the lower frequencies and red and blue knobs the higher ones. Tuning the sets accurately to the required en-route frequencies was not always straightforward. If possible, we listened out for a transmission from the ground station, turned the 1155 volume right down and then carefully tuned the receiver as accurately as possible. We then tuned the 1154 to the receiver frequency. To enable the signaller to obtain maximum performance from the 1154/1155 installation, the Valetta was fitted with a trailing aerial. We always used it for the lower frequencies, and often needed to for the higher ones. We wound out the calculated length of wire to permit the transmitter to radiate at maximum power. Most importantly, we had to remember to wind the thing in before the aircraft landed.

Made by Marconi, the 1154/1155 installation incorporated a Type 52 resistance. This device, because it got so hot, served as a heater for soup. A small can of Heinz tomato soup, with the wrapper ripped off, fitted neatly into the shroud around the Type 52. Tipped the wink by the older hands, I had learned how to open the can without the expanded air, and scalding soup, bursting out through the hole. Somewhere over the endless miles of the sand and rock of Arabia, en route to Bahrein via Salalah and Sharjah, the navigator declared that he was ravenous and desperate for his soup.

With my right hand still bashing out a message on the Morse key I handed him the piping hot can. I did not see exactly what he did, but out of the corner of my eye I glimpsed the emergency fire-axe swing gracefully down onto the unsuspecting soup tin. A second later I heard a loud cry of anguish. The navigator, unskilled at Valetta catering, had savaged the can, which had then erupted all over his station, his maps and his charts, and him. Hot tomato soup, looking remarkably like blood, oozed everywhere. I thought it inopportune to explain that there was a better way to open a can of hot soup at 8,000 feet above sea level.

One of my early flights was known as the RSM. The three places visited were Riyan, Salalah and the island of Masirah, at which we night-stopped. Most months we were the only visitors to the small RAF outpost just off the coast of Oman. Normally, the Valetta crew would take on the combined Officers' and Sergeants' Messes at darts and other games. Whoever lost had to drink an extra beer or two. It was fortunate that the return flight did not leave before sun up, but even so it took a while for our heads to recognise the new day. A unique feature of the flight away from Masirah was the unusual service provided by the lone ATC officer. After the Valetta was established in the cruise and I had sent off the W/T departure message, I called Masirah Approach to announce that we were ready for the first offering. Over the international VHF approach frequency wafted the opening bars of our first tune. Yes, music. The ATC officer had a small selection of records in his Tower. From his menu, we requested our favourites. A very unofficial service, but a most acceptable one.

Squadron operations around the Arabian Peninsula were not accident free. In May 1957 one of our Valettas crash-landed on the beach just north of Riyan. The aircraft was carrying a full load of passengers, a detachment of the Aden Protectorate Levies (APL). There were no injuries to anyone on board. The signaller later told me that everyone vacated the Valetta in an orderly fashion, and ran away to a safe distance. The thirty APL soldiers suddenly stopped running turned about and galloped back to the Valetta. They had left on board about the most valuable piece of kit they would ever own, worth about a year's pay – their Lee Enfield .303 rifle. Rifles retrieved, the APL doubled off for the second time and awaited orders.

Another flight, an air test, was rather more exciting. Many of the squadron captains were quite young. Invariably, before converting to the Valetta, they had been fighter pilots, either in the UK or in Germany. Flying a transport aircraft was, by comparison to rushing around in a fighter, dull. They looked upon an air test as a bonus. As far as I know it was not possible to turn the 'Pig' upside down but other thrills could be found. The usual routine was to head east up the coast, away from the Colony. If required, engines were shut down and then restarted. Flying controls, trims, electrical services and radios were all tested. About thirty minutes after take-off, it was time to head for home. This particular air test was on a Sunday. The captain announced that he intended to carry out a low-level join, instead of the more usual, sedate, rejoin at circuit height. When the air test captain said low level, he really meant *low*. The skipper brought the Valetta right down to the deck, lower than I thought possible. Surely the propellers would carve a groove in the sand. No, they did not. The return route was along the beach, which, as we descended to it, seemed to be moving. There were swarms of crabs everywhere, making the beach look like a moving carpet. We were so low that, from my seat next to the pilot, I could make out individual crabs, barely an inch across.

The beach we were flying over, or in, also served as a road, the sand being firmer than inland. Looking ahead, all three of us on board could now see a black dot. It grew bigger as we got closer. In less than a minute we were almost on it. 'It' was a large, black, official-looking sedan, the driver of which would undoubtedly have been expert at maintaining passage on the best tract of sand. He would be following the outgoing wave closely, and would then turn away from the sea to stay ahead of the incoming wave. His eyes would be focussed no more than thirty yards ahead of the gleaming black bonnet. There was no reason at all why he would have expected 16.5 tons of Her Majesty's air force to appear at three miles a minute over that bonnet, thus spoiling his view. We were so low, the driver must have thought his time was up. He was not to know that my captain was about to pull up to a more respectable height. Self-preservation demanded action. Suddenly, the sedan turned right, straight into the Indian Ocean. We flew on. After landing, we taxied in, shut down and climbed out. Unusually, the Station Commander's car drew up. 'Get in', said the Group Captain to the young captain. The car sped off. The navigator and I went off to change into our khaki drill and head off for a meal. Before we left, our captain walked in, looking very crestfallen. 'Guess who was in the car?' he said. 'Out for his usual Sunday afternoon drive, with his wife, was the Governor of Aden.' Bloody Hell, we thought. 'And guess who has just collected one month of Orderly Officer duties?'

I was always happy to carry APL soldiers. They were not quite so easy to cater for when rationing-up, because of their religion, but I felt they were a good insurance policy. Lunch boxes were not in vogue in those days. The signaller collected a variety of victuals from the ration store and, with the help of one or two of the passengers, made sandwiches, doorsteps more likely, to go with the tomatoes and other delicacies. With the APL aboard it was not unheard of for the aircrew to catch a whiff of charcoal burning. The Arab troops often carried their own rations, and occasionally made a small charcoal fire at the rear of the aircraft to heat up the food.

Issued to us before making our first flight from Khormaksar was a 'blood chit.' Printed in Arabic on the small card was a statement that the British Government would pay a grand sum of Maria Theresa dollars in return for the safe return of the card-carrying British airman. My colleagues told me that the card would not save anyone from the fiercer of the marauding Bedouin. They told gory stories of how the females of the tribe would first emasculate the downed airman, then sew the family jewels into his cheeks. The hapless infidel would then be staked out on the ground to be fried to death in the sun. In addition to the 'gooley chit', as we called the card, aircrew were issued with small arms for most up-country flights.

In 1958 the Chief of the Imperial General Staff (CIGS), Field Marshal Sir Gerald Templar, flew out to Aden on a farewell tour of British bases in the Arabian Peninsula and East Africa. On 29th March with Len Taylor as captain, we took the CIGS and his party to Nairobi, Kenya, in Valetta VW 859 and returned to Aden on the 31st. That visit went smoothly; one of the others did not.

The itinerary of the CIGS included a visit to two up-country airstrips: Lodar and Mukieras. The latter was situated on top of an escarpment, at an altitude of 4,000 feet or more. Manned by a few British troops, there was also a considerable number of APL camped there. After a brief tour of inspection, the Field Marshal boarded for the thirty-minute flight back to Khormaksar. Acting as second pilot for start up and take-off, the normal routine, I gave the thumbs up to the captain, 'Clear starboard.' He looked left, released the parking brake and we taxied off. The small parking area was on a down-slope and a left turn was necessary to head for the sand runway. 'Checking brakes' called Len. A quick squeeze on the pedals was followed by 'They've failed. Neither brake is working.' There was no emergency back up in the Valetta. That meant the aircraft could only be controlled directionally by varying the engine power. By this time, however, it was too late. The edge of the parking area, a dried out ditch, was almost upon us. Len stopped both engines to slow the Valetta down. Sadly, and ever so gently the aircraft rolled on, ending up in the ditch.

I nipped back to brief the Field Marshal. He was not too pleased; he had a tight schedule to follow. On the wireless I explained the problem to HQ at Khormaksar. Message understood. All we had to do now was wait for an aircraft to bring up the spares and a working party. In addition, one other small problem to overcome: how to shift the Valetta out of the ditch. That was solved in Boy Scout fashion. The APL officer established where it was safe for his men to push on the aircraft and then set to. Out of nowhere came dozens of APL soldiers. A brief explanation by their officer, a loud shout of encouragement and in no time at all VW 859 was back on firm ground. Waiting in the cool air of Mukieras was pleasant. If Aden, with its enervating high humidity in summer, its hazy and leaden skies, was hell, then Mukieras, the capital of the Audhali Plateau, was heaven. Aden was virtually barren, whereas the land around Mukieras supported crops of wheat and barley. There were lush grassy valleys and produce in the markets included locally grown plums, apples, peaches and apricots. The privileged few were able to go on shooting parties, seeking out hare, pigeon and chikor (greater hill partridge). I whiled away the time by leafing through the strip-briefing sheet for Mukieras. One passage caught my eye. 'In the event of an engine failure at the latter end of the take-off run, the

Lord's prayer is recommended.' Rescue came. We exchanged aircraft with the incoming crew and took-off, without the need of a prayer, into the gathering dusk for Aden.

On one VIP sortie to Nairobi I recall that the VIP passengers were Air Vice-Marshal Johnnie Johnson and his wife. On another flight to the Kenyan capital we carried the AOC on his annual inspection of air bases. The flight to and from Nairobi usually stopped off at Hargeisa, the capital of British Somaliland, to refuel. The only RAF presence at Hargeisa airstrip was a leading aircraftman acting, unpaid Sergeant air radar mechanic. He was there to look after the BABS/Eureka beacon, the primary navigation aid for the airfield. In addition, he supervised the firetruck, which was manned by Somali auxiliaries. During the five-hour flight from Nairobi to Hargeisa we had flown through a cloud of locusts. The captain's forward view was completely blocked by the multi-coloured mess on his windscreen. He was forced to slide open the direct vision panel in order to see sufficiently well to make the approach and landing. Our Valetta, with thousands of squashed locusts spread over it, was looking very grimy. The AOC told the young Sergeant that instead of responding to a surprise fire drill, the normal practice in an AOC's inspection, he would like the firemen to demonstrate their skill by washing down his grubby aircraft. 'Right Sir' replied the sergeant. Off he went, gathered his crew together and briefed them. Standing well clear, the aircrew and the AOC watched. 'Now', in Somali, came the shout. From the hose nozzle came not a gigantic plume of water but an all-enveloping dollop of foam. To the aircrew's amusement, and the AOC's well-controlled anger, the Valetta's nose section all but disappeared under the stream of custard-like mess. In Somali came the shout 'Stop' and a few other words. The stream of foam died. With much shouting and arm waving the Sergeant was hopeful that his men would now pull the correct lever. Hooray! This time out flooded the water. Having regained our composure and with a near-sparkling aircraft, we were now ready to embark the AOC for the ninety-minute hop to Aden.

At the end of April 1958 the fort at As Serir, near Dhala, close to the border with the Yemen, was under siege. Dhala was frequently the scene of military activity. Like Mukieras it sat on a plateau more than 4,000 feet above sea level. Smaller aircraft could land at Dhala but we could not. Army friends told me that the road from Aden to Dhala was a bit like the Khyber Pass in the days of the Raj. The Valettas were called upon, with aggressive support from the cannon and rocket-firing Venoms of 8 Sqn, to drop supplies to the beleaguered troops. Twelve sorties were mounted, of which I flew on three. The first was a drop to a convoy of British troops heading to Dhala as reinforcements. The other two were to drop bundles of barbed wire close to the fort. Skimming the drop zone fifty feet above the sand was almost as exciting as the earlier air test, ignoring the odd bullet or two that probably came our way.

In mid-1958 a number of Beverley transport aircraft joined 84 Sqn to boost the load lifting capacity enormously. Sadly, within a few months, a Beverley crashed at Beihan while attempting a landing there after it had suffered an engine failure shortly after take-off. The Beverley also featured as a key player in the subduing of a rebellion in the Muscat and Oman. The Sultan of those territories had close relations with the British. His royal residence was in Salalah. Every so often he would fly in one of our Valettas to Aden and back. At the end of each flight an aide reached into a battered leather case and handed a Rolex watch to each crewmember. I received mine in July 1958. My son now wears it and it still keeps good time.

Since 1957 the British had been assisting the Sultan to suppress the rebellion. Ground forces had gradually pushed the rebels onto a formidable redoubt. Some six to seven hundred rebel troops became firmly ensconced on the Jebel Akhdar, or Green Mountain. Politically, with Colonel Nasser parading as the Arab saviour, the British believed that a full-scale military assault on to the Jebel would be out of the question. The Special Air Service (SAS) was called upon to deploy a squadron into the area. The first SAS soldiers, including one Captain de la Billière, landed on the island of Masirah on 18th November 1958, having been flown in from Malaya. From there a Beverley of 84 Sqn flew them to the dirt strip at Azaiba, a coastal landing strip close to the present day airport of Seeb. Their target, the Green Mountain, was formidable. Topped by a plateau about the size of the Isle of Wight and some 8,000 feet above sea level, it featured precipitously steep sides. There was no road to the top and just a handful of tracks led up from the wadis to the plateau. Each track could easily be defended by a small number of adoo, Arabic for enemy. Air support was going to be crucial to the success of the mission. Shackleton aircraft, detached to Masirah, flew many missions over the Jebel, dropping 1,000lb bombs on to water tanks, dams and aqueducts used by the rebels. RAF Venom fighter-bombers unleashed their rockets on more military-like targets, as did Venoms and Seahawks from a Royal Navy aircraft carrier. Muharraq/Bahrein became the airhead for transport support. Through December 1958 the campaign was nearing its climax. My contribution was tiny. I arrived in Bahrein on 5th December and spent the next two weeks shuttling supplies and manpower through Sharjah, Firq and Azaiba, often encountering poor weather. On 22nd I was recalled to Aden, there to spend a very quiet four weeks. The SAS had a tougher time of it, soldiering in the heat of the day and the cruelly cold nights.

It became obvious that things were hotting up because a string of VIP flights suddenly appeared on the Squadron task board. On 24th January I flew straight to Azaiba. Meantime the Shackletons were bombing sangars and caves used by the adoo, and our Valetta detachment at Bahrein was reinforced for some forthcoming air drops. After dropping our VIP back at Aden we snatched a short sleep and a change of clothes. Then, in VX 579, we set off direct for Bahrein, a hop of seven hours and fifteen minutes. Whilst I was enjoying the luxury of the long cruise, popping foul-smelling boiled eggs out through the Verey pistol mounting, D day had already arrived on the Jebel. The SAS troops were poised for the final assault, and our VIP wanted to be in the area for the culmination of the campaign. The next morning, at 0645 local time, three of our Valettas made an air drop of much needed ammunition and victuals. The victorious, but parched, troops especially welcomed the fresh water. Within three hours of the drop we were on our way back to Aden. The long-term result of the operation for the SAS was that it secured their future. By the end of February I had flown twenty-nine VIP sorties on the trot. A few days later, with nearly 1,500 hours in my logbook, I was on my way home in a DC-6A of Eagle Airways.

After a couple of months with the Ferry Communication Sqn at Benson, I set off on my brand new AJS motorcycle to South Cerney for twelve weeks of officer training. Training complete, next stop was Tern Hill, to start pilot training. My first instructor was an ex air signaller and had served on 84 Sqn, flying Brigands in Malaya. One problem I had in the early days of training was that I did not like flying upside down. 'Curly', my bald flying instructor, effected a simple cure. At 2,000 feet he suddenly inverted the Piston Provost. All the accumulated bits of dust and rubbish floated up and sat on the canopy. 'Pasco, you have control. Carry on straight and level, upside down.' After a while, 'Turn left onto south.' Gradually I felt more at home. Curly directed me to repeat the process a number of times. My fear of being the wrong way up evaporated. Problem solved, I felt very happy. In those days, if a student pilot had not flown solo by about twelve hours of dual flying training, it was the 'chop.' As my course had already dwindled from nine to five, I was very relieved that my problem was behind me. By July 1960 I had completed my basic flying training. My course was destined for either Transport or Coastal Command, which meant that we all set off for Valley, on Anglesey Island, to do the Vampire and Varsity course. Valley had been the first recipient of the Vampire T11, in 1952.

DH VAMPIRE T11. Two-seat advanced trainer. One 3,200lb thrust DH Goblin 3 jet engine. Span 38 feet. Length 34 feet 6 inches. Maximum loaded weight, with rockets and drop tanks 13,600lb. Maximum airspeed, at 20,000 feet, 540mph. Time to reach 30,000 feet (clean) 12 minutes. Built as a private venture, it first flew in November 1950. There were over 500 in RAF service. Of interest, on 23rd March 1948, John Cunningham set a world high altitude record, in an extensively modified Vampire Mk 1, TG 278, of nearly 59,500 feet. The area used for the flight was between Cambridge and Lakenheath. At full power the jet engine of the T11 gobbled nearly 4,000lb fuel per hour at sea level and burned 700lb of fuel (out of a total of 2,550lb internal) in the climb to 30,000 feet. It ended RAF service in January 1968, but served with Marshall at RAF Shawbury until 1969.

At the end of September 1960 Ron Williamson, my instructor, had a very near miss. The weather was claggy, too poor for student flying, so Staff Continuation Training was authorised. Ron went off with another instructor in a Vampire to hone up his instrument flying skills. An hour or so later, Ron came back to the crew-room looking like a man who had stared death in the face. He had been flying the instrument approach procedure from overhead the airfield, using the onboard Rebecca radar homing device. During the rapid descent away from Valley he glanced at the swiftly unwinding altimeter, which he mistakenly read as 10,000 feet. At that very second, his fellow instructor shouted, 'Pull up.' As he did so, recognising the urgency of the call, the Vampire broke out of cloud. At the bottom of the descent Ron spied, just a few feet below the aircraft, the wave tops. He kept climbing. What he had seen as 10,000 feet was, in fact, just 1,000 feet. In May 1961, after a total of one hundred and forty-eight flying hours, I gained my wings and went straight to Colerne to be attached to 24 Sqn. The reason was that the military leaders of Iraq, just three years after seizing power, were threatening Kuwait with invasion.

Part of the British assistance was to airlift troops to Kuwait through El Adem and Aden. My part in the airlift was to fly as second pilot to Flt Lt Barry Northwood in Hastings TG 606, leaving Colerne on 9th July. We dropped our troops at Bahrein then flew home via Aden, Khartoum and Malta. Immediately afterwards, I left Colerne for Dishforth, to convert on to the Hastings. Course completed, I joined 202 Meteorological Reconnaissance Sqn as a co-pilot. Arriving at Aldergrove, Northern Ireland, on 11th December 1961 I was greeted by the sight of a still smoking, wrecked Hastings. It had crashed on take-off that morning. The co-pilot on board for its final attempt at flight told me that after the Hastings, TG 621, had come to rest he escaped through the clear vision panel alongside his seat. No mean feat since the panel was barely big enough to get your head through.

HANDLEY PAGE HASTINGS C1. Long-range transport. Four 1,675HP Bristol Hercules 106 engines. Span 113 feet. Length 82 feet 9 inches. Loaded weight 80,000lb. Maximum airspeed at 22,000 feet 345mph. Cruising speed 300mph. Maximum range 4,250 miles. Entered service with 47 Sqn in 1948, and took part in the Berlin airlift. It had an excellent safety record. Metal fatigue caused it to be withdrawn from transport use in 1968, to be replaced by the Lockheed Hercules. Handley Page converted the last six Hastings Mk 1s to Met Mk 1s for use by 202 Sqn. A pretty cumbersome radar altimeter was fitted on the flight deck, alongside the co-pilot. Other modifications were a host of meteorological instruments, filters for measuring air quality including radioactivity, and a hatch at the rear of the cargo compartment for dropping flares. We once carried a member of the WRAF on a flight. The flight engineer told her that the flare hatch was the loo. The Met Mk 1 entered service in 1953 and stayed with 202 Sqn until it disbanded on 31st July 1964. Two of the original six crashed on take-off and were replaced.

The secondary task for 202 was to act as the transport squadron for Coastal Command and the primary task was to fly Bismuth sorties. On a typical

Bismuth flight, most of the flying was at 1,500 feet. A portion of the flight was spent climbing to a pressure level of 500 millibars, about 18,000 feet. Before and after the climb we made a descent to exactly two hundred feet above sea level for a few minutes to record meteorological data. The whole flight was flown manually as the autopilot had been deactivated. Two air meteorological observers took reams of meteorological data throughout the flight while the two air signallers radioed back the data by W/T. A flight engineer and a navigator completed the crew.

A Bismuth flight went off every day except Wednesday and Sunday, usually for about eight hours over the Atlantic. My captain was a solidly built Pole, Flt Lt Ignatowski. Iggy had been in the Polish Air Force when the Germans invaded his country. Pushed back by the overwhelming strength of the German onslaught, Iggy was captured by the Russians when they, too, invaded Poland. After a spell in a Russian prisoner of war camp, surviving on dogs, rats and whatever else could be stolen and eaten, Iggy escaped. He made his way to England via the Mediterranean area and joined the RAF. Our first flight together was on 16th December 1961. A more memorable one came the following year.

In October 1962 the Beatles exploded into the charts with 'Love me do.' It was also the height of the Cuban missile crisis, potentially a vastly greater explosion. Soviet surface vessels were in transit to and from Cuba, carrying surface-to-surface missiles and bomber aircraft. Also active along the route were numerous Soviet submarines. At the end of the month we were, unusually, sent out over the Atlantic towards a large area of high-pressure air. Normally, the Central Met Office sent us through the worst of the weather, into areas of low pressure, to help predict the likely weather heading towards the United Kingdom. On one of the descents to two hundred feet, an unexpected meeting took place.

The weather over the Atlantic was superb, a light breeze, excellent visibility and no turbulence. Not our usual experience at all. Having just levelled off at two hundred feet, Iggy shouted 'Submarine.' His wartime years in Coastal Command meant he could smell a sub before the rest of us could see it. The squadron motto Be Always Vigilant was surely written with him in mind. Sure enough, first a periscope then a conning tower appeared as the submarine surfaced. It was dead ahead but some way off. Iggy flew the Hastings straight at it. As we bore down on the sub the hatch atop the conning tower opened. Out popped the head of a Soviet submariner, no doubt savouring the sensation of all that ozone-fresh air. 'Hell's teeth' he must have thought when he saw us racing straight at him. Iggy wrenched the Hastings into a steep turn for a second run. The sub, meanwhile, was already in 'Dive, Dive' territory. By the time we got round for a second pass, great plumes of water were gushing up as the Soviet vessel rushed back below the surface. As Iggy flew, I scribbled. With no camera aboard, I did my best to sketch what I saw. The sea was so calm and clear that we could follow the submerged path of the sub with ease.

It was a chance encounter in a million. All we had to show the Intelligence boys back at Aldergrove would be my sketch of what we saw. We never did find out the precise model of that sub nor were we issued with a camera. A pity, because a few months later the sharp eyes of Iggy spotted another Soviet submarine sheltering underneath a thunderstorm just off the coast of Ireland.

Increasing technology, especially satellites, caused the demise of 202 Sqn. Weather forecasting no longer needed our input. The final Bismuth was flown on 31st July 1964. My captain on that flight was Frank Radina. A Czech, Frank had followed a similar path to Iggy's before joining the RAF. Included in his wartime experience was a spell in the French Foreign Legion in North Africa. While flying he never ate, he just drank tea and smoked lots of Woodbine cigarettes. His last Bismuth was his four hundred and forty first.

After leaving Ireland, I spent five months at Little Rissington, the home of CFS. Graduating as a qualified flying instructor (QFI) in January 1965, I headed for Church Fenton to join 7 FTS. My first two flights there were both air-tests, with me acting as scribe to the unit test pilot, Flt Lt Jackson.

I should have known that when the flight commander pops into the crew-room and calls for two volunteers to do a bit of instrument flying training on a murky July day, something is being hidden. The 'something' was that Jet Provost XR 651 also needed an engine slam check at 30,000 feet, to complete an air-test flown the day before. John, another new QFI, and I headed out towards Whitby. As we climbed, the whole time in cloud, we each practised turns. Eventually, we levelled off at 30,000 feet. Running over the required procedure before attempting it, we were both happy that we knew what to expect. As I throttled back, John counted down 'Three, two, one, Now.' I slammed the throttle forward and John started the stopwatch to record the time the engine took to accelerate to 95% RPM. He need not have bothered. Instead of winding up, the engine wound down. It had flamed out. We looked at each other. 'What now?' I said. 'Well, you're the captain' said John, helpfully. Adopting the glide, I initiated the hot relight drill. The engine stayed dead. Time was on our side. It would take nearly half an hour to glide back to earth. We headed for base. There were other airfields around, but we had height in hand, and the weather was no better elsewhere. Having declared an emergency, radar directions relieved us of the need to navigate. With a dead engine, however, we soon started to feel the cold. Being summer, we were not wearing all the layers of clothing that would have been appropriate for a winter's flight. However, the air at altitude was just as cold in summer. Working from Flight Reference Cards, we carried out the recommended drills. The engine stayed quiet. Our plan was to fly to overhead Church Fenton, then spiral down, close to the airfield, to carry out a dead stick landing. The cloud base was a worry, because it had stayed annoyingly low. John suggested that we should have another go at a relight when we were in the thicker air at a lower altitude.

Still in cloud as we descended through 10,000 feet, I re-tried the relight drill with success. A huge feeling of relief filled the cockpit, and so did some very welcome warm air. Despite the live engine, we carried on with the glide approach, just in case. Safely back on the ground, we decided it was someone else's turn to finish off the air-test.

HUNTING JET PROVOST T4. Two-seat basic trainer. One 2,500lb thrust Viper ASV 11, Mk 202 turbo-jet. Span 37 feet. Length 32 feet 6 inches. Loaded weight 7,400lb. Maximum airspeed 410mph at 20,000 feet. Maximum rate of climb at sea level 3,400fpm. Climb to 20,000 feet took about eight minutes. The Mk 4 entered RAF service in 1961.

Just after my 28th birthday I was airborne in a Mk 4 Jet Provost with a member of 13 Course. The OC of my squadron was leading the formation, and he was doing precisely what he had briefed. We changed formation from line abreast to line astern, and, on a beautiful day, got stuck into a tailchase. A couple of wingovers then up into a loop. It was normal to slip back a little near the top of a loop, and then regain the lost distance on the way down. Suddenly, however, the lead aircraft filled the windscreen. With one hand up to shield my face from the seemingly inevitable collision, I snatched the control column from the student and pulled hard right. It worked; we missed.

No more frights came my way and I stayed with 7 FTS until it disbanded in November 1966. Destined for the Hawker Siddeley HS 748 Andover transport aircraft my next stop was Abingdon. I married Judith, my first wife, in June 1967 and one month later we flew out to Singapore to join 52 Sqn, based at Seletar. The commanding officer of the squadron was Barry Northwood, whom I had last seen at Colerne in 1961.

HAWKER SIDDELEY HS 748 Andover C1. Medium-range transport aircraft with STOL (short take-off and landing) capability. Crew of four. Two Rolls-Royce Dart Mk 555 turbo-prop engines. Span 98 feet 3 inches. Length 78 feet. Maximum take-off weight 51,000lb. Could carry up to 44 troops. A unique feature was the kneeling undercarriage. By pumping out hydraulic oil, the main undercarriage legs sank, to lower the rear ramp to ground level. Maximum cruising speed 260mph. Service ceiling 25,000 feet. Range with maximum payload and fuel reserves 810 miles. Maximum ferry-range 2,700 miles. Entered RAF service in 1966 as a Valetta replacement. The last Andover, an E3, was retired from RAF service in October 1996.

The primary task of 52 Sqn was to fly into short airstrips, drop supplies to Army units in the jungle and perform a number of schedules and specials all over the Far East. Places visited included Thailand, to air bases like Udorn, Takhli, and Korat, all used by the USAF for operations into North

Vietnam. We had reckoned that it would be possible to fly the Andover direct from Singapore to Darwin, Australia, with the two internal ferry tanks fitted. HQ did not much like our suggestion of a jolly to 'Oz' to prove it, so they sent us around the South China Sea instead. Naming each turning point after an Australian town, we made the first ferry-tank flight on 21st June 1968 in XS 613. The flight lasted eight hours, and in addition, greeted by a big cheer from the four of us aboard, we coaxed the Andover all the way up to its maximum altitude of 25,000 feet. Fourteen years later, in response to a certain South American General's invasion of the Falklands, I met up again with those very same ferry tanks.

Late at night on 28th October 1968 I received a telephone call to mount a flight as soon as possible to Seria Anduki, in Brunei. Landing at Anduki in the dark was not possible because the grass airstrip had no lighting. Early on the 29th we set off from Seletar in XS 637, complete with a medical team. The reason for the flight was to rush the baby son of a Gurkha family to the military hospital at Changi. The poor lad had a very distended stomach and needed urgent medical attention. We landed just after dawn and took on board the boy and his mother. The flight back was into foul weather. Barely an hour away from Singapore, in torrential rain, there was a loud bang. The intercom, the radio system and the rest of the electrical system went dead. We were left with just a few key items powered by an emergency supply. Navigation was now by dead reckoning as all the electronic aids were dead too.

After a radio failure in a radar environment, the drill was to fly a triangle. In theory, ground radar observers would spot the triangle and render whatever assistance was possible. Unable to communicate with Singapore ATC, we decided to fly an emergency triangle. We then managed to get one of our radio receivers to work so we now hoped that someone down below would understand what was going on and transmit on the most likely frequency: 121.5 MHz. Hopefully the ATC wallahs would then direct us to an airfield, using the speechless procedure. We were wasting our time; the radar observers did not spot our predicament. I put the Andover into a descent, well out to sea, and the navigator map read us to Changi. Waggling our wings to indicate no radio I joined the circuit at low level and landed. We taxied in, shut down and arranged for the Gurkha boy to be whisked away to the nearby British military hospital. A most irate wing commander then stomped aboard. 'How dare you land at my airfield without permission, and without telling anybody. What do you think you are up to?' I explained what had happened. 'That's no excuse. I want a full incident report as soon as you get back to Seletar.' We left the stricken aircraft at Changi, and went by road to Seletar. I made the report and forwarded it through the usual channels. From the wing commander we heard no more. The Gurkha boy, unfortunately, died a few days later.

In September 1968 I was lucky, in that I flew a party from the Imperial Defence College on an end-of-course tour of Malaysia, Indonesia and

Australia. By then I knew that the squadron was soon to move base. In early
1969 the RAF handed Seletar over to the Singapore Air Force and 52 Sqn
moved the few miles to Changi. My final year in Singapore was taken up
almost entirely with converting some of our co-pilots to captaincy. Included
in the training task was the full gamut of tactical air support: low flying by
day and by night, dropping parachutists and various stores on to training
drop zones, DZs. Of all the different tasks that came my way in the RAF
flying tactical support missions was easily my favourite. Exactly one year
after the hospital flight to Anduki came the call to drop supplies to some
SAS units training in Malaya. What an ideal way to increase the experience
of the new captains, I thought.

Right from the start, we guessed all might not go well. The Army drop-
signal gave details of what to drop, where and when. Plotting out the grid
reference, the navigator said 'They must be joking. The first DZ is in the
middle of Kuala Lumpur.' A recheck of his plotting confirmed that he was
right. 'Terribly sorry,' said the Army body; 'we have reversed two sets of
numbers.' Having got that key information sorted, we flew up to the Royal
Australian Air Force base at Butterworth, close to Kuala Lumpur. After a
refuel and a final briefing with a representative of the ground unit, we took
off for the drop mission. Different from the normal run of supply drops, the
task called for us to home to the dropping point for a blind drop. The loads
being dropped, from about eight hundred feet, were quite small. Suspended
below a single parachute on a long line, the 'chute would hang up on the
treetops. The load would then free-fall and dangle by its line close to, or on
the jungle floor. The system was called Jungle Line.

Each of the three or four ground patrols was detailed to operate a VHF
radio beacon at a precise time. The supplies were to be dropped at exactly
five-minute intervals. Each ground patrol was to switch on its beacon thirty
seconds before drop time and switch off by sixty seconds after. Fitted to the
aircraft was a radio device that incorporated a homing needle. The DZs
were quite close to each other. Adherence to the briefed procedure,
especially the timing, was vital for success. The ground beacons had a
speech facility, to be used only in emergency. It was vital that only one
beacon was transmitting at any one time, otherwise it would be impossible
to home the Andover to the required drop point. All the beacons operated
on the same frequency. It seemed like a straightforward task.

Homing in to the first DZ, we were thrilled to see the needle of the
aircraft homing indicator come to life within seconds of the briefed time.
'Good old SAS' shouted someone. I lined the aircraft up, keeping the
needle centred. 'Red on' called the navigator. We could smell success. The
Army despatch team steadied themselves to heave the load out. 'Green on.'
'Load gone.' Brilliant. 'Well done everybody. Prepare the next load.' The
co-pilot and I exchanged a grin as we manoeuvred for the second run in,
just a mile or so away. 'Hold it steady,' called the navigator. At that very
moment the homing needle went mad. Left, right, it swung crazily. Up

piped a voice 'We're over here, you've flown past us.' Another voice butted in 'We can see you.' And so it went on. The DZs were so close to each other that we needed to circle around to get the dropping run lined up correctly. All of the patrols hidden in the jungle below could hear us above, and perhaps see us too. However, unless they shut up and transmitted as briefed, we would never be able to drop in the right position. And so it turned out. We dropped only to the first patrol. The rest of the loads stayed aboard. Back to Butterworth we flew, off-loaded the supplies and headed home to Changi.

Judith gave birth to our son, Nicholas, in Changi hospital on 8th October 1969. In December 52 Sqn disbanded, a consequence of the British Government's decision to withdraw British forces from Singapore. On 6th January 1970, in Andover XS 608, I left Changi for Kemble, Gloucestershire. Fitted with one internal long-range fuel tank, our route home took us through Colombo, Bombay, Sharjah, Luxor, Cyprus and Malta. After forty hours and fifteen minutes flight time, we handed XS 608 to the maintenance unit at Kemble. It was another three years before I returned to flying duties.

Anna, our daughter, was prematurely born in Hitchin hospital in the early hours of 1st January 1971. In early November that year I flew to the Italian Air Force base at Pisa. Now a squadron leader, I was in charge of the operations room to co-ordinate RAF Andover and Hercules aircraft on a joint RAF/Italian para dropping exercise. The paratroopers for the exercise were all Italian, based at nearby Livorno. Well before dawn on 9th November 1971, three waves of three Hercules took off. Their mission, the first of the detachment, was a low-level night formation flight, to parachute troops on to a drop zone in Sardinia. Not long after the last aircraft had left, reports started to come in of an explosion just off the coast near Livorno. By dawn it was established that one of the Hercules had crashed in to the sea. There were no survivors. Six RAF crew and sixty-five Italian para-troopers died. By agreement with the Italians, the joint exercise continued as scheduled. Months later, accompanying Air Marshal Crowley-Milling, the AOC of 46 Group, I attended the most moving ceremony of my life. Flying to Rome in a Comet of 216 Sqn we shared the sad and harrowing experience of the close relatives of all those RAF personnel that had died two days before Remembrance Day.

After a refresher course at Oakington in early 1974, flying the Varsity, I moved to the Hercules conversion unit at Thorney Island. Immediately after the acceptance check flights with 30 Sqn at Lyneham in July 1974, I was at work flying between Lyneham and Akrotiri, Cyprus, to bring home British families affected by the Turkish invasion of that island.

Later that year I made my first flight to the USA. Having travelled to Gander, Newfoundland, as a passenger in a Hercules, I then flew XV 292 to Ottawa, Canada. The next leg, to Dulles airport, Washington, was quite a short one at less than two hours. The main feature of the pre-flight briefing was the high risk of thunderstorms (CBs). The meteorological officer warned us of considerable CB activity, but indicated that the storms were well spread out, which would allow us to fly round them. Ensuring that our load of freight was tightly secured, we launched off to the south. The climb to 30,000 feet was without incident. The aircraft radar showed many CB returns, but gaps were apparent all around. I decided that we would press on, but conscious of the fact that no large aircraft is built to withstand the extreme upsets that are possible within a CB, I did not make the decision lightly.

Halfway through the flight the situation suddenly changed. As if by some grand design, within just a few minutes the gaps between the CBs closed up. We were surrounded. Running swiftly through the 'pre-thunderstorm' drills, all the internal lights were switched on and a further check of the freight was carried out. A loose item of freight could spell disaster. Selecting a flight path to avoid the heaviest cells we reduced from cruising to turbulence speed and sat tight. Outside the cockpit it became as dark as night, punctuated by vivid displays of lightning. As far as we could tell, we were not struck by lightning. The turbulence, however, was at times extreme. The Hercules was tossed around like a rat being savaged by a Jack Russell terrier. Unable to maintain our authorised cruising level, we alerted ATC and just hung on as we lurched up and down at the mercy of the elements. I looked round at one stage to check how the young flight engineer was coping. His face would have made a good advert for a washing powder. It was white, apart from his brown eyes that stayed glued to the engine instruments. A strange, calm feeling came over me. It could shortly be the end; several Hercules aircraft have been downed in CBs. There was nothing I could do except try and maintain as steady a flying attitude as possible and hope for the best. ATC cleared us for descent; Washington was now, thankfully, only fifteen minutes away. I called for a lower power setting, reduced speed a little and lowered the nose. The seventy-five ton aircraft should have descended. Nature decided otherwise and up we went. To increase drag, and our chances of descending, I called for partial flap and then for gear down. Still the Hercules climbed. Suddenly, like rushing out of a long, dark tunnel, we were in clear air. Now we came down, like a brick. I kept the nose of the aircraft down to maintain airspeed. We were all overwhelmed by a huge feeling of relief. For a while no one spoke. Then, the nightmare behind us, we reverted to our normal, rational routine. The landing came as a welcome end to a memorable flight.

It took several hours for the flight engineer to return to normal. By late evening he was not only well recovered but also highly exuberant. So much so, that he agreed to our suggestion to be transformed into a female. A televised beauty contest was being staged in the hotel. We got chatting to one of the contestants; she was about the same size as our young engineer. She agreed to help with the transformation. On with the make-up, a quick brush and spray of the hair, a fetching one-piece dress and a pair of high-heeled shoes did the job. Now looking quite the part, he sidled up to the edge of the stage. Just before he could waltz on in front of the cameras, a loud 'What the hell is that?' ended his bid for Miss Whatever. We all felt on top of the world; it was a marvellous end to 3rd September 1974.

All my flights through the United States were associated with unusual happenings. The next adventure occurred in 1975 in Hercules XV 220. Two crews were sharing a round the world flight through the USA, Hong Kong, and then on home through Singapore and the Arabian Gulf. On 18th November I was captain for the leg from McClellan Air Base, California, to Hawaii. Conditions were nigh on perfect in the cruise at 32,000 feet. The entire flight was over the Pacific Ocean. About two hours out from Hickam Air Force Base, Honolulu, the flight engineer chirped up 'Captain, the windscreen has cracked.' And so it had. Tough though the windscreen is, a crack straight across one panel is not a happy event. The problem associated with the crack is that excessive pressure inside the aircraft, due to internal pressurisation, could cause the panel to push outwards. 'Captain to crew, oxygen masks on.' Within a minute everyone had checked in. 'Flight engineer, commence depressurisation, not too fast.' We commenced a slow descent wondering if our windscreen could be replaced at Hickam. By good fortune, the USAF had a spare Hercules windscreen in store. The cracked one was removed and the new one was installed. As luck would have it the glue that secured the screen to the frame needed three days to dry. We saw a lot more of Hawaii than we had expected to.

One of my last training flights at Lyneham, however, made me sweat a little. In the gathering gloom we launched down the main runway at the start of a two-hour night sortie. I became vaguely aware of a shape in front of us on the runway, which, as we approached one hundred knots, clarified itself as a double-decked bus. Closing the throttles, hammering the brakes, and putting the propellers into full reverse failed to avoid a collision. Crunch, we boarded the bus without a penny between us for the fare. Peals of laughter came from the supervising aircrew behind us. They had arranged for the vehicle to appear on the runway. Fortunately, on this occasion we were in the simulator, but the shock of hitting the Dinky toy was very real.

With just over 7,500 flying hours in my logbooks, six months passed before I found a suitable job in Civvy Street. I joined Marshall of Cambridge in March 1977. My first six days were a whirl of activity. Off to Dinard and back in an Aztec with John Preece, then to Stuttgart and back in a Citation, two Hercules air tests with Doug Page, and seven instructional flights in a Cessna 150. Life quietened down after that, until the cadet season arrived in June. However many flights we fitted in there was always an expectant young face waiting to become airborne. The pattern was repeated every summer until well into the 1980s.

1981 was a relatively quiet year. There was little Hercules flying and not much in the way of visits in the Aztec or Citation. One student that arrived in May stands out in my mind. Wilbur Nyabongo, a charming, shy and intelligent young Ugandan, arrived for flying instruction. The lady who accompanied him was anything but shy. Sweeping into the Control Building waltzed this stunning and elegant beauty. Only years later did I discover that the two were man and wife. The lady was Princess Elizabeth of Toro. In the 1960s she studied at Girton College, Cambridge, and qualified as a lawyer in 1965. She became the first woman to be called to the bar in her country, Uganda. In 1974, not yet thirty, she became Idi Amin's Foreign Minister. Princess Elizabeth and Wilbur escaped together from Uganda in 1981, travelled to London and were married shortly after. Wilbur came to the CAC to start on the long road to becoming a commercial pilot. His career was not a long one, however.

Teaching someone to fly who was shy but determined was a pleasure. Never afraid to say that he did not understand something, Wilbur and I worked together for two months. By the middle of July, having passed his final handling test, Wilbur left us to continue his commercial pilot training elsewhere. I heard no more of him until July 1997, when the *Daily Mail* featured Princess Elizabeth in a three-page story. I read that Wilbur had achieved his ambition to become a commercial pilot. At the end of 1986 he and Elizabeth planned to return to Toro for a family wedding. Flying as co-pilot in a private jet, Wilbur was to fly to Uganda via Nigeria and Casablanca. After Elizabeth had arrived in Kampala, she heard the terrible news. Wilbur's aircraft was waiting in the holding pattern for permission to approach and land at Casablanca when it ran out of fuel. The aircraft crashed and sadly there were no survivors.

If 1981 was quiet, the following year was anything but. On 2nd April 1982 General Galtieri sent Argentinean forces to the Falklands to remove the islands from British sovereignty. He had reckoned without the resolve of Margaret Thatcher, and that determination was swiftly turned into action. Before many days had passed Marshall was once again contracted to assist the British Armed Forces to do their job. That was the start of a hectic few months. So much happened as a consequence of our involvement in air-to-air refuelling that I shall cover the story in a later chapter.

On the bitterly cold night of 7th February 1983 I was playing badminton at Bottisham when I felt what seemed to be a kick from my doubles partner. It turned out to be an Achilles tendon giving way. The untimely injury grounded me for three months and led to the Company recruiting another Hercules captain, Rob Butterworth, because my injury meant that only John Preece was available as a captain.

One consequence of my leg injury was that I was able to devote more of my time to a project that I had long felt overdue. Because of the nature of our test flying, we instructors sometimes had to leave our Aero Club students in the lurch. I had long held the view that students would benefit if some specific aids to learning to fly at Cambridge were put on paper. I started along that road by producing a host of questions and answers for

use by CAC students. It took five years to achieve the end result, the
Cambridge Flying Guide, but it was well worth the effort. I was always
impressed by the effort that most of the CAC students put into their desire
to become pilots. Fitting in flying lessons around family, work, the weather,
and not always being 'lucky' to find an instructor available, they achieved
their goal in a way that I knew would have been difficult for me. How
fortunate I had been to receive RAF training, full time and all paid for.

Some instructional flights did not go as expected. One man 'froze'
during a spin recovery. I had to wrench his hand off the throttle, which he
had pushed fully open, to regain control of the Cessna. He probably still
has the two scratch marks visible on the back of his right hand. On another
occasion I was instructing a lady in the art of navigation. She was learning
to fly without the knowledge of her husband. Unusually, she had not made
any reference to her map during the whole of the first leg. As this was her
third navigation sortie I left her to get on with it. At the start of the second
leg I said 'Let us have a look at your map.' She replied 'It's in my
handbag.' 'That's alright, just take it out.' 'I can't' she said, 'I've left my
bag in flight planning.'

Learning how to land in a safe and dignified manner is, perhaps, the
most difficult part of the course for most students. Some students just
could not achieve this very important step. One hopeful, who came over
from Amsterdam once a month, did not seem to have the gift. Her
spectacles and my headset would often end up on the cockpit floor on
some of her firmer landing attempts. Fortunately I have no false teeth.
I told the lady that I felt she had best take up sailing. She persisted, 'As
long as I can pay, may I continue to try?' One year later she had mastered
the art of touching down safely and went on to get her licence. Some
students were not so lucky. The ATC cadets who came to us for their
scholarship training had the constraint of time to contend with. If they
were unable to achieve a safe landing technique after about twelve hours
dual instruction they were removed from the course. Sadly, at least one a
year had to pack his bags and go home early.

Just briefly, I should mention that QFIs have to satisfy a civilian
examiner every two years that they are still competent to teach. This
involves a flight, with the examiner playing the part of a student, and a
grilling on the ground to check that knowledge of the academic subjects is
still adequate. In addition, if we were teaching students on the RAF
scholarship course, a CFS examiner would come to Cambridge once a year
to put us through our paces. Other exams came our way too. Every thirteen
months we had to renew our commercial Instrument Ratings with a CAA-
approved examiner. The authority to fly certain aircraft, like the Aztec and
Citation, had to be renewed every thirteen months by undergoing a flight test
with a Flight Examiner. The initial test of competency to fly the TriStar was
flown in the aircraft, at Shannon, Ireland, but the thirteen-month renewals
were conducted in a British Airways simulator at Heathrow airport.

My Achilles tendon injury put me off playing competitive badminton. I returned to ballroom dancing and, in 1991, met my second wife, Margaret. We married in 1992.

In 1996, after almost twenty years with the Company, I retired, thinking that my flying career was over. Two years later I felt a strong pull back to the air. In December 1998 I took the air and ground examination to regain my flying instructor rating and rejoined the CAC as a part-time instructor. If I were asked would I follow the same profession again if given a second chance, I would say 'Yes.' My forty-seven years of flying, especially the years with Marshall of Cambridge, have been interesting, sometimes exciting and always rewarding.

Chapter 11

Tim Mason

On one memorable exercise in 1959 after a take-off in the small hours, we and over one hundred other Canberras flew out to Norway, turned round and formed a two-level, V-bomber above Canberras line of advance with aircraft a few miles apart. As the sun rose behind us there were vapour trails as far as I could see to left and right – very impressive. On another similar occasion when, as usual, timing was of the essence, we needed to slow down to achieve our ETA when one engine surged and it had to be shut down. We descended, inevitably, and relit the engine at, I think, 25,000 feet. We did an orbit to lose time on the climb back to our appointed height, 40,000 feet, and place in the scheme of things. After landing we were left in no doubt about our error of judgement in making the orbit in the face of hundreds of incoming aircraft and for destroying the whole carefully planned exercise. One learns, perhaps, not to mention such excursions to one's superiors.

Apparently my father threatened to put me back when he saw my pointed head at birth on 27th August 1937 at Haslemere, Surrey. My mother failed to see the necessity and worried about the practical details. Things soon settled down and I grew to know my parents well over the next half century – their devotion to the needs and well being of others, particularly their three children, was an inspiration and example I have been unable to emulate.

I was three years old when my data bank started. I recall my mother singing at the sink, my aunt Dodo, whose house we shared when the Admiralty commandeered ours, radiating terror as we cowered together under the stairs during an air raid. Stroud school was a short daily bus ride away, sometimes driven by my grandfather, doing his bit for the war effort my mother said. Being in the southeast of England the school was felt to be in the way of Doodlebugs, the V-1, and it moved to Zeals in Wiltshire. And so, in 1948, I graduated to Guildford Grammar School.

I could not believe the huge class sizes (thirty) and the freedom after school every day. Trains were *the* big 'thing' then and only a little initiative was needed by yours truly to spend ecstatic days at Woking station watching the great belching monsters hurtling down the straight from West Byfleet. The odd day of hooky became two and eventually three weeks. The ensuing enquiry after my health by the school secretary was entirely predictable, as was my father's reply. He stressed that I was at school *every* day. Oh well, I thought, another of those bruising close encounters with the Head. But, no! He was amazingly calm and, he said, he just could not understand why I had rejected his school or how I had managed to travel the length and breadth of Southern England by train with no ticket and without getting caught – maybe he wanted a few tips. Anyway, we parted amicably, I thought, and I never looked back – only forward to the day I could fly those wonderful machines I had seen screeching past in the rain at the Farnborough Air Show. I have missed only one year's show, 1956, since 1948. A Flying Scholarship produced a PPL and a passenger: my father. His pilot son had thirty-one hours in his logbook.

Having failed twice to join the RAF via a cadetship at Cranwell, my distinguished schooldays ended with a summons to report to Cardington on 28th October 1955. Our hut NCO was a wizened man who had his own tiny room, unventilated, but adorned with choice pictures of bare ladies. He rejoiced in the name of Corporal Balloch; no prizes for guessing his sobriquet, but, yes, he had a brother. We sprogs thought they would make a right pair. At Kirton-in-Lindsey the only relief from marching, night guard duty, bulling our boots and barrack block was on a bright sunny day when an 'old boy' gave us the 'low-show' in an F-86 Sabre; what a tonic. Half of my course was sent to Tern Hill and I joined the select mob going to Canada for flying training.

A first class passage to the New World, courtesy of SS *Empress of Scotland*, found the very green group of sprogs 'Oh, you poor boys, are you from England? Are things real bad over there?' at London, Ontario for three weeks indoctrination. I missed ten days of this by volunteering to test a new high altitude pressure suit, for a secret fighter. Never having even seen an oxygen mask, this spacesuit was fitted to my pink young body and up I went, with supreme faith in both the kit and those men in white jackets peering in through the portholes of the chamber. Any slight anxiety and discomfort was all worthwhile on rejoining the others at London. My upper chest was covered with hundreds of tiny red spots – 'Oh, it's alright, blood boils at 120,000 feet and the spots are areas not covered by the pressure suit.' This was to be twice as high as I ever went again, whether in a chamber or aeroplane. Sort of reached the pinnacle of my flying at eighteen years of age.

Station London, as the Royal Canadian Air Force (RCAF) referred to it, had the reception area for North Atlantic Treaty Organisation u/t aircrew and also the reserve squadrons – one Mustang and one Mitchell as I recall. Station Centralia, about thirty miles north of London, on the other hand, had just Harvards, about eighty in bright yellow lines on the day I arrived. My course had two Danes and fourteen Brits. The Brits were in bad odour as the previous week a RAF student named Bates had been 'chopped.' He immediately took off and beat up the camp for over an hour, causing a mite of anxiety to the management – to the extent of the commanding officer alerting the nearby Mustang squadron to shoot him down. Did the new boys want some of the action?

Our course was No 2 of 1956, the first to be issued with bonedomes and we celebrated the fact with a course badge in appropriate shape. The fourteen tyro pilots were soon down to eight. The Harvard proved too big a handful for the remainder, who had had no previous flying experience, and who could not be sent off solo within the stipulated thirty hours of dual flying. Chipmunk aircraft appeared after a few months to provide a gentler introduction for later courses to the fine art of mastering a flying machine.

NORTH AMERICAN NA-66 HARVARD. Two-seat advanced trainer. One Pratt and Whitney Wasp R-1340-49 engine. Span 42 feet. Length 29 feet 6 inches. Maximum take-off weight 5,250lb. Maximum level speed, clean, 205mph at 5,000 feet. Service ceiling 21,500 feet. Built under licence by Noorduyn of Canada.

After one hundred and eighty airborne hours, Canadian National Railways whisked us in two and a half days to the unbelievable cold of Winnipeg for nearby Macdonald, where flying had stopped as the chill factor was over the prescribed limit. Jets at last. At age nineteen I had been waiting a lifetime, and I was generally not disappointed, although on an early aerobatics sortie the instructor grabbed the stick, shouting 'Don't push the stick forward, you'll flame the Goddam thing out.' That, and the film that showed the propensity for the T-33 to tumble, gave me a healthy respect for the beast throughout my time on the course. In retrospect, the course was not designed to produce an aggressive fighter pilot – more a smooth instrument 'trucky' [transport pilot]. Most flying took place in clear skies, over a snow-covered landscape, but one flight stands out in my mind. I entered cloud at about 1,000 feet and emerged at 36,000 feet. Then I had to get back down. The instrument training paid off, but at the time it felt a wasted sortie.

NORTH AMERICAN T-33, or T-Bird. The Canadian version, built under licence, was termed the Canadair CL-30. One Rolls-Royce Nene turbo-jet. Span 37 feet. Length 37 feet 9 inches. Maximum take-off weight 18,400lb. Maximum level speed, without tip-tanks, 570mph at sea level. Climb to 20,000 feet eight minutes. Service ceiling 47,000 feet. Entered service with the then RCAF in 1953.

My roommate was a Dane called Koch. He was on the course ahead of mine and he was killed about this time doing aerobatics below the authorised minimum height – another lesson. Almost my own last training sortie was a land-away flight via airways. After a totally inadequate briefing I found the air traffic clearance over the radio was completely incomprehensible to me; a fact not lost on my instructor whose verbose and fortissimo debriefing was at least comprehensive and clear. Anyway, all the junior courses, and the long-suffering station personnel, were on parade to see me get my wings, in May 1957. After a survival course at Namao, in Alberta, during which my lack of hunting skills made the enjoyment of venison, after four hungry days, all the more exquisite, and another week first class at sea back to the UK, I had to report for a Canadian Acclimatisation course.

A culture shock is a barely adequate description of the new world I found myself in. First, arriving at the railway station on a very misty day I heard a jet at low level overhead. 'Poor sod' I thought, 'lost in the fog.' Then another and another jet flew by. 'What is going on' I wondered? The answer? It was a perfectly normal day's flying at nearby 4 FTS at Worksop, in weather even the instructors in Canada would eschew. The next shock was the Officers' Mess (I was a real Pilot Officer by now) located in a wartime corrugated-iron Nissen-type hut, with Seco huts about half a mile distant for sleeping, and with ablutions a further one hundred yards away. Our mounts were Vampires and we were soon disabused of our trucky aspirations. 'Don't pussy foot around lad' said my instructor on an early trip as he whanged the stick to one corner and the rudder to another. We instantly completed about five snap rolls. 'Won't it flame out, sir?' 'No it wouldn't bloody dare lad, and you won't get shot down either.' To my astonishment the engine whined on sweetly and the wings were set at the same angle that we had started with. The single-seat Vampire 5s and 9s were a delight. You strapped them on your back and went flying. Suitably acclimatised, Hunters beckoned. Disappointment followed when Canberras were ordained to be my tipple. It could have been worse; others were awarded Hastings co-pilot postings. We went over to the next hangar for asymmetric training on Meteors – a strange aircraft at first, with incredible stick forces in the spin and an impossibly heavy rudder at low speed using only one engine. It was an excellent introduction to the 'gotchas' of twin-engine flying, emphasised by one instructor whose favourite trick was to slowly close one throttle while flaming out the other engine. He did not kill anyone, but I, like other tyros, had been warned before experiencing this Machiavellian event. So, it was goodbye Worksop, and its characters. An ex-Swift pilot, with two ejections to his credit, one Pissy Rimmington, had, it was said, a horse trained to find its own way home at closing time from the pub to the Rimmington hut.

Hello Bomber Command. I dropped one hundred and eight practice bombs on Wainfleet and Misson ranges from Varsities, and six dummy radar bombs from an Avro Lincoln, both from Lindholme. Then to Bassingbourn, home of the Canberra conversion unit. Easy peasy on one engine after the Meteor, the electric rudder trim beat the multi-turn manual device in the Meteor. And a crew: John Keable, the plotter, and Mike Jones, the bomb-aimer, of whom more anon. After Bassingbourn we went to the holding unit at Coningsby for more Canberra B2 flying pending a posting a month later. With five hundred and twenty four flying hours to my credit and a few days before my 21st birthday, *the* crew joined *the* squadron: No 12, at Binbrook. We flew the Canberra B6, plus a few B2s while the B6s were progressively modified, largely by Marshall of Cambridge, for the low level bombing role. For us, the junior of twenty crews, there was as much flying as we could wish for ('we' is the Royal usage; John and Mike saw little point in starting a two hour sortie at 1530 on a Friday afternoon). Wartime techniques, visual and GEE-H blind bombing, broad-front attacks, radio jamming, BABS approaches after 'Trombone' holding patterns, were our tipple for the first year. Thanks to Mike's skill we soon featured among the most accurate in both visual and blind bombing.

1959 saw two major developments: my nuptials and the squadron's change of role to low level, involving nuclear training, low flying and LABS. The last involved cantering along at 430 knots at a height of two hundred and fifty feet, pulling up into a loop and rolling off the top; the bomb was released automatically halfway up. With frequent day trips to Germany for low flying, detachments to Idris, in Libya, for LABS and occasional high level exercise, not to mention the novelty of matrimony, life was good. After the squadron had moved to Coningsby two things spoiled the euphoria: QRA (quick reaction alert), with the American 'little-E' nuclear bombs guarded by USAF policemen, a minor irritant, and, then would you believe it, getting caught for unauthorised low flying? The good citizens of Brighouse, where Mike Jones's intended lived, objected to our visit and my court-martial ended with the words 'Severe Reprimand.' The court was composed of very understanding pilots whose sympathy was palpable. One result was cancellation of my posting to CFS to become an instructor. Instead I was sent to the mighty 'Detergent' (Deterrent) Force: Avro Vulcans. They had no identification markings under the wings, unlike the Canberra's nine-foot high characters that had led to my fall from grace.

Sent to Finningley to learn Vulcan, my immediate impressions come back to me, how serious everybody took things and the unique and unpleasant smell of the new ground school building, which produced more paper than I knew existed. Flying was strange at first although the simulator, as the Link trainer was known, helped familiarity. We mounted the beast one and a quarter hours before take-off, waded through a monstrous checklist and then flew seemingly endless circuits and bumps at the end of each sortie. As a so-called co-pilot, my duties were, in fact, those of airborne clerk – rations, in-flight paperwork, radio and watching the fuel being, oh so slowly, consumed. My captain, Wg Cdr Mallorie, was not amused one day when he called for the crew to check in 'Captain', 'Radar', 'Nav', 'AEO', and then 'Clerk' said I. Soon thereafter I became a spare 'bod' and was posted to Scampton; both 83 and 617 Sqns were kind enough to say after my two months stint that they found my presence helpful. Blue Steel was the new toy in 1961, and new aircraft modified to carry the missile arrived every fortnight. My only trip with one involved a dummy, I was pleased to note. The real thing seemed to involve a lot of unpleasantness and men wandering around encased in rubber overalls – denied to aircrew. We flyboys had our own, fatherhood-threatening kit. Tight pressure jerkins, tighter g-suits and space helmets (very soon abandoned) made flying a tedious business and smoking was actively discouraged.

I moved back to Coningsby as part of the first crew on the reformed 9 Sqn, whose bat emblem was a prescient choice for our nocturnal aviating. I did not enjoy operational life on Vulcans. The aeroplane was okay, particularly when we received the up-rated Olympus 301 engines; at low weight it went like the proverbial off the shovel. The serious business of deterring war was not intended to be enjoyable; we spent at least one twenty-four hour period per week on QRA in full flying kit, with target study and the endless routine of Training Profile Flights. These were all at high level and frequently in the dark air, when I had an extra duty: 'Shall I put the navigation lights on, Captain?' One reflection, sobering then, and more so with the passing years, was that if the aircrew had an unexciting existence, then the ground crew's lot was a continuous grind. Their routine was an endless round of inspection, refuelling and a long list of items to be fixed after every flight. And yet there was always laughter and banter, attributable in large measure to outstanding senior NCOs, particularly the aircraft crew chiefs. All ranks realised the seriousness of the job, and the word 'professional' was aptly used in describing and measuring performance. For example, aircrew tried very hard to take-off precisely on time, to the extent of adjusting brake release to compensate for headwind and aircraft weight, and, on taxiing in to dispersal, of opening the entrance door to view the nosewheel in the final inches on to the picketing point. We all realised that the better we were, and seen to be, at our jobs then the more effective our peacekeeping role.

AVRO VULCAN B2. Medium-range strategic bomber. Five crew. Engines were initially four Bristol Olympus 200 series of 17,000lb thrust; later 20,000lb thrust Olympus 300 series. Span 111 feet. Length 100 feet. Maximum take-off weight 204,000lb. Maximum authorised airspeed .93 Mach at 55,000 feet. Service ceiling 56,000 feet. Maximum unrefuelled range at low level 3,450 miles. Weapons: 21x 1,000lb iron bombs or one nuclear free-fall weapon carried internally, or one Avro Blue Steel Mk1 stand-off bomb carried externally. First flight of production B2 – August 1958. First squadron to be equipped was 83, in July 1960. Eighty-nine B2s were built. Tim Mason delivered XM 657, the last production B2, on his final trip in Bomber Command. From 1966 onwards the B2 squadrons became fully operational as a low-level penetration force using special terrain-following radar. For the Falklands war, Carousel inertial navigation equipment was installed, and six B2s were converted as AAR tankers. They did not see service in the war, but remained in use until the VC-10 tanker was introduced.

I returned in July 1963 to Coningsby for the fourth time, to join 35 Sqn as captain of their fifth crew. Two parallel developments added interest: change to low-level operations and the introduction of rapid starting facilities. The latter enabled four aircraft, with checks complete and crews ready to go on the readiness platform, to be airborne in the magic four-minute warning that was expected of incoming missiles. It became a standard item at displays. The event, and its inevitable practices, was fun and impressive as sixteen Olympus engines wound up to full power, belching black smoke and more than a tad of noise. On the subject of fun, a rare experience in the Bomber Command of the early 1960s, one of my most enjoyable trips followed a diversion from the intended destination, Offutt, Nebraska, on one of several 'western Ranger' flights to the USA. We landed instead at nearby Lincoln Air Force Base, which featured no less than one hundred and sixty-five Boeing B-47 Stratojet bombers. It was the last operational base so equipped, and had more crews on QRA than all of Bomber Command. The next day we completed the journey to Offutt. I had the delightful pleasure of taking-off, at very low weight and with the high power Olympus 301s, (soon after derated), from a base equipped with aircraft having a notoriously long take-off run. So, full power against the brakes, heave-ho at rotation speed, up like a dart to be at 5,000 feet by the end of the runway. Oh, I enjoyed that. After landing, my euphoria evaporated. The crew chief said that the aircraft may have to be grounded – it had been overstressed on take-off! Luckily, all was well. There were no wrinkles on the wings and a chastened young man returned gently to Coningsby.

Low level flying in the Vulcan was, in 1964, a comparative term – five hundred feet above the ground by day, and one thousand feet by night, at two hundred and fifty knots, with a 'dash' of 330 knots to the target. Daylight flying at low level was quite enjoyable for the pilots, but not for the three guys facing rearwards in the back, and without ejection seats, whose stygian gloom was unrelieved. Equipment designed for high level was woefully inadequate for low level navigation at night. All crews, in my squadron at least, made a generous allowance for mum and the kids when deciding on heights to fly on the pressure altimeter, in order to avoid going bump in the dark air. A chum, John MacDonald and his crew died on a Welsh mountain, but in daylight; bad weather prevented them seeing the high ground. After six years in Bomber Command it was time for a change. I could apply for the instructor's course, or test pilots' course, or exchange with the USAF or anything. Gerry Goodyer, my navigator and flight commander advised me to apply only for the job I wanted most. It was the most significant advice I ever heeded, and determined the course of the next thirty years of my life. To my surprise I was posted to the 1965 course at Farnborough to join the test pilots' empire. My delight was tempered by learning later that selection was from a poor and very small set of applicants.

The course was the most intense and hard working ten months of my life. My enthusiasm never waned, but confidence soon took a knock as I struggled to master the new world of handling, stability, performance and systems assessments. Cancellation of the TSR 2, which I saw as a large part of my future, added to my woes in the mid-course. The flying was great; fifteen types of aircraft, including, at last, the Hunter, a helicopter and three gliders, and I learnt a great deal about joined up writing. Of the thirteen pilots who started the fixed wing course only eight graduated and a ninth finished the course without graduating. My posting came through to Boscombe Down: 'The best flying club in the world' said Ray Watts, the Commandant of ETPS, on my departure. So it proved over the next three years on B Sqn, which tested bomber and maritime aircraft.

Six flying squadrons: A – fighters; B; C – naval; D – helicopters; E – transport; and a handling squadron – had several dozen aircraft of many different types. 'How many can I fly?' was my first thought on arrival. With my background I became the Vulcan project pilot, after a period as sidekick, but otherwise the 'available Joe.' My first flight was in an Armstrong Whitworth Argosy tanker for another Argosy 'prodding' from behind – a novel feeling, then some Canberra armament work dropping bombs in Lyme Bay, which must be almost full up with Boscombe's detritus. Next, I did some asymmetric work on a heavy Vulcan. What a joy, and what a difference from Bomber Command, was Vulcan flying on B squadron. Thirty to forty minutes from changing room to airborne, with a short walk out to the aircraft, and checks reduced to the safe and sensible minimum. Six to ten different types per month became the norm, including those scrounged from other squadrons, and also acting as co-pilot. Much flying was CT (Continuation Training) – a euphemism for pleasuring myself, usually over the glorious countryside of southwest England. There always seemed to be more aeroplanes serviceable than crews to fly them; it was wonderful. Report writing occasionally interfered with flying, but by and large pilots decided their priorities on a daily basis.

I remember my first trip in a Javelin – having to fly around with one engine idling to balance the fuel as one belly tank had smoke fluid in it, and also keeping under 1,200 feet as the aircraft was not allowed into cloud. The navigator was an understanding soul. Other odd memories include the Scimitar, XD 217: a naval fighter, which reached four hundred knots by the end of the runway on the take-off, and the Lightning, XL 629: having to half-roll to level off at 36,000 feet because of the steep climb. The Sea Vixen, XJ 488, induced an odd feeling while holding off bank when turning finals to land, and the Lockheed F-104, 57-1316, when accelerating from low speed to Mach 1.6 in a gentle push-over manoeuvre, and lowering the undercarriage *after* rounding out from a deadstick approach. In the Boeing B-52, 52-003, we had to carry a crew chief in the bowels of the machine to change radio frequencies. One day I flew over to Pershore in Bristol Freighter XJ 470 and had a couple of flights in Hermes II, VX 234.

Among the more interesting trials were the Vulcan autoland, including checking individual aircraft at Scampton, Vulcan two-engine-out take-offs at maximum weight at Boscombe Down and Edwards Air Force Base, and an overloaded Canberra with a full bomb load, full fuel, two missiles and two rocket packs. Two particular events come to mind concerning the heavy (60,000lb) Canberra, WH 967, both during hot weather trials at

Wheelus Air Base in Libya. One measured take-off, loaded to the gunwales, in 104°F ground temperature, took 3,000 yards to unstick. Later analysis showed an average three-knot tailwind. This was the standard length of concrete of a V-bomber base. A few days later, during single-engine climbs, the starboard aileron became detached with a sharp crack, and after flying around to examine the possibility of landing, I decided to take the Martin Baker option (eject) over the sea. Pull the stick-disconnect and then the seat handle, a sharp pain in the back, the parachute opens, pull the inflation knob for the Mae West: nothing. A few quick puffs into the inflation tube and splash into the warm Mediterranean. Find the dinghy inflation device, tug: nothing. 'Oh dear' or words to that effect, not my day at all. After I had floundered around for several minutes without success, a helicopter hove into view and whisked me away to the USAF hospital at Wheelus. Pidge Holme, the navigator, was uninjured and soon flew home. Many visitors making suitable clucking noises helped, but the poor sod in the next room screaming all day from fatal burns received at a desert oil rig depressed me no end. After a few days nurses strapped me prostrate and profane to a stretcher for the journey, via the Malta Communications Sqn Valetta and then a Britannia, to the military hospital at Wroughton in Wiltshire. Reunification with my family was sweet indeed and it is amazing what can be achieved in the back of a Mini. A brief sojourn at the RAF rehabilitation centre, Headley Court, was followed by the inevitable sick leave on light duties, i.e. no gardening.

My return to flying, with no ejection seats for another three months, started at 0900 with my first trip in a Shackleton. At 1700 I was a fully signed up captain and the following day carried eight groundcrew passengers. Little did they know, or maybe they did. The three months of non-ejection seat flying offered plenty of scope: Andover, Anson, Argosy, Beverley, Meteor, lots of Shackleton, and helicopters. Restoration of a full medical category broadened the scope, and life was full.

Stupidities during my next two years flying at Boscombe were few. Maybe I *was* learning. Two I remember, the first in a single-seat Hunter which I cranked up to maximum speed at about 2,000 feet on the way home, and on passing my home throttled right back and popped the airbrakes for maximum wonder on the ground. I was completely unprepared for the switchback ride when the airbrakes extended – entirely self induced as I pumped the stick out of phase with the pitching aircraft. The other occasion was in India, en-route to Singapore in a Canberra T17, WJ 977, for trials connected with the planned, but never realised, squadron there of this electronic jamming variant.

Before departure, Jim Watts-Phillips had adjured me to 'Bring it back this time, Tim.' Anyway, due to the short range of the T17 and our slow progress eastbound, we had conceived a plan to take-off from Bombay at 0400. Bureaucratic formalities that my worst nightmare had not prepared me for, a temperature of about 90°F and 99% humidity (it seemed) had tested my temper and delayed our arrival at the aircraft, which was sitting in almost pitch dark and covered in heavy dew. Needless to say I was a wet, grumpy, almost sightless lump as I tied myself into the aeroplane. I had asked the 'Perspex wallah' to make sure that the outside of the canopy was wiped clean. This he did. I started the engines, and looked out only to find that the canopy was again entirely covered with heavy dew. I undid my straps, reached my hand through the small direct vision panel and cleared a tiny, asymmetric area that gave me a small cone of vision to the left. With judicious swerving and frequent wiping I was able to proceed, mostly, on the ill-lit taxiway, but in conditions of blind faith that made me shudder on reflection later. The ensuing four weeks in Singapore were memorable for water-skiing with water snake accompaniment, a nine-ship formation trip in Javelin XH 446 one Saturday morning, and, on a later occasion, flying through the worst thunderstorm of my experience.

The good life continued through 1968. Ange and Jacque were happy at the village school, where I was secretary of the Parent Teacher Association; Penny and I loved our small bungalow, Winterslow was where we wanted to be, and the job of an RAF test pilot at Boscombe Down was almost too good to be true. And so it came to pass in the thirty-second month of my tour that the blow fell. My posting to HQ Air Cadets, in October, was announced. The news was particularly painful, if not entirely unexpected, as the year had been very busy, including a challenging yet enjoyable month in California at Edwards Air Force Base with Vulcan XH 539 on 'hot and high' trials including chopping two engines on take-off at maximum weight. The RAF had decided some twelve years after the Vulcan entered service, that a single, catastrophic engine failure could cause both engines on one side to fail. The most critical phase of flight was on take-off. After a gradual reduction in 'chop' speed on successive take-offs and an incremental increase in weight, a trial at Boscombe had shown that, suitably handled, a double failure could be safely accommodated on the ground at speeds too high to stop. I am glad 1968 was so full of good flying – including my first flight in the Piasecki H-21, Sioux helicopter, Varsity, Bristol Freighter, Pembroke and others, to make forty-one different types of aircraft in my stay at Boscombe Down – indeed the best flying club in the world. The OC, John Wilkinson, even put out a note which started, 'Some pilots are hogs.' I cannot think to whom he was referring. He made the point that it was not possible to retain a sufficient depth of knowledge for safe concurrent flying of many types.

I set off to the HQ Air Cadets at Brampton in a fit of depression. My job was to visit schools in northwest England that had RAF sections to their cadet forces. At the time of the Farnborough Air Show in 1970 the powers-that-be told me to present myself for interview for a job with the NATO Multi-role Combat Aircraft (Tornado) management team, which I had not previously heard of. Ignorance did not prevent me from being posted to Munich, south Germany, as Staff Officer to the Deputy General Manager

(SO DGM), an Air Commodore. I was soon known as SOD GM. My productive work was virtually nil, and my career, defined by promotion, stopped. However, everything outside was more than compensation. The pay was good, tax-free income based on international civil servants' rates, friendships made have lasted a lifetime, and Munich was, and is, a great city in a beautiful part of the world.

After more than three years there, and to my joy, I was posted – a good term, like being put in the mail – back to Boscombe Down as senior pilot on E squadron (transport aircraft). Sadly, it disbanded just as I arrived in early 1974 after a course of refresher flying at Leeming, in Yorkshire. 'Never go back' is an apt aphorism to describe my initial impression on return. Things had changed. There were far fewer aeroplanes and two of the earlier five test squadrons had disbanded. However, I was older now, thirty-seven, and soon realised that an enjoyable if not very challenging time was in prospect, as I was transferred to my old B squadron where the only new type was the Nimrod.

An early trial involved flying from Kinloss, north Scotland, to the North Pole to test a new secure communications system. Two memories persist. Fuel was in short supply due to Middle East difficulties and escalating price problems. On our first sortie the test kit failed. To reduce weight for a prompt landing I jettisoned tons and tons of fuel. The RAF station commander was not amused, and could not understand why we did not use the fuel for endless circuit training. He could not grasp the need to get the test kit on the ground at the earliest moment for rectification. The other memory concerns turning round at low level near the Pole, at 0200 in broad daylight, when I decided to take a couple of photographs. I became a little concerned as the bank angle increased and we started to descend alarmingly. On castigating my co-pilot for this dangerous manoeuvre, he merely said 'I thought you were flying the aircraft.' Of such mis-understandings are accidents made.

Anyway, we survived and the rest of the tour was fairly uneventful with occasional 'whizzes' in the Jet Provost and Hunter to shake out the cobwebs. I was in a position to select the Air Loadmaster that produced the best rations (catering) for long Nimrod and Comet trips; not exactly gastronomic heaven, but eating made an important contribution to my well-being. In 1976, towards the end of my second stint at Boscombe, I wangled myself as third pilot on the squadron's Britannia, XX367, that was used to support the far flung RAF following the disbandment of many of its own transport squadrons. We were taking helicopter rotor blades to Hong Kong, and the crew had become past masters at using statutory rest days at the most salubrious places on the most scenic routes. We went west about, and had three nights at Honolulu and also at Hong Kong; the trip took over seventy flying hours.

Penny and I lived from 1974 in Salisbury with Angela, Jacque and, by then, Julie in a house under the disused Harnham chalk pit. We liked

Stratford-sub-Castle, also in Salisbury, and eventually moved there in November 1980.

After two and a half years at Boscombe the RAF said 'Ministry of Defence for you, Squadron Leader.' With great misgivings I started work in London in November 1976 in the Directorate of Flying, Procurement Executive. The job involved staff work connected with the flying at Boscombe, Farnborough and Bedford. We worked office hours, 0900 to 1730, unlike colleagues in Main Building, the real powerhouse of the MOD. They were often working until 1900 hours or later. With the Cold War dominating military activities, two of my responsibilities were the preparation of war plans and discussions with people at our three airfields for use by the USAF, and the building of hardened shelters for aircraft. In London, my regard for civil servants took a dive; they seemed obsessed with the regulations, particularly those relevant to their pensions and pay and with petty things in general.

In 1980 I went back to Yorkshire to be refreshed for another flying job, this time as the OC of the Experimental Flying Sqn at Farnborough. My speciality was flying the larger aircraft: Comet XV 814, BAC-111 XX 919 and Andover XS 646, but we also had a couple of two-seat Hunters that I flew at first. Although familiar with the type, I was not comfortable flying them and stopped doing so as captain, although I did join in with trials as required. One involved a new sort of anti-gas mask that doubled as an oxygen mask. It involved an unbelievably close fitting, air tight rubber helmet and face piece, which required a hand-held air supply to walk out to the aircraft, followed by awkward strapping-in procedures and then the most exhausting one-hour flights. On two of them the object was to maintain six or more g for as long as possible. This was achieved in a turning dive. I was shattered after two consecutive such flights and people said I had aged ten years with my grey complexion deeply lined with the marks from the oxygen mask. I believe that front-line pilots regularly use this kit; good luck to them. The squadron's task included some quite 'hairy' night flying in helicopters and fast jets, testing equipment which projected an image in front of the pilot, who also had very early night vision goggles. I made one flight with goggles on and that in our staid old Andover. I was interested to see how many details could be seen but I thought there was a lack of depth perception and a very limited field of view. Once again, front-line pilots later used developed night goggles.

The even tenor of life at Farnborough was disturbed in 1982 by a series of interrelated events. A friend at Bedford needed a BAC-111 pilot for a European tour demonstrating some new kit on board, the 4D management system. This equipment accomplished navigation left, right, up, down and made speed adjustments to achieve accurate 'slot' times. I jumped at the chance, and, although incompletely briefed, enjoyed ten days at the expense of, I think, Smiths Industries, staying in good hotels, but spoilt by my recurring but undiagnosed gout. No sooner was I back home than

General Galtieri invaded the Falklands, and I was whisked off to Waddington, the last Vulcan base, to test an aircraft fitted with a Martel missile, both handling and firing. It was very enjoyable, even though it had been about ten years since my previous flight in a Vulcan, XM 597. In the event the Americans made the Shrike available and Martel was abandoned. The last event to make 1982 unusual for me was the Army's autumn exercise in Germany, for which the RAE provided an aircraft in which to mount various types of sensor equipment intended for unmanned drones to find both moving and stationary tanks. The Dakota, ZA 947, was chosen on account of its ability to loiter at about ninety knots, and to provide space for the kit and boffins. People at Gütersloh, where we were based for a couple of weeks, evinced little overt interest in the World War Two relic – the Dakota, not me. It was good to live in a gasthof again.

The next two years passed with plenty of routine flying, including ten-hour epics in the Comet, refuelling at Kinloss, on BAINS trials (British Advanced Inertial Navigation). One of these gave me my worst moments in an aircraft. The sortie profile included high and low level, and extended into the dark air. On this moonless but generally clear night, somewhere over the North Atlantic, we were climbing through isolated cloud when the airspeed fell to zero and the altimeter stuck. The radio altimeter reached its upper limit of, I think, 5,000 feet, and the boffins said that all the BAINS had stopped indicating height (they were gated by altimeter pressure). No sweat, I thought, just set climb power and aircraft attitude, but there was no horizon or light to be seen. I felt uneasy at the complete lack of external reference, although I could see the stars. Then two things happened which terrified me. A voice from the back said 'I think we are descending', and at the same time the radio altimeter needle gave a kick as though confirming a descent. I thought we were so iced up that we were going down but in a nose-up attitude. None of us in the crew had a clue what was actually happening. The anti-icing was fully on and the pitot heaters were on and using a healthy current. Just before I ordered ditching stations the radio altimeter needle returned to its maximum position and I remembered the odd indications that sometimes occurred. I then glimpsed some lights well below us. We made a 'Pan' (emergency) call, which brought a pair of Phantom fighters alongside. Their pilots told us our speed and altitude and on the last part of the descent to Leuchars the instruments read accurately again and we landed. The terror was caused by apparent aircraft behaviour contradicting experience and common sense. Fortunately the latter prevailed in the crucial one to two minutes.

DH COMET C Mk 4. Medium-range transport. Crew of five. Four 10,500lb Rolls-Royce Avon R A 29 turbojets. Span 114 feet. Length 118 feet. Maximum weight 162,000lb. Maximum speed 500mph at optimum altitude. Service ceiling 39,000

*feet. Range 2,650 miles. In 1956 216 Sqn started the world's first military jet
transport operations with the Comet Mk 2.*

Among my last trips at Farnborough was a ride in the two-stick Buccaneer,
XV 344, except that the second stick had been removed. It was, I believe,
the first flight of the so-called '1553' bus that was a sophisticated
information highway later in general use, and which was curtailed by a
hefty birdstrike over Devon. This flight, and others in Hunters, gave me
great respect for A-Flight pilots doing night low-level with early night
vision goggles or experimental infrared information or both on the head-up
display. This highly demanding and risky flying was largely unrecognised,
with only one or two awards of the AFC over several years. The small
number of pilots involved at any one time always seemed to be posted as
they were at their most proficient and thus most productive.

After a very ill advised agreement by me, while my OC – David Scoular
– was away, for a pop star and his Harvard and Tiger Moth to film at
Farnborough, David was incensed when he found a low aerobating Harvard
over his airfield, about which he knew nothing. My career had stopped
some fourteen years previously and whatever hopes I had of restarting it by
being the only one qualified for a wing commander's job at Boscombe were
dashed by this attempt to help our crooning brethren. The situation was
saved by the telephone ringing shortly before Christmas 1983. A voice said
to this forty-six year old 'Would you like a job flying in industry?' I quickly
recovered my wits and after a minute or two replied 'Tell me more.' The
upshot was that Marshall of Cambridge (Engineering) Ltd made me an offer
I could not refuse, and the RAF, at a time of shortage of aircrew, let me go
without a murmur.

I had heard very little of this long established aircraft engineering firm in
Cambridge, except that I had once landed there in a black Canberra, and my
steep take-off had, I later discovered, impressed the observant Sir Arthur.
My ignorance was soon overcome, and the reason for recruiting a
grandfather (I claim to be the first grandfather to join a British company as
a test pilot. What a claim to fame – almost dead before I started) was, of
course, General Galtieri, whose Malvinas adventure led directly to the RAF
acquiring Lockheed TriStars to support the Falkland Islands. Marshall had
the contract to convert six aircraft to tankers. It had chosen from a large cast
of two or three, John Blake and me to join the flight test organisation to test
the said TriStars as tankers. Apart from this 'proper' test flying there were
on offer Hercules post re-assembly air tests, communications in the Citation
and Aztec and instructing in the Cessna 152 and Rallye Minerva. The flying
promised, and later proved, to be varied and interesting. Perhaps most
important, the people were both capable and amicable and it was my good
fortune to work among a great bunch of people. If I was happy at work, and
with an ideal bungalow nearby, Penny made friends and enjoyed her garden

but did not feel settled in the Cambridge area. She never once suggested leaving and, when appropriate, encouraged my work. A great wife.

On 31st July 1984 I joined seven other pilots (soon down to five) at Marshall's, and set about getting my ATPL and instructor's rating. The former was tedious but straightforward, and the latter interesting and initially frustrating as I had to wait a month even to take the exam which permitted me to start the instructor's course. This was at the Rural Flying Corps at Bourne. At first sight the set-up at Bourne was quite different from Cambridge. There was a single, short, licensed strip on a long abandoned wartime airfield, a Seco hut as clubroom, offices, ATC (not manned), a schoolroom and an open-ended corrugated-iron hangar. Getting the fuel out of the underground petrol storage tank involved hand-cranking a prehistoric diesel engine while standing on oil-stained concrete. The appearance of the place, however, belied the completely dedicated and professional way that David Hughes went about instruction.

With an instructor's 'ticket' and a civil licence, flying could start in earnest at Cambridge. Instructing dominated my aerial activities; it was a new and initially very satisfying experience. I am convinced that there is such a thing as natural ability in aviating – some people seemed to be able to fly accurately and well while maintaining good awareness right from the start. Others achieved a very creditable standard by intelligent application over time and others seemed never to develop a feel for aviating no matter how long they, and I, tried. Among the most natural pilots was Mark Ambrose, a young Air Traffic Control assistant, who could repeat perfectly any manoeuvre after a single demonstration, but who, in spite of my encouragement to take his flying further, was content in his job. In the second category was another young man, Ben Bussey, whose constant questioning and application was both a challenge and an inspiration. Among the third category was a middle-aged customer who paid a great deal of money but showed little aptitude for flying. He also paid for his competent daughter. When told that he was unlikely to achieve the standard required for a PPL he promptly removed himself and his daughter from the scene.

He had given me a moment or two of extreme alarm. I eventually convinced him that judicious forward movement of the control column would avert a stall. On this occasion he pulled hard at the 'moment critique.' The aircraft dropped vertically down and he rammed the stick fully forward using both hands. Inverted flying in the Cessna 152 was a new, if extremely brief, experience for him, and me. Anyway, both the aircraft and I were strong enough to recover the situation and that incident concluded the exercise, the flight, together with his and his daughter's aviating careers.

With the passage of time my enthusiasm for instructing waned, due partially to my increasing sloth, partly because pupils made the same mistakes, and by the increasing bureaucracy and regulations of the syllabus laid down by the CAA. From my observation of a few other instructional establishments I believe the standards set and maintained at Cambridge were second to none, and that the experience of the instructors was probably among the broadest in the country. But we had other, primary, calls on our time.

John Blake and I, together with Tim Gooch who doubled as aircraft inspector and flight engineer, had done the British Airways TriStar ground school and simulator training at Heathrow before we completed our conversion on a flight at Brize Norton before John and I left the RAF. My second flight piloting a TriStar was over one year later, in ZD 950, the first tanker conversion. The intervening period had been fascinating as I watched the various new parts, particularly the HDUs (Hoodoos) and extra fuel tanks being installed. It remains a mystery to me, even after eleven years with the Company, how aircraft and their components are designed. I watched many engineering draughtsmen at their boards and it was soon apparent what they were drawing. The difficulty I have is comprehending how draughtsmen know where to put access, fixing and other details such as reinforcing frames so that the item fits – as it usually did. Of course the hangar engineers soon returned to the drawing office items that did not match their intended location, but by and large the whole process is a black art to me. Two relevant thoughts stay with me – at Marshall, alone of several factories I had seen over the years, there were very few people *not* actively working in hangars whenever I visited. Secondly, and more reassuring to a test pilot, the aerodynamicists, stressmen, avionics and system designers together with the hangar supervisors, inspectors and engineers gave me absolute faith in the serviceability of aeroplanes I was given to fly; the system worked. Of course, there were frustrating delays, and our flights revealed shortcomings such as misting up of the TV cupola, leaky bellows round the HDUs and the need to adjust HDU settings to cater for higher speeds when trailing the hoses. But I feel that Marshall took a superb aircraft, the TriStar, and made a thoroughly professional job of conversion. In particular, the freight door was, and is, a masterpiece of engineering. There was a lot of breath holding during the first cut in the fuselage and during the proof pressure testing. Lockheed admitted that the conversion was better than the one designed by their subsidiary and subsequently took a manufacturing licence.

In view of the foregoing, it is hardly surprising that my pulse-enhancing moments in the TriStar were due to my own ignorance or stupidity. During a series of stalls, after we had abandoned trying to determine the clean (flaps and slats retracted) speed because of airframe buffet like I had never previously felt, I positively opened the three throttles to gain speed. One wing engine gave an almighty bang but seemed thereafter to be running normally. What I did not know at the time was that I had exceeded the N1 (low-pressure) limit or maximum speed on the other wing engine. This was found on reading the 'tape' after landing and both engines had to be returned to Rolls-Royce for examination. No damage was discovered with one but the other was found to have a seal rub, which caused a surge on acceleration. Ignorance of the implications of the absence of RPM limiters had led to the unnecessary engine removal.

So much for the 'lowlights.' Apart from early landings on Cambridge's 6,400 feet runway, I always enjoyed my flying on the TriStar. I was captain on a long sortie with Boscombe Down aircrew (Contractor/Joint trials, as they were known) to clear the aircraft as a receiver to maximum weight. Sqn Ldr Bob Tuxford was responsible for the 'prods', and he put up an impressive performance. We needed two VC-10 tankers to meet our almost insatiable needs, and we eventually reached a gross weight of just over 245 tonnes – the heaviest RAF aircraft ever. As far as I know the RAF has not flown any aircraft at this weight since. It is a sobering thought that the maximum fuel load of one hundred and forty tonnes is over 39,500 gallons, or two lifetime's worth of average motoring.

The length of Cambridge's runway restricted the weight of TriStar taking off, but by using reduced power we gained a useful addition to the permitted fuel load. The reason for this apparent contradiction is connected with the yawing (turning) force in the event of a wing engine failure at maximum power just before take-off. Even at the lower power rating a steep climb angle could be achieved by holding the aircraft at the minimum safe climbing speed. The performance of the TriStar was always reassuring. At average operating weights it was possible to fly a one-engined approach, abandon it and climb safely away. We practised that emergency situation every time we did our simulator training at Heathrow. How different from the poor performance of multi-engined aircraft of an earlier generation.

Perhaps of equal interest to the tanker programme was the one-off Pegasus TriStar conversion flying in 1993. Modifications, to carry a rocket weighing up to 80,000lb designed to launch small earth satellites, were extensive. We first had to test the aeroplane as a flying machine, and then check handling, airflow, stress and vibration with a 50,000lb rocket underneath – but did not get to launch it.

Airflow and stress needed attention, but using tufts to visualise flow and a chase aircraft, a Hawk, the problems were soon solved, but not before a report had been sent to the CAA: 'TriStar N140SC – during testing with dummy rocket fixed under fuselage, eight items fell from the aircraft.' The largest was a long piece of the lightweight fairing between the aircraft belly and the rocket, and the smallest a VHF radio aerial under the rear fuselage. None was found. Orbital Sciences Corporation, the company managing the Pegasus project, subsequently made the first successful launch on 3rd April 1995, in America. At the time of writing the aircraft is back at Cambridge for further modifications for a new rocket: the X-34, a re-usable launch vehicle.

The TriStar and instructing on little 'whizzers' occupied sixty percent of my effort. Of the remaining forty percent, Hercules air test and deliveries, for which I reverted to Vulcan co-pilot priorities and arranged the flying rations, were fairly routine – one engine fire warning (spurious) and a pressurisation failure were the only two untoward incidents that I recall.

Another one-off trial, with intermittent flying lasting eighteen months, was of a Meteor U16, WK 800, for which I was the only pilot old and ugly enough. Various installations for intended future target aircraft were fitted, the most important of which was RVMDI (Radar Vector Miss Distance Indicator) with one transmitting aerial above and one below the fuselage, and eight receivers at the four extremities. The idea was that missiles under development would be programmed to miss the target aircraft, and the RVMDI would record the exact miss-distance, and even give the attitude of the missile as it passed by. I believe the trial was successful; the equipment was certainly sensitive. One trial involved flying accurately along the edge of the two miles of Bedford's runway. Every metal drain cover was faithfully recorded, as was the test object on an eighty-foot pole, so placed as to miss the wing tip by what seemed like inches.

The final trial was a most relaxing three weeks at Llanbedr. Only one flight was at all alarming. Things were going so well that, because the weather reports for Llanbedr transmitted by the range controller remained favourable, I decided to complete the optional test points at the end of the flight. Tests complete, I set heading for Llanbedr with sensible minimum fuel for a visual rejoin and landing but was appalled to learn that the weather was deteriorating rapidly. The cloud base had reduced to just two or three hundred feet, which meant that a radar approach would be necessary. The reassuring radar controller did the proverbial cool, calm and collected talk-down literally on to the runway, although I picked up the lights, dead ahead, at about half a mile.

At the end of 1993, with Pegasus TriStar finished, life was reverting to routine, except that I had been deputy airport manager for a few years. For various reasons there seemed more and more to do in this 'secondary' duty, even though my boss, David Bywater, spared me the more onerous duties. Nevertheless, on 20th December 1993, a Sunday, I was due to go to work, but Penny thought that I was being even more stupid and for longer, than usual. My poor old brain had suffered a TIA, or minor stroke. Sympathy from the CAA, understanding by my colleagues and a family's love could not undo the effect. My medical category was withdrawn, which meant no flying licence, which meant my flying career was at an end.

Chapter 12

The Falklands War and Aftermath

BY DENNIS PASCO

In 1981 Tim Gooch, our youngest flight engineer, had discovered a wing rupture on Hercules XV 204 in an area surrounding a fuel tank. An adjacent fuel tank had, seemingly, ruptured, damaging the wing. The RAF tasked Marshall with air testing another Hercules, XV 211, to endeavour to pinpoint the likely cause of the rupture. Bob Smythe and John Preece enjoyed themselves throwing the thing around in all sorts of manoeuvres during the half-dozen flights generated. Apart from that prospects for 1982 looked bleak for air test personnel. Had we known a bit more about some goings-on way down south we might have thought differently.

In early 1982 General Galtieri, head of the ruling Argentine military junta, had stated that the UK and the Falkland islanders would not celebrate the 150th anniversary of British settlement of the islands. Instead, he promised to possess the Malvinas islands, as Argentina called the Falklands, before 3rd January 1983. In March 1982 the Argentines had even asked the UK if they could buy some Avro Vulcan bombers scheduled to be phased out by the RAF. Did they have a specific target in mind? General Galtieri pushed the button that, on 2nd April 1982, launched the invasion of the Falkland Islands. The Falklands lie 52 degrees south of the Equator; by co-incidence Cambridge is 52 degrees north.

On 5th April the largest British force since World War Two launched from Portsmouth and headed south for a journey of over 6,000 nautical miles. Sitting halfway between South America and Africa, about eight degrees south of the Equator, lies the British Island of Ascension. On it, constructed by the Americans in World War Two for the Americas to Africa ferry route, sits the airfield of Wideawake. RAF transport aircraft were soon shuttling south to start the build up on Ascension. Over the weekend of 17/18th April the first Victor tankers arrived at Wideawake. By the end of the month the first of the 'up for disposal' Vulcan bombers was on station at the airfield.

For Marshall pilots April was occupied almost exclusively with instructional flying in the Cessna 150s. Across the Newmarket Road, however, life was getting ever more hectic. Having been instructed late afternoon on 15th April to 'Give the RAF Hercules an Air-to-Air Refuelling (AAR) capability' the Marshall machine went full speed ahead to convert the first six aircraft to Modification 5308; the first metal was cut on Saturday 17th April in advance of drawings. A Design Office Instruction (DOI) gave the bare bones of the work needed. A Mk 8B probe, surplus to

V-bomber needs, would connect to a three-inch diameter pipe, allowing fuel to pass through some non-return valves into the aircraft's ground refuelling pipe. The ground-refuelling panel would be repositioned inside the cargo compartment on the starboard side. A crewmember would operate the panel, talking to the pilot through the intercom system. This was purely a temporary fit. The production standard called for a refuelling panel to be installed above the navigator's station. The test schedule was circulated on 22nd April and called for two flights; probe installation was completed on 25th April and essential ground checks followed. That same day Royal Navy helicopter aircrew sighted and attacked the Argentine submarine *Santa Fe*. The damaged vessel ran aground on South Georgia Island, some eight hundred miles from the Falklands. By the following day British troops had wrested the island from the Argentines. British morale rose markedly.

On the morning of 28th April final clearance checks were made on Hercules XV 200 and the all-important Form 1090 was issued. With Bob Smythe as co-pilot, Dave Ryding and Tim Gooch as flight engineers, I lifted XV 200 off the runway at 1445 hours for its first test flight. Mixing the new items with the standard schedule we carried out stalls in straight and turning flight in a number of flap and gear configurations. We then flew a simulated approach to land, plus a go-around manoeuvre, all the while checking whether XV 200 behaved any differently from an unmodified Hercules. It did not. The rock n' roll of lateral and directional stability, plus sideslips at high angles of bank, were all carried out safely and satisfactorily. After a flight of four hours and fifty-five minutes we landed back at Cambridge.

Technicians worked throughout the night to cure a handful of defects and handed the aircraft back to us the next morning. Plagued by umpteen developing showers, we headed south for better weather. At an altitude of 4,000 feet in the vicinity of Farnborough we carried out the minimum-airspeed checks. As Fred Moss, Marshall chief of aerodynamics, had predicted XV 200 behaved just like a standard Hercules. At 1330 we landed the first C Mk1P at Boscombe Down and handed it over for the A & AEE experts to launch their own test programme. This they did on 1st May. The next day Sqn Ldr John Brown, with Group Captain David Bywater – a future Director of Flying at Marshall's – as co-pilot, flew XV 200 to Marham. After a briefing with the Victor tanker crew, John and David spent the next couple of hours working through the AAR test programme. Placing the refuelling probe into the refuelling receptacle, or basket, is known as prodding. David made the very first prod. On 5th May, with the test programme completed, A & AEE handed XV 200 to Lyneham for operational use.

The standard navigation fit of the Hercules was not accurate enough for the many hours to be spent over the South Atlantic, especially since linking up with a tanker aircraft required precise position fixing. A new navigation aid was needed. Modification 5309 called for the fitting of Omega, a navigation system that relied on very low frequency (VLF) signals from a network of transmitting ground stations. As pilots, our first task was to learn how to use the new equipment. Next, we produced an idiot's guide in time for the first Hercules to be fitted with Omega. That was XV 179, the second Hercules to be fitted with a probe; John Preece air tested it on 12th May. Eventually all Mk 1 and Mk 3 Hercules were fitted with a probe and Omega. Many of the VLF stations were de-commissioned by 1998, thus creating a demand for another navigation aid.

One major problem soon came to light when a Hercules refuelled from a Victor. As a Hercules took fuel on board it became heavier. More power was then needed to maintain height and speed. Eventually there was not sufficient power available to maintain formation, speed and height. The cure was for the Victor tanker to initiate a descent at about 500 feet per minute. This allowed the Hercules to reduce power and still stay in formation at its ever-increasing weight. RAF aircrew called this procedure a toboggan. There were at least two problems resulting from a toboggan. Firstly, the Hercules had to use many gallons of its newly acquired fuel to regain the lost height. Secondly, it was not unusual for the descent to drop the aircraft into poorer weather, including icing conditions, which invariably forced early termination of the refuelling process. Ideally, the RAF would have liked a Hercules tanker. On cue the MOD duly instructed Marshall to convert four Hercules to tankers, Modification 5310, on 30th April. Also on that day General Haig, the United States Secretary of State, announced that the USA would now abandon its neutral position and supply the UK with whatever military equipment it needed.

The first Hercules tanker airframe, XV 296, arrived at Cambridge on 1st May for conversion. Four ex-Andover ferry fuel tanks, including the two that I had used in June 1968 over the South China Sea, were already installed in the cargo compartment. Within a couple of days the Design Office issued details of the conversion lash-up installation.

A HDU, made by Flight Refuelling Ltd, was to be installed on the cargo ramp at the rear of the aircraft. Wrapped around the drum unit was the fuel hose, eighty feet long with an internal diameter of three inches. Attached to the fuel hose was the drogue, or basket. When wound in, the basket would sit within the drogue deployment box that was to be fitted under the ramp and door. An air intake, manually operated from inside the aircraft, would feed ram air into the drogue box to eject the basket. A hole was to be cut in the cargo door to allow the hose to pass to the outside world. The air turbine within the HDU needed bleed air that would be tapped off the tailplane de-icer supply. As this was very hot, a heat exchanger would be needed to cool the bleed air to below 250°C for safe operation. The heat exchanger would be fitted just aft of the starboard para door; external ram air for cooling it would enter via an intake fitted within a window blank immediately ahead of the starboard para door. It would exhaust overboard. Another ram air intake would be required for directing cooling air to the auxiliary components of the HDU. This intake would be fitted just behind the starboard para door. The HDU also needed a vent pipe, to accommodate over-pressurisation and expansion of fuel. A control panel would be fitted to the tubular framework of the seats just forward of the port para door. Wiring for all the electrical items, which included a control panel at the navigator's station, was also needed. Of interest, Flight Refuelling Ltd had done a tanker conversion study for the RAF, in 1970. That study envisaged the use of external Mk 32 refuelling pods for fighter aircraft. In 1969 Marshall had done a project study for fitting the Hercules with fuselage tanks, but the tanks were not Andover ones. Finally, on XV 296 only, some instrumentation was needed to record temperatures, pressures and fuel and airflow rates. To give the pilots some idea of what might happen in flight Leslie Worsdell produced a 1969 letter from MOD that gave details of behaviour of a hose and drogue underneath a Victor tanker.

On 1st May the Argentines received first hand experience of the effectiveness of the Avro Vulcan bomber. At 0235 local time Vulcan XM 607 took off from Wideawake airfield for the longest-ranging bomb raid in aviation history. It dropped twenty-one half-ton bombs on Stanley airfield, a few miles from the Falklands capital, causing damage to the runway. The Vulcan was refuelled many times in flight by Victor tankers, whose home base was Marham. To get XM 607 to the target it was supported by one other Vulcan and eleven Victor tankers. British Special Forces raided Pebble Island airfield on 14th/15th May, destroying eleven Argentine aircraft on the ground, and British troops landed on the Falklands on 21st May.

To get up to speed on the use of the HDU and standard RAF AAR techniques and procedures, Marshall pilots and flight engineers went to Marham for a one-day course. Our instructor, a navigator, did a first class job in no time flat. Sadly, in 1991, he was killed in a RAF Tornado during the Gulf War. On return from Marham the pilots produced another idiot's guide for trailing and winding the hose, and a host of recording sheets for the forthcoming test of the Hercules tanker. Ground checks, including a transfer of fuel through the HDU into a receiver Hercules, were completed on 6th June. The 7th June was taken up with final inspections, checks on the aircraft, parachute drills and some 'what-ifs.' What if the hose could not be wound in, or what if it fell off? Umpteen pounds of hose dropping at high speed could spell disaster to people and property on the ground. One RAF tanker, not one of those we flew, suffered a rupture of the main driving chain within the HDU. The hose ran out and fell away. All our trailing and winding was, therefore, to be done over the sea. Waddington, which was used to tanker operations, agreed to act as our diversion for the first flight.

With John Preece flying XV 296 from the left-hand seat and myself conducting the programme from the right-hand seat, we took off at 1700 hours on 8th June and headed east for the North Sea. Dave Ryding, Tim

Gooch, Mick Milne, Karl Chapman and Ron Henson, of Flight Refuelling Ltd, completed the crew. Bob Smythe and Doug Page flew alongside us in the Company Citation, G-BFRM, with Norman Harry, the Company Chief Designer, a photographer and a RAF test pilot aboard, to witness at first hand how the hose and drogue behaved. In addition to the standard post-major inspection tests there were specific tests for the HDU installation and some extra aerodynamic tests identical to those on XV 200 in April. The hose tests were first to be carried out at 10,000 feet and then, if successful, at 20,000 feet.

Settled into a steady racetrack pattern at 10,000 feet over the largely fog-shrouded sea my thoughts were probably no different from those of the other eleven bodies cruising around at 220 knots. Would it all work? With just a little anxiety, we worked through our checklist and waited for the first countdown. 'Three, two, one, now' called the flight engineer. At first, nothing happened. Ron said 'Don't worry, there's a built-in delay. It'll go.' As if by magic, rather like a suspicious rabbit emerging at dusk from its hole, out popped the drogue from its container and began its slow trail. There was much jubilation on the flight deck. We wound in the hose and then re-trailed at speeds of 180, 200 and 235 knots. Two more trails, one with No 1 engine shut down, and the other with a bootful of rudder on to give a decent sideslip angle, were both successful. Modification 5310 worked successfully at 10,000 feet; now for the climb.

In the thinner air at 20,000 feet we needed to don oxygen masks because for hose operations the aircraft remained de-pressurised. With once-familiar voices sounding like Daleks, we trailed at 200 knots and wound in at 220. 'That's enough' called Norman Harry from the Citation, 'let's go home.' John Preece landed XV 296 back at Cambridge at 2000 hours. At Bluff Cove, on the Falklands, four Argentine aircraft attacked and hit two landing ships, *Sir Galahad* and *Sir Tristram*. The ensuing British casualties made this the worst day of the war. Our triumph over the North Sea was tinged with sadness at the cost of the operations far to the south.

Hercules XV 296 made a second flight, with the cabin pressurised, on 10th June. Next day John Preece delivered the Hercules to Boscombe Down. Mick Milne and I travelled by road to continue the flight testing with Boscombe Down test pilots over the next two days. The Pope visited Argentina and endeavoured to persuade General Galtieri to withdraw from the war with honour. Galtieri declined the Papal offer.

During the Boscombe flights, which included a more extensive schedule of tests at higher speeds, two problems came to light. The first was that at higher speeds there was some buffeting of the elevator, almost certainly due to disturbed airflow from around the drogue box. Secondly, the HDU ran too hot. To cure these problems, XV 296 was returned to Cambridge on 15th June. Arthur Marshall called a meeting late the same night. The only sure way to cure the problem of overheating was to increase the amount of cooling air passing through the HDU. It was decided to give each of the three components that needed a flow of cooling air its own air supply. The night shift got on with the job straight away. By 17th June the aircraft was ready to fly. The fitting of two strakes to the cargo door was expected to relieve the buffeting. The strakes worked. Four flights later, on 21st June, XV 296 gave away its first fuel. Over south-west England the RAF's first turbo-prop tanker successfully transferred 5,900lb of fuel into a Buccaneer, callsign Evergreen 26. We were treated to a very appropriate victory roll as the Buccaneer roared off to its base at Boscombe Down. The next day, while John Preece and Colin Rudder air tested NAF 910 (the Nigerian Hercules) Bob and I delivered the tanker to Boscombe Down. On 14th June the Argentines surrendered. The war was over, but the military effort and consolidation continued apace.

RAF test pilots continued with their sequence of flight trials, which included successful prodding by a Sea Harrier, a Phantom, a Nimrod and a Hercules. On 29th June John Preece and Colin Rudder flew XV 296 the thirty minutes to Cambridge for completion of outstanding work. American Independence Day saw John and I transfer fuel into Hercules XV 210. RAF Lyneham received XV 296 for operational use the following day. During late evening on 8th July a wing commander flying on board the second tanker – XV 201 – suffered a problem that no refuelling pilot would ever wish to experience. While taking fuel from another tanker the refuelling hose became hard, whipped about violently and broke off the tip of the probe. Fuel spray splashed all over the windscreen. The probe tip stayed in the basket of the tanker. While on a training sortie Hercules XV 211 suffered a worse problem. A couple of disconnects (the receiving aircraft disengaging from the tanker's basket) made by the trainee prodding-pilot had not gone quite as expected. The RAF instructor pilot took control and had a go, only to find that on his disconnect the probe tip broke off, dropped onto the fuselage, bounced off the starboard side and hit No 3 engine's propeller. Vibration and fluctuating propeller RPM immediately followed. The crew managed to shut down the afflicted engine.

Cooling the bleed air within the HDU continued to be a problem. On Sunday 11th July while airborne in XV 201, giving away 33,000lb fuel to XV 211, we had to shut down the HDU turbine pump because of excessive bleed air temperatures. In a bid to cure the problem once and for all, a modified Nimrod heat exchanger was fitted into XV 201. Fingers crossed, we took 201 airborne again on 13th July. At 10,000 feet we happily gave 23,000lb fuel to XV 296; temperatures stayed well below those recorded on the previous flight. Would it work at 20,000 feet? At 200 knots, taking just five minutes to pass another 15,000lb to 296, the answer was 'Yes.' All four tankers – 192, 201, 204 and 296 were delivered to Lyneham before July was out, complete with new heat exchanger.

One feature of the AAR trial programme was that the Hercules receiving fuel would often finish up heavier than the authorised landing weight. There was no option but to dump fuel overboard through the integrally fitted dump pipes. Marshall flight engineers became experts at carrying out the dumping drills. During one of the flights, recalls Tim Gooch, his Hercules tanker seemed to have given away too much fuel and finished up needing to land in a hurry. The problem was that the fuel carried in the ex-Andover fuselage tanks was not coming out as quickly as anticipated. Suspecting an air lock Tim unscrewed the filler caps on all four tanks. He could then hear fuel gurgling out of the tanks. Happiness returned to all on board. After a hectic two months, which generated forty-eight test flights plus much instructional and communication flying, air test activity suddenly faded.

Now with the RAF, the four Hercules tankers were really earning their keep. In order to get one Hercules to the Falklands from Ascension Island, with adequate fuel reserves on arrival, it took one Hercules and two Victor tankers to support it. A Hercules, with two auxiliary fuselage tanks fitted, would take off from Wideawake with the Hercules tanker in close pursuit. One Victor topped up the other Victor and then returned to Wideawake. After about four hours into the flight the Hercules tanker transferred about 23,000lb of aviation turbine fuel to the other Hercules. One hour later the Hercules tanker topped up from the Victor, which then flew back to Wideawake. The two Hercules continued south, with the tanker topping up the other before it, too, turned for Wideawake. The lone Hercules then flew on to reach the Falklands after a flight of about thirteen hours.

For their efforts in leading the Marshall design team so successfully Roy Gates, the Marshall executive director, engineering, and Norman Harry were awarded the OBE in 1982 and 1984 respectively. The RAF ordered two more Hercules tankers, and Marshall duly modified XV 203 and 213.

In October 1982 the RAF decided that it needed some new, bigger tankers. Government finance was available for the purchase of a handful of aircraft. The RAF specification for its new tanker included the need to carry forty-five tons of fuel in the cargo bay and two HDU units, one as a back up, located at the rear of the aircraft. The two choices were the McDonnell Douglas DC-10, already in service with the USAF as the KC-10, or the Lockheed L1011 TriStar. British Airways was in the market to sell six L1011-500s. RAF pilots from Boscombe Down flew a variety of aircraft behind both contending tankers during feasibility trials. They concluded that the Hercules had considerable difficulty maintaining the likely AAR position behind both contenders. On 11th December I arrived at Boscombe Down to sit on the flight deck of Hercules XV 205 while Sqn Ldr Tony 'Banzai' Banfield, a Boscombe test pilot, spent over four hours of energetic flying behind a TriStar and a Victor tanker assessing the difficulty of maintaining the refuelling position. He had already done a similar exercise behind a KC-10.

I was able to glean some useful information, but whenever the chat turned towards direct comparisons I was asked to take my headset off. Even though I had secreted a small tape recorder inside my flying suit, linked to the aircraft intercom, I gained nought. On playback all I got was a loud squeal. Justice, really. Marshall, supported by Lockheed, put in a bid for the conversion of six L1011s before the deadline of 22nd December 1982. On 2nd February 1983 the decision was made and Marshall got the contract to convert six TriStar-500s into freighter-tankers. Construction of a large new hangar, No 17, started immediately. The TriStar tanker conversion turned out to be the biggest flight test programme in my time at Marshall's. However, before flying commenced on the new aircraft, a string of Hercules modifications came along.

As a staff officer at Upavon in 1973 I had gone to the USA to inspect and report on the system that the USAF used to fly parachute-dropping aircraft in formation, day or night. Part of the equipment was called SKE: Station Keeping Equipment. Electronically the lead aircraft could signal its intentions to turn left or right and the following aircraft had electronic guidance as to spacing left, right, in trail, up or down. It seemed to work well, and my boss recommended it for purchase by the RAF. There were no funds available at the time but nine years later the Falklands war changed that. Money was found to equip twenty-three Mk 3 Hercules with Modification 506, or SKE.

The radar items were to be fitted in the roof rack, two antennae would go below the fuselage, and indicators and controls would all go on the flight deck. The pilots' ADF controller was removed to make way for the new items and a new altimeter, which incorporated a height encoding facility, would replace the navigator's instrument. Delivery to Boscombe Down was scheduled for early October 1983. Having checked out the equipment on the ground we were ready to fly XV 188 and 197 by September. We were briefed that it was not our job to assess accuracy, just to check that the equipment worked as advertised. Photographers flew in one of the aircraft. Their job was to record the change of airflow expected around the circular antennae, which had been surrounded with dozens of wool tufts. Five flights in five days, starting on 22nd September, proved that the equipment worked, but it was clear that accuracy was awry. Since one of the tests to be carried out at Boscombe was accuracy it was a waste of time to give them aircraft that were not producing the goods. New, factory-calibrated and aligned units were needed. They did not arrive in time to meet the hoped for delivery date, so we were ten days late flying the two aircraft to Boscombe. The equipment is still being used successfully today.

No sooner had we finished with SKE, than out of the hangar popped XV 177, specially modified to act as the test bed for the HDU destined for the RAF's TriStar tankers. The HDU was fitted to a spare ramp and exchanged with the ramp of XV 177. On 31st October Colin Rudder and I flew to south-west England to spend a couple of hours navigating between TACAN beacons at Yeovilton and Lands End while our basket was prodded by a receiver aircraft. There was no fuel connection to the HDU in XV 177 since all refuelling contacts were to be dry. The idea was to observe hose and basket behaviour at anticipated TriStar refuelling speeds. It was the start of many flights across the south-west of the country. A specially adapted Canberra from Boscombe Down did a lot of the initial prodding. The first Hercules-to-Hercules activity took place on 3rd November 1983. Unfortunately, having borrowed XV 200 from Lyneham with strict instructions not to break it, the Boscombe Down pilot, Sqn Ldr John Brown, suffered a whipping hose, which broke the probe tip clean off. We handed the broken XV 200 back to a grumpy RAF team and removed the probe tip from the receptacle of XV 177. On 21st December 1983 the Boscombe Down Canberra broke its probe tip behind XV 177. It was not such a Happy Christmas for the RAF.

In June 1983 the Defence Minister announced that a new airfield, capable of handling wide-bodied jets, would be constructed on East Falklands. Much larger than Stanley airfield, Mount Pleasant would allow aircraft like the TriStar to fly direct from Ascension without needing to refuel in flight.

Her Majesty the Queen was scheduled to fly in a British Airways TriStar to Jordan in April 1984. British newspapers reported that safety checks were being carried out on her TriStar, G-BBAI, because of a sudden de-pressurisation of another TriStar when flying between Delhi and Dubai. More sinisterly, they also reported that secret RAF equipment was being fitted to G-BBAI to ward off any incoming missiles. The papers did not say that Marshall's would be doing the work. A temporary Marshall registration, G52-16, was painted on the aircraft. Because the TriStar was now Marshall-registered, I found myself captain of the flight tests. I did not fly the aircraft but I did have to sign for it. Two test flights were needed to prove the efficacy of the installation. The Queen got her aircraft on time.

It had become apparent that Hercules tankers operating in the Falklands area needed a radar surveillance capability, as relying on visually spotting ships was not sufficient. The RAF ordered that its Hercules tankers should be fitted with a radar device known as Orange Crop. The Marshall modification was called MAROC (Marshall Orange Crop). Within a few weeks the first Hercules tanker to be fitted with the kit was ready to fly. To flight test the equipment we needed an area that would be free of all ground-based radar transmissions. Nessie was in the news at that time. Where better to fly than along Loch Ness, protected by umpteen miles of best Scottish granite to ward off any incoming radar signals? On 9th May 1984 we flew XV 206 along the Loch, telling the inquisitive that we were searching for Nessie. It was a clear and peaceful day, with excellent visibility and hardly a breath of wind. Flying at just two hundred feet above the smooth surface of the loch was quite magical. 'Up there' said Dave Ryding, the flight engineer, pointing to a hotel above us, 'is where we spent part of our honeymoon.' Just then the RAF navigator, brought along to work the magic radar box, shouted 'Captain, we are being tracked.' The MAROC was responding to an incoming signal in our six o'clock position (behind our tail). 'It's overtaking us' the navigator called. Every head was on the lookout. Rocking its wings as it roared past was the culprit, an F-111 of the USAF. We put an extra tick in the tested box. Down below, Nessie remained dormant.

In February 1985 we finally got our hands on another, much delayed, Hercules test flight spawned by the Falklands conflict. The maximum permitted all-up weight for the use of autopilot was 155,000 lb. Many flights since April 1982 had, of necessity, been made at higher weights. In the simulator at Lyneham we had practised the routine for a take-off at weights above 155,000lb to prepare ourselves for the new event. With a well-ballasted cargo compartment, topped up oleos and tyres, an extra 5,400 gallons of Avtur poured in at Boscombe, XV 210 was ready for us to test at weights up to 175,000lb. At normal air test weights Fat Albert would sprint down the runway like a champion greyhound. On 7th February XV 210 performed like a drugged cow. There was almost time for a cup of tea before it got airborne. Finally the ground fell away and the overweight lady crept upwards from the Wiltshire test centre. An engine failure here could have led to a most unwelcome descent. The only way to reduce weight would be to dump lots of fuel overboard. Dave Ryding, the flight engineer, was poised to hit all dump switches in a trice. We finally made it to operating height, carried out the necessary tests, and were able to report that the autopilot behaved sufficiently well for the RAF to clear it at the higher weights.

On 1st May 1985 a TriStar of 216 Sqn made a route-proving flight to Mount Pleasant airport and on 12th May HRH Prince Andrew performed the opening ceremony. Hercules tanker aircraft were based at Mount Pleasant to support a detachment of McDonnell Phantom fighters. The Hercules and Phantom detachments continued until 1996 when VC-10 tankers and Tornado fighters replaced their elder brethren. While in the Falklands Hercules tanker XV 206 had a narrow escape when it clobbered a Sea King helicopter and suffered damage to the port wing tip and the MAROC pod. The follow up was that we were tasked with flight testing the Hercules to quantify any handling or performance differences between an undamaged model and one with a damaged port pod, caused, for example, by a birdstrike. Once again Fat Albert showed that it could take just about anything in its stride. There were negligible differences in performance between the two versions.

By the end of June 1985 the first of the RAF's TriStar tankers, ZD 950, was nearly ready for flight. On 9th July 1985, with Lockheed test pilot Bill Weaver at the controls, ZD 950 made two flights at Cambridge. After one of them he treated the multitude of spectators to a fast and low fly-past along the main runway at Cambridge. Bill had a very good reason for enjoying life. He had had more than a normal ration of good luck nearly twenty years before ZD 950's first flight. On 25th January 1966 Bill was flying the super-fast-and-high 'spyplane', the Lockheed SR-71A.

Travelling at Mach 3.0 at 80,000 feet above New Mexico, a number of things went wrong simultaneously. The end result was that the front end of the aircraft detached itself from the main body. Shortly after, Bill went unconscious from the high G forces involved. Coming to, Bill thought he had passed into the next world. His frosted up visor prevented him from seeing anything. His main parachute was scheduled to open at 15,000 feet, if the barometric device worked properly. It did. Pushing up his visor Bill had time to enjoy the incredible view in the clear air of the afternoon. He could also see the 'chute of his crew mate, Jim Zwayer, quite close. With freezing hands, Bill was unable to steer his 'chute to the best looking terrain below. Despite that he landed without breaking any bones and turned his thoughts to survival. To his amazement he heard a voice say 'Can I help you?' Walking towards him was a man wearing a cowboy hat. A short distance away stood a helicopter. By sheer co-incidence the ranch-owning helicopter pilot was flying in the area and had seen Bill and Jim descend. Sadly, Jim had not survived the descent.

LOCKHEED SR-71A. Reconnaissance aircraft. Two Pratt and Whitney JT11D-20B turbojets of 32,500lb thrust each. Span 55 feet 6 inches. Length 107 feet 6 inches. Take-off weight 170,000lb. Maximum airspeed 2,000mph.

Flight-tests with TriStar ZD 950, most of them conducted from Boscombe Down with joint Marshall and A & AEE crews, continued apace. The first transfer of fuel from the RAF's newest tanker was approaching, albeit hindered by some poor refuelling-hose flight characteristics. From an on-board tape recording, here is an edited record of part of those tests:

> 'No cloud, no appreciable turbulence. We'll do this fairly cautiously Dennis' said Sqn Ldr Bob Tuxford, the prodding pilot, 'as it's the first time around. Here we are at long line astern, in free airflow. Take the power settings Engineer.' 'Torque 12,000, TIT 880.' 'Marshall One Four from Two Zero, clear to close up'. The R/T callsign of the TriStar was that of Tim Mason – Marshall 20; the Hercules callsign was Dennis Pasco's – Marshall 14. 'Slight buffeting appearing about forty feet below the line of the basket, about sixty feet astern; we have the line of the hose; the basket is nice and steady, just the occasional wriggle. About twenty feet low now and about thirty feet astern and marked jiggling from the rear end of the Hercules. A slight bit of directional instability there.' From the TriStar: 'Event 3.1, 230 knots, scoop setting two.' 'It's totally undamped at the moment, this directional instability. The slip ball is in the middle. About thirty feet astern now and the wriggling from the rudder, the aeroplane

apparently wholeheartedly moving left and right. Let's have a
look at a little bit of rudder to correct it. It's very easy to set
up a swinging directionally, more in yaw than in roll. A small
amount of rudder corrects the yawing. About twenty feet
astern the basket. There is constant play on the rudder. Oops!
The aeroplane moved about ten feet to the left there, with no
control input. The slip ball is way out at the moment. We'll
move further astern now and try again. Right, I am going to
put my feet on the floor now; you do the same please. I shall
do this with aileron alone. We are about forty feet from the
basket and fifteen feet low. The aircraft is just going sideways,
with no feet on the rudder pedals. I can't permit that; it is
unacceptable with rudder free. I am back on the rudder pedals.
I have to put constant little left and right rudder inputs in,
approximately one centimetre. And now stabilising somewhat
better, about twelve feet from the basket. Taking larger aileron
inputs this time to stop it wandering away. Whenever the
aeroplane is central I am getting a moderate buffet over the fin
surface, and it is just destroying the directional stability of the
aeroplane. We'll have a look a little closer this time. There is
continuous lateral activity, plus and minus about twenty
degrees on the stick, and little left/right rudder pedal
movement. Amber light is on. We'll have a look at a contact
this time.'

'Marshall Two Zero from One Four, closing up. Getting a
little easier now, as I get more familiar. Slight rim contact
between refuelling probe and basket edge, at five o'clock.
Closing up again. It needs very tight control to keep the
aeroplane straight. The aircraft stops dead just there, an
apparent increase in drag just before the basket. Touching the
basket, I think it's contact.' 'And you're five feet in', calls
Marshall Two Zero. 'Wandering a little again, just look at that
ball, the slip indicator. Its now better in contact with about
forty-five feet of hose out, the lateral wandering has stopped.
It is a normal contact in all senses. What's the next serial?'
'It'll be 210 knots, with zero flaps.' 'Right Dennis, your turn
for a little station keeping, if you are happy. You have control.'

'General movement around a simulated cone is not too
bad. At forty feet it is quite reasonable directionally and
laterally. Tell him it is satisfactory, moving starboard. Backing
off. Overall, with flap it is a better environment. Let's try the
next serial, with fourteen degrees of flap, speed 200 knots.
Moving forward. Contact. The hose is just hanging there. Ooh,
a little wiggle there, but I think we've got away with it. Oh, no
we haven't. Coming back, we've broken contact. It had the

indications of a partial hard hose.' 'Blackbox Lima (the photographic Hawk) from One Four, did you get that one on film?' 'Affirmative.'

The cause of the poor hose behaviour was finally tracked down, by trial and error, to the baffle within the fluid drive of the HDU. The baffle was increased slightly in size, which resulted in much improved hose characteristics.

By early October 1985 we were ready for the first attempt at a transfer of fuel from the TriStar tanker into a receiver aircraft. The designated receiver aircraft was Hercules C Mk1 (P) XV 210. Scheduled for 3rd October the link up with a TriStar could not take place for the oldest of reasons – the weather. A too-strong crosswind caused the delay. Conditions were just right on 5th October, so the flights were launched. With me on board Hercules XV 210 were Frank Heap, flight engineer, Dave Woods, fourth crewmember and Keith Ingle, photographer and video operator. Representing the RAF, and doing all the prodding, was Sqn Ldr Bob Tuxford. We lifted off Lyneham's runway at 1430 BST, and half an hour later, overhead Yeovilton, linked up with TriStar tanker ZD 950, captained by Tim Mason. After a spell of dry contacts (no fuel passing to the receiver aircraft) it was time to make history.

> 'Our weight is now down to about 100,000lb', said Bob Tuxford. 'We are using about 4,500lb fuel an hour. The ball is reasonably in the middle now. Trimming nose down. We have taken a little fuel. I think we've got the first wet transfer out of a TriStar.' 'Marshall One Four from Two Zero, Carter pumps coming on shortly.' 'Roger.' 'Just for my own interest, I've got no vertical or lateral line-ups, but there have been no problems in turns. At night that might present a problem in terms of how far in or out you are.'
>
> '240 knots, scoop setting two.' Moving in. 'Slightly right, slightly right, in line, spark. Oops, what's that? Is there any fuel in the hose? I think I'm in again. I'm going to have to go; I don't like that wriggling in the hose.' 'Two Zero from One Four, check that there is fuel in the hose.' 'Stand by.' 'Ooh, just got out in time, as the hose wriggled even more. The hose is probably empty of fuel, and the wriggle got out of hand. I sense that the hose emptied. We need to ensure that the hose stays full of fuel at all time, otherwise I stand a chance of losing the probe tip that could then fly off and hit one of our propellers. That was a ripple in the classic sense. It should make good viewing on the video. The hose went sloppy after initial contact. It's approaching five fifty-five local time; they both – the TriStar and the photographic Hawk – wished to land

in daylight. We'll carry on as long as they are happy.'

'Repeat serial 5.14, 240 knots.' 'Clear in', calls Marshall Two Zero. Stabilised refuelling position, 240 knots, 11,000 feet; power settings please.' '16,400, 16,400, 15,700, 15,600. TITs 1005, 1000, 995, 1005.' 'Carter pumps off, all eight booster pumps on, we'd like you to break contact' calls Marshall 20. 'Roger.' 'London, this is Marshall Two Zero, we'd like to turn right now, 060, for Lyneham. We'll carry on to Cambridge, One Four will land at Lyneham.' 'Two Zero from One Four, we'll move starboard and adjust C of G, dump some fuel.' 'Fuel flowing from both wings' says Dave Woods. 'We'll go for the final point now, serial 5.20, and 240 knots. Closing up. Slightly right. In line. Contact. Pushing in, wiggle, pre-check prime, flow confirmed. Emergency break next. Three, two, one, now. All throttles to idle, running it, hard snap, hose is firm. Nice clean break. Moving starboard. You have control Dennis, let's land at Lyneham.'

At 1930 BST we touched down on Lyneham's runway 25 after a very successful day's work.

LOCKHEED TRISTAR K Mk 1. Long-range transport and tanker. Basic crew three. Three Rolls-Royce RB211-524-B4 turbofan engines each of 50,000lb static thrust. Span & length (without the probe) are 164 feet 3 inches. Airspeed limit 375 knots above 8,000 feet. Maximum cruising speed 0.87Mach. Maximum take-off weight 540,000lb. Maximum altitude 43,000 feet. Lockheed built 250 L1011 TriStars; the prototype first flew on 16th November 1970. The flight control system was very advanced for its day, in that it incorporated Direct Lift Control (DLC) spoilers. With landing flap (33 degrees) selected, four spoilers on each wing move in response to pitch inputs from the pilot or autopilot. The DLC spoilers then vary the lift demanded without changing the pitch attitude of the aircraft. RAF Mk 1 TriStars have eight fuel tanks: two in each wing, two in the wing centre-section and two under the cargo compartment floor. Total fuel capacity 176,534 litres (310,695lb).

One by one the problems in the new system were identified, modified and cured. It was discovered, for example, that the Mk 17B drogue, with a different centre of gravity and more drag than the Mk 17T, proved to be more stable. On one flight in the TriStar a loud clacking noise became apparent in the passenger area. Careful listening tracked it down to an area where the fuel vent line was sited. Alarmingly, the surrounding panelling was getting scorching hot. Fuel plus heat equals a nasty mix. Too heavy to land, another bowser-load of Avtur, twelve tons, was quickly dumped. The cause of the trouble was identified as a vibrating nylon blank, smaller than a saucepan lid.

During another flight, transfer of fuel into the receiver aircraft was going well. A relaxed feeling was spreading around the flight deck until the flight engineer piped up 'Cargo door unsafe warning.' The crew thought that the cargo door had, or might, come adrift. The crew of the receiving aircraft inspected under the belly of TriStar and reported that nothing seemed amiss. However, to be safe, a landing was called for. Overboard went another deluge of fuel in order to get down to landing weight. It turned out that there were two panels missing from within the HDU. This allowed air pressure to escape, which in turn caused the cargo door to move inwards, which activated the cargo door warning.

Marshall handed over the first production TriStar K Mk 1, ZD 953, to the RAF on 24th March 1986. It was the RAF's first genuine multi-role air-to-air refuelling tanker/transport and it would enable the RAF to mount operations at short notice almost anywhere in the world.

In addition to testing the TriStar in the air it was necessary to conduct some taxiing trials at high weight, which places a great strain on the tyres, causing them to heat up to a dangerous level. In September 1986, using ZD 950, taxi trials were conducted at Boscombe Down. A take-off at high weight, 518,980lb followed the taxi trials and finally a landing was made at higher than normal weight. The latter was needed to provide performance data for crews faced with an emergency that demanded a heavyweight landing.

Buffet and vibration on Hercules tankers still caused some concern, primarily with regard to a shortening of the fatigue life of the airframe. In September 1985, using XV 203, another set of flight trials was conducted to examine the problem. The results were inconclusive.

During 1986 a Mk 1 Hercules, XV 218, was instrumented to enable a more comprehensive record of stresses and strains to be made in service use. The aircraft was fitted with a Plessey Structural Usage Monitor System (SUMS), a QAR cassette deck, a control unit and a circuit breaker assembly. Certain events were connected to the autopilot, a fatigue meter was connected to the weight-on gear oleo and three accelerometers were fitted on the front spar of the wing. Sensors for altitude, airspeed, cabin pressure, elevator-trimming tab and flight control angles were also fitted. A number of strain gauges were fitted around the aircraft. The resulting recordings would give the RAF adequate data to assist with assessing fatigue life of their Hercules fleet. We flight tested XV 218 at Cambridge in October and November 1986 and then handed it over for operational use.

In early 1987 a meeting was held at Marshall's as a further consequence of concern over stresses on the Hercules airframe and engine propellers. The problems were a follow-on from the much higher number of high weight take-off and AAR behind large tankers. Buffeting of the fin and engine nodding had been observed on numerous occasions. The cause of the phenomena was thought to be the disturbed airflow emanating from the wing of the big tanker aircraft during AAR. MOD agreed that trials were needed to investigate the problem.

The OLM Hercules, XV 218, would be used for the trials. In addition to the OLM instrumentation it would be fitted with a Dowty Rotol system for measuring propeller stress and a Chadwick-Helmuth system for recording engine gearbox vibration. A cupola would be fitted in place of the crew escape hatch to permit visual observation of any fin movement or engine nodding. During service with the RAF a number of aerials had come adrift and some fin brackets had broken. The HF radio aerials would be removed and replaced with high strength cables and new profile masts. The propellers of 1 and 3 engines were fitted with strain gauges and the anti-icing elements were removed. Flight in icing conditions was now prohibited.

Vibration of No 1 engine, the port outer, manifested itself as hard-edged knocking felt through the engine throttle lever. From the astrodome the engine had been seen to execute a nodding motion at a frequency of about 5-Hertz, with the propeller spinner tip moving about plus or minus one inch. Initial flights would be flown in the refuelling position behind a TriStar, a VC-10 and a Victor tanker. A qualified AAR pilot, Sqn Ldr Bob Tydeman, joined us for these flights because we were not AAR-qualified. Flights behind the TriStar and a heavy VC-10 produced evidence of fin buffet and throttle knocking. It was not until 1989, however, that a full trial was undertaken.

On 14th October 1988 TriStar ZD 948, the first KC Mk1, made the world's first L1011 freighter flight, beating the parent company – Lockheed – to the occasion. Another first, of a less satisfactory kind, came on 27th November 1988. During a five-hour air test of a TriStar, flown out of Brize Norton because of a high take-off weight, Tim Gooch, the flight engineer, was aware of what seemed to be a contrail from behind the centre, No 2, engine. The presence of a contrail, ice crystals, is not unusual at high altitudes. This one seemed to be rather persistent, and, seemingly unconnected, Tim was also experiencing problems with the fuel system. He was quite often obliged to transfer fuel from one tank to another to maintain the necessary balance. Again, this was not exceptional, as fuel migration did sometimes happen. While inbound to Brize to land, ATC reported the presence of something flowing, or leaking, from the TriStar. The penny dropped; there was a fuel leak. After landing we witnessed the entire Brize crash and rescue fleet following us down the runway. We turned off at the exit near the end of the runway, stopped, shut down all three engines and evacuated the aircraft. Fuel was still streaming from the nacelle of No 2 engine, up in the fin, and was pooling on the tarmac. Crash crews soon cleared up the mess. The tarmac surface of the turn-off had, however, become contaminated and was put out of action for some months. We later referred to that turn-off as Marshall corner. The leak was traced to a tiny O ring in the fuel line, which had ruptured and allowed twelve tons of fuel to leak away. Tim Gooch again featured when the first ever TriStar-to-TriStar AAR fuel transfer took place in early July 1989. B Squadron at Boscombe found itself short of a flight engineer and had borrowed him for a few days.

Just before that event the RAF had tasked Marshall with flying Hercules XV 218 behind all four of its tanker types at various altitudes, speed, weights and flap configurations. The first problem was that John Blake had not refuelled since his Buccaneer days and I had no experience of flying as a receiver pilot. The cure was easy; do the course. Lyneham provided us with the theoretical training and, later, A & AEE provided a pilot for airborne practices. The RAF pilot, whose nickname was Rambo, showed us the ropes in Hercules XV 218 on 26th July 1989.

My first attempts were pathetic. Despite advice to the contrary, my eyes always moved to the swaying basket at the crucial moment, which meant that invariably, I missed it. With the whole crew watching my feeble attempts I felt despondent. Rambo looked me over and said 'Dennis, you have got to change up a gear. Make your feet and hands work quicker, with smaller movements of the controls. Keep your eyes on a reference point on the tanker and ignore the basket.' Putting his advice into effect my next attempt at spearing the basket worked like magic. The huge cheer from the watching crew would have silenced Wembley on Cup Final day. From then on John and I needed only to be shown, and practice, moving to the extremities of the safe refuelling envelope, up, down, left and right of the central refuelling position. The next few weeks turned out to be as busy as at any time in 1982. During one flight back to Cambridge, while we were over the North Sea, the radar controller asked us if we would mind being embellished by an air-defence Tornado fighter. 'What does embellish mean?' we asked. 'It means that the fighter pilot wishes to use you for a practice interception and he has live ammunition aboard.' 'Yes, that's fine. Just tell the young man to keep his finger off the button' we replied. I completed ninety-six contacts during the hugely satisfying and successful test programme.

The C-130 Hercules has never been granted the necessary clearances to be put on the British civil register. However, on 23rd February 1986, G52-17 took to the sky from Cambridge. The aircraft was surplus to the requirements of a Middle Eastern air force, and we were asked to flight test it for a potential customer. As luck would have it, one of the landing lights fell off and the crew had to file an Incident Report. A second Hercules, G52-18, followed the path of -17. Both were sold to Canada, I think.

John Brownlow had joined the Company in December 1983 on retiring from the RAF in the rank of Air Vice-Marshal. John's first contact with Sir Arthur had been in 1952. He was ADC to the then Air Vice-Marshal Dermot Boyle, who had participated at the 1929 opening of the first Marshall aerodrome, and had made contact with the Cambridge Aero Club for Anthony Boyle, Sir Dermot's elder son, to take up his RAF Flying Scholarship with the club. Contact was renewed much later during John's and the Company's involvement with modification of Canberra bombers to provide them with a LABS. As Director of Flying, Production Executive,

John was responsible for approving aircraft industry test pilots to fly government-owned aircraft, and providing airfield and ATC approvals for government test flying. In this role John had frequent discussions with Sir Arthur, Leslie Worsdell and Doug Page. He made air staff inspection visits to Cambridge on many occasions and first flew from Cambridge on 30th October 1954 when Mr Jeffrey checked him out in Auster V G-AIGH. At that time this flight provided some light relief from converting to the Canberra at the nearby 231 OCU at Bassingbourn. As Assistant, and later Commandant, of RAF College, Cranwell, John remained in close touch with the Company on matters relating to Cambridge UAS.

Much of John's RAF career was spent as a practising test pilot at Farnborough and Boscombe Down. He became OC Experimental Flying Department at Farnborough in 1971, and Commandant of the A & AEE at Boscombe Down in 1977.

On joining the RAF in 1947 John first trained as a navigator. During this period, whilst serving as ADC to the AOC 1 Group, Bomber Command, Air Vice-Marshal D A Boyle, he was fortunate enough to take part in the goodwill tour of South America, Operation 'Round Trip,' as the AOC's navigator. This tour included the first jet crossing of the South Atlantic, both westwards and eastwards, from Dakar in French West Africa to Recife in Brazil. Both crossings were by day on 23rd October and 2nd December 1952 and took four hours and thirty minutes and four hours respectively. The only navigation aid available for most of the crossings was a periscope sextant with which shots of the sun and moon were taken. Each of the four Canberra B2s on the tour was fitted with a 300-gallon reserve fuel tank in the bomb bay in order to extend range sufficiently to make the crossing with a small reserve.

John took over the Company position of Airport and Flight Operations Director from Leslie Worsdell in January 1987. Most of his work was administrative but he maintained currency as a flying instructor with the Cambridge Aero Club, flew the Aztec whenever possible, and took part in test flying Service Chipmunks and Bulldog aircraft. The Company was contracted to complete an anti-corrosion and recovering programme on the Chipmunks, which involved collection and delivery of the aircraft from their home bases. Since this involved ferrying Chipmunks over considerable distances, and Service Chipmunks were not equipped with navigation aids, John devised a hand removable mounting for a Garmin GPS 100, fitted to the cockpit frame. This worked well and provided a much-needed back up for dead reckoning and map reading on long collection and delivery flights. GPS, or Global Positioning System, is a highly accurate navigation system that uses signals beamed down from a couple of dozen satellites.

The Chipmunk flight test schedule called for a one-hour proving flight, including eight-turn spins in both directions and a dive to maximum permitted indicated air speed. The Bulldog contract called on the Company to fit avionics suites to the fleet of some one hundred and twenty aircraft, including a new type of UHF/VHF radio, secondary surveillance radar transponder radio, and a VOR/ILS set, all with associated cockpit displays. Testing involved flying a schedule to check the functioning of this equipment, which all worked well, to provide a welcome and long overdue updating of the Bulldog's training and navigation capabilities.

Almost exactly one year after the completion of the prop-stress flight trials the military rulers of Iraq again impinged on my life. Instead of just threatening an invasion of Kuwait, as in 1961, Iraqi troops poured across the border on 2nd August 1990. The coalition build-up to eject them started almost immediately.

Over the next few months a flood of work was generated within the Company. The RAF placed an urgent requirement to provide some state of the art navigation equipment to those Hercules used by the Special Forces aircrews. Decisions and actions flowed swiftly. A special configuration navigation system (SCNS) was selected and fitted in short order. SCNS was a computerised system fed with signals from a GPS receiver and was shoehorned into the now crowded navigator's station. We were told that the manufacture would provide a skilled operator, and the RAF would provide a navigator as a back up. There was, therefore, no need for any of us to learn how to programme and use the equipment. Had we not heard that one before? John Blake, our chief test pilot, wisely decided that, especially with Christmas just a few weeks away, one of us should learn how to operate the SCNS. His finger pointed at me – signaller, pilot, air quartermaster and now navigator: promotion at last.

The first SCNS flight, in Hercules XV 200, took place on 1st December 1990. John Blake and I flew it locally to check that the new black boxes worked as advertised. They seemed to and the RAF collected the aircraft so that their selected crews could familiarise themselves with the new kit. The second and third flights of SCNS were in XV 179 on 2nd and 4th December. Flying it from the left-hand seat was a young RAF Special Forces pilot. The briefing was 'to fly the mission as if on a real operation'; that meant fly it low. The RAF Flt Lt certainly did that on both flights. Neighbours of mine in Cherry Hinton told me that the Hercules seemed to go round St Andrew's church, not over it. A visual impression, this, in that the larger the aircraft the lower it seems to be. With a monitoring team from Boscombe Down in the cargo compartment, our route took us to Blakeney Point on the Norfolk coast, over the North Sea, across the Yorkshire moors, around Newcastle, across to Wales, through a string of valleys, across south-west England and back to Cambridge. Rarely has seven and a half-hours gone by so quickly. On 18th and 23rd December the wisdom of being self-supporting paid off. With John Blake and Daz James, our newest, ex-RAF, test pilot, up front I made myself at home at the navigator's station for the flight tests of two more SCNS aircraft, XV 298 and XV 205. By the end of January we had tested and delivered all the modified Hercules.

On the night of 16/17th January the coalition forces unleashed an air war against Iraq. I was unaware of it at the time, being lost in a deep sleep. On waking at 7 o'clock I noticed the red light on my answer-phone flashing. The voice of Spike (Ron Spinks), from 17 hangar, said 'Dennis, 216 Sqn wants one of its TriStars back as soon as possible.' I got ready, called Tim Mason at home, and raced to work only to find that there was now no rush for the TriStar. I also discovered that a Marshall security man had visited my home in the early hours, rung the doorbell, threw stones at the window, hammered on the door, all to no avail. The same had happened at Tim's bungalow. What a dozy pair. A little later we learnt that a rather more alert John Blake had been at work since 0300 that morning, and had already gone home. The TriStar that the RAF had called for at such an ungentlemanly hour was one of a pair that the Company hand-painted a fetching shade of pink. The new and unusual colour scheme was selected to make the TriStar less obvious when standing on the desert airfields of Arabia. Inevitably, RAF personnel named them Pinky and Perky.

The crews of 216 Sqn were all committed to flying their steeds up and down the route to the Gulf so we were rewarded with a steady run of collecting and delivering TriStars. Overnight on 24th February 1991 the ground war crashed into action and, brilliantly planned and executed, lasted just five days. General Sir Peter de la Billière was Commander of British Forces Middle East, a big step-up from his 1958/9 adventure.

In 1992, up to 14th July, almost all air tests had been of the Hercules, either RAF or Swedish Air Force. The pattern was broken that day when Daz and John stepped inside a Tardis time machine that deposited them at Finningley to collect the first of eleven Hawker Siddeley Dominie T1 aircraft, XS 728. The Company, teamed with Thorn EMI electronics, had won a contract to completely upgrade the navigation equipment by fitting a super-searcher radar, new radios and mission navigation computers. Future students would be able to use up-to-date 'black boxes' similar to that found on military aircraft like the Tornado.

HAWKER SIDDELEY DOMINIE T10. Navigation trainer. Up to six crew and students. Two 3,310lb thrust Bristol Siddeley Viper 301 jet engines. Span 47 feet. Length 47 feet 6 inches. Maximum loaded weight 20,500lb. Climb to 25,000 feet 13 minutes. Maximum cruising speed 470mph at 25,000 feet. The Dominie superseded the Meteor NF 14 as the RAF's standard navigation trainer for advanced pupils. Entered RAF service in 1965 at Stradishall, Suffolk (now Highpoint Prison). The programme stretched to 1997 before Daz James handed the final modified Dominie, XS 727, to the RAF College at Cranwell.

On 1st March 1993 John Blake and I had the privilege of making the first flight in a RAF C Mk 2A TriStar: ZE 706. An ex-Pan American Airways aircraft, it was one of three bought from Pan Am and had spent nearly nine years in storage at Cambridge. At the end of March we flew this C2A to Marham to become one of many RAF aircraft participating in the RAF review, attended by HM the Queen. Possession being nine tenths of the law, Marshall operated the aircraft on behalf of the RAF. We flew it to Brize Norton on 2nd April to formally present it to 216 Sqn.

In mid-July 1993 John and I chalked up another TriStar first, in N140SC. During 1992 the Orbital Sciences Corporation (OSC) of the USA had chosen Marshall to convert a TriStar to carry a Pegasus rocket under the belly. Hitherto OSC had launched the satellite-carrying Pegasus rocket into low space orbit from below a NASA-provided Boeing B-52 bomber. However, the bomber was approaching the end of its life and the L1011 was selected to be its successor. The Pegasus launcher-rocket weighed over 40,000lb, was over fifty-two feet long with a wingspan of twenty-two feet, or seven metres. In order to carry the necessary fuel for a long flight most of the test flights were mounted from Brize Norton. The Pegasus rocket carried on the air tests was a dummy, but that did not stop speculation that the RAF had contracted Marshall's to build and test an air-to-ground ballistic missile. Representing the Federal Aviation Authority for many of the tests was Bill Weaver. On 29th October 1993 he and I took off from Bedford on a performance-measured take-off run just a few days before that aerodrome closed down for good.

Air Commodore David Bywater replaced John Brownlow as Director, Airport and Flight Operations in January 1994. After joining the Company with 4,500 flying hours and two decades of involvement in test flying to his credit, David has been unable to fly as much as he would like. The demands of a busy office have had to take precedence. He does, however, participate in the ab-initio pilot training of CAC students, and flies Company personnel to UK destinations in the Piper Aztec.

1995 brought yet another first for Marshall's when, on 11th August, John Blake and I flew TriStar N102CK for the maiden flight of a civilian TriStar freighter. Ordered by Connie Kalitta's American International Airways (AIA) in 1994, N102CK was the first of a number of ex-British Airways L1011-200s bought by AIA to be converted by Marshall. Earlier in the year a quite different flight programme had come our way.

The Royal Netherlands Air Force had placed a contract with the Company to install and test an electronic suite that would warn the crew of hostile radar transmissions and approaching missiles and, if missiles were detected, fire off a cloud of small explosive charges. As well as Company aircrew and design staff, the C130 H-30 would have three other nationalities aboard, both civilian and military. Extensive co-ordination would be required between the four nations involved, the low-level agencies at home and abroad, the UK air defence organisation because of radar-jamming tests, civil and military ATC agencies and the photographic chase aircraft. Last, but certainly not least, there was a considerable insurance requirement in the event of accidents. It had all the makings of a monumental can of worms.

Against the odds, the programme went like clockwork. This was very largely due to the tireless efforts of Bob Fox of the Marshall Design Office. The first flight, in early 1995, did not get the programme off to an encouraging start. A lightning strike caused a low-oil quantity warning light to illuminate. The fault could not be cleared so it was necessary to abort the flight and return to Cambridge. On a later flight I encountered a basic design fault of the Mark One eyeball.

We had taken the Hercules to Holland and were engaged in flying the aircraft against a ground electronic facility situated on a very low-lying, almost featureless sandy island. The programme called for us to fly at three different altitudes, starting at five hundred feet above the sea on dead straight tracks some ten kilometres long, spaced exactly 750 metres apart. Similar, I imagine, to the conditions that Flt Lt Kinkead experienced in 1928 over the Solent, it was a hazy day with the sun low on the horizon. Some aircrew use the expression 'flying in a gold fish bowl' to describe such conditions. On one reversal of heading at the end of a ten-kilometre leg, I rolled the Hercules out of the turn at five hundred feet altitude at a speed of two hundred plus knots, looked ahead, and saw nothing. 'Where's the island?' I said. 'Dead ahead' the crew assured me. I could still see nothing. I was grateful for years of training, which allowed me to realise that I should now revert to basic disorientation technique. Glance in, use the instruments to fix the aircraft in a straight and level attitude, inform the crew of my situation to give the co-pilot a chance to take over the flying if I did something silly, glance out, and so on. Suddenly, the island and all its features registered in my partially addled brain and my eyes locked on to it straight ahead. Empty field myopia, the medical types call the situation. A very unpleasant experience when close to the earth's surface.

The RAF retired its Hercules tankers in March 1996; some of the airframes now (February 1999) sit like rejected cast-offs on the edge of Cambridge airport. On 19th July 1999, work started on one of them to prepare for service with the Air Force of Sri Lanka.

Back in 1994, in a joint venture with Lockheed, Allison, Dowty and Westland, the Company had demonstrated the replacement power unit of the new Hercules – the C130J. Hercules XV 181 was leased from MOD, one T56 engine was removed and a new Allison 2100D, driving a six-bladed Dowty propeller, replaced it. Other changes included a new engine nacelle, made by Westland, a new fuel-cooled oil cooler, fly-by-wire technology and a glass cockpit fitment to display the new engine's parameters. The first flight of the SED (single engine demonstrator) with John Blake and Daz James up front was on Saturday 19th March 1994. One week later the Swedish Air Force gave us permission to use one of their Hercules E models, which needed a test flight, as the photo-ship to allow the Lockheed team to take air-to-air video of the SED Hercules. On completion of the demonstrations, XV 181 was demodified and returned to the RAF. Lockheed flew the first of the RAF's thirty C130Js in 1996 and delivered the first of many to Cambridge in October 1998.

The OSC TriStar returned to Cambridge in late 1998 for modifications to allow it to carry the larger Pegasus, the X-34. It flew back to the USA in February 1999 crewed by Tim Gooch, Daz James and John Blake, who, I am delighted to record, was awarded the MBE for services to test flying in the 1999 New Year's honours list. Flight testing of the X-34-carrying TriStar began in June 1999.

Appendix One

List of
Marshall of Cambridge Test Pilots

BEADLE Ted. Died while air testing Venom WK 427 that crashed near Chelmsford in the spring of 1954.

BLAKE John David. (Marshall 13). Born in August 1939, John joined the RAF after failing to get a job with the South Eastern Gas Board. He trained with the RAF/NATO scheme in Canada, flying Chipmunks, Harvards and the T-33. After an acclimatisation course on Vampires at Valley, John joined 203 (Shackleton Mk 3) Sqn at Ballykelly, Northern Ireland. In November 1962 he was posted to 7 FTS at Church Fenton as a QFI on Jet Provosts. Moving to Linton-on-Ouse in June 1965, John added the Chipmunk and Vampire to his instructional repertoire. A further instructing tour came along in June 1967, this time at CFS, Little Rissington, which lasted until 1969. The next three and a half years saw John at ETPS, where he won the Patuxent Shield on 28 course in 1969, and A & AEE, Boscombe Down, where he flew the Canberra, Nimrod, Shackleton AEW2, Vulcan, Hunter and Buccaneer. He escaped from Boscombe in May 1973 to be let loose on Hunters and Buccaneers with 12 Sqn at RAF Honington. Sixteen months later John, now a Sqn Ldr, found himself piloting a mahogany bomber at MOD in London. In September 1977 he renewed his acquaintance with ETPS, and added the Jaguar, Lightning, Basset and Hawker Siddeley HS 748 Andover to his growing list of aircraft types. All that ended in February 1981 when he was detached to the aircraft industry to assist with the introduction of the Tornado simulator to RAF service. Responding to an opportunity at Marshall's, John joined the Company in May 1984. He was appointed Chief Test Pilot in February 1987, became Chief Pilot and Chief Flying Instructor in October 1996 and was awarded the MBE in January 1999.

BROWNLOW Bertrand (known as John since childhood). Born January 1929. Served on 12 Sqn, Lincolns, as navigator. Remustered to pilot and served on 103 Sqn (Canberra B2s). Graduated from 17 ETPS course in 1958. In the mid-60s served a ground tour at Lyneham as OC Operations Wing, operating two Britannia squadrons and 216, Comet, Sqn. Was Defence and Air Attaché at British Embassy in Stockholm, Sweden from 1969 to 1971. John flew some 8,000 hours in one hundred and ten aircraft types, including gliders, while in the RAF, not all as a pilot. While with the Company John was asked to flight test kit and plans-built aircraft constructed by enthusiasts for type under regulations delegated to the Popular Flying Association (PFA) by the CAA. The first few of these aircraft were constructed by their owners in a workshop on the south side of Cambridge airport. Until his retirement from the Company in January 1994 John made the first flights, and tested to Permit-to-Fly standard, twelve aircraft in this category.

Following his retirement from the Company John joined the CAA Board as a non-executive director where he represented the interests of general and business aviation; he retired from this appointment in December 1996. In recent years John has devised, obtained CAA approval for, and put into effect the PFA Pilot Coaching Scheme aimed at encouraging the highest standards of airmanship and flight test safety among PFA members. He is currently PFA National Coach, responsible for implementation of the coaching scheme, a full category gliding instructor, self-launching motor glider instructor and examiner, and a member of the CAA Panel of SMLG Instructor Examiners. In 1983 he was awarded the Royal Aero Club Silver Medal for services to British Gliding, and in 1996 the PFA's Pete Clark Trophy for his contribution to air safety. John became Liveryman at GAPAN on the day of Sir Arthur's speech in May 1997. He remains an active part-time flying instructor and examiner with the CAC.

BUTTERWORTH Robin John. Born 16th December 1944. Ex-RAF Hercules pilot with 30 Sqn at Lyneham and the RAE at Farnborough. Joined Marshall in March 1983. Involved with TriStar and Hercules projects, including the SKE modification. Left in July 1987 to join Brymon Airways to fly Dash 7s.

BYWATER David. (Marshall 10). Graduated from 23 ETPS course in 1964, winning the Patuxent Shield. David joined the RAF as a cadet at Cranwell in 1955. In 1958 he was posted to Cottesmore to join the newly formed 15 Sqn, which was equipped with the Victor Mk 1 V-bomber as that aircraft entered service. He became the youngest Victor captain at the age of twenty-four. After graduating from ETPS in December 1965 he spent four years on B Sqn at A & AEE, Boscombe Down. During this time he was involved in flight refuelling trials and the introduction of terrain-following radar in the Victor and Vulcan Mk 2. On returning from HQ RAF Germany he spent one year at Farnborough, as OC Radio Flight with a fleet of two Comet 4 aircraft, a BAC 111 and an Andover. As a Wg Cdr he spent three years at the RAE as OC flying, during which time he qualified as a helicopter pilot.

In 1952 he returned to the A & AEE in the rank of Group Captain as the Superintendent of Flying. He supervised the establishment's test flying in support of the Falklands emergency. David left Boscombe Down in 1984 for the RAF Staff College at Bracknell. As an Air Commodore he returned to Boscombe as the Commandant of the Experimental Establishment. He was able to fly a large number of foreign aircraft, including the Saab Viggen, the F15, F16, F18 and, in a USAF T38, simulated space-shuttle glide approaches from 20,000 feet to land at Edwards Air Force Base, California.

CARPENTER David William. Born September 1946. RAF Hercules pilot and graduate of ETPS. Test work on Hercules and TriStar at A & AEE Boscombe Down. Joined the Company in February 1988 and left in December to fly Boeing 757s with Monarch Airlines.

ELSE Peter. Featured in Part 1.

EVANS Mark. A RAF Hercules captain, he joined the Company in 1997 and left after an eighteen-month stay.

FLIGHT Ron. Was possibly on 3 ETPS course in 1946. Stayed with Marshall for a couple of years in the 1950s. Flew the Venom. Went to Australia as Flight Inspector.

FROST Ronald Nelson. Featured in Part 2.

HEALY David. Ex-RAF, with five years in Air Traffic Control and seven in Supply, mainly on VC-10 support. Obtained his PPL in 1994 at Halton. Completed commercial pilot training and IRT at Oxford in the summer of 1996 after leaving the RAF in the March. Joined the Company in April 1997. Flew the Cessna 152 with the CAC, the Citation and Aztec, and as second pilot in the Dominie and Hercules. He left the Company in June 1999.

HUBBARD Horace Gordon. Born August 1909. Owned a chicken farm at West Malling and pre-World War Two owned a Spartan aircraft, in which he gave joy rides from sandy strips along the south coast. Joined Marshall in January 1938 with the RAF expansion scheme. Posted to RAF CFS with Leslie Worsdell on Instructor Wartime Course No 4, both as sergeant pilots. Rejoined 22 EFTS, Cambridge, in March 1940 and was commissioned by mid-1942. Posted to an operational Beaufighter Sqn in Cyprus. On return to UK did an advanced instructor's course, attended 7 ETPS course in 1948 and joined the staff at the school. Rejoined Marshall as an instructor and test pilot in November 1945. He was deputy to Leslie Worsdell and with him performed some memorable aerobatics displays at the annual Volunteer Reserve 'Open' days. In a target-towing version of the Venom he returned to Waterbeach unable to jettison the cable and target, and thought he would fly low over the airfield and drag the target along the ground in the hope that the cable would break. ATC called in Norman Harry who was able to suggest a successful alternative way of releasing the cable and target. His last test flight before retirement was in a Canberra B8, XM 265, on 13th October 1964. (Has since died).

JAMES David Anthony Zenthon. (Marshall 16). Born in April 1944, Daz flew the Chipmunk on the RAF Flying Scholarship scheme in 1961. He then joined the RAF and flew the Jet Provost and Folland Gnat trainers at Cranwell and Valley. In 1965 Daz arrived in the hot spot of Aden to fly the Hunter, firstly with 8, and then 43 Sqn. Khormaksar was by then the busiest RAF station in the world, with two Hunter squadrons and 37 Sqn Shackletons forming the Khormaksar Strike Wing. The British left Aden, after one hundred and twenty-eight years of occupation, on 29th November 1967. Daz came home to Cranwell to fly the Jet Provost as a QFI on the Basic FTS. After a spell with the Officer and Aircrew Selection Centre at Biggin Hill, he flew the Hunter at Chivenor and Brawdy, from January 1974 to November 1975. For the next four years he flew at RAF Wittering, with 45 Sqn (Hunter), 1 Sqn and 233 OCU (Harrier). January 1982 saw Daz arrive at ETPS for 41 course, on which he won the Sir Alan Cobham Trophy. He stayed for a year then moved to Bedford, where he did test work on the Harrier, Tornado and BAC-111. Almost five years later Daz joined the staff at ETPS, Boscombe Down, where he again flew many types. He joined Marshall in April 1989 and has been involved with TriStar, Hercules, Bulldog, Dominie and other work.

JONES Robert, AFC. Trained with the US Army Air Corps in 1940. QFI on Tiger Moths, Oxford, Wellington & Halifax. After WW II flew the Dakota with the Indian Air Force. In Transport Command flew Halifax, Dakota – in Berlin AirLift – and Hastings. Last military tour was with Royal Australian Air Force on the Hercules. Then flew with Short Bros, Marshall (67 to 69), Airwork in Saudi Arabia, Lesotho & Yemen, plus flying clubs in Jamaica & elsewhere.

MARSHALL Sir Arthur. Featured in Part 1. Sir Arthur's awards include: OBE and Coronation Medal for services to the Air Training Corps, Knighthood for services to the RAF, Hon. Old Cranwellian, Hon. Fellow Jesus College Cambridge, the Order of Istiqlal 1st Class (Jordan), Companion of the Air League. In 1998 was awarded the Masefield Gold Medal of the British Association of Aviation Consultants.

MASON Timothy. Featured in Part 2.

O'ROURKE Kenneth Vincent. Born 12th March 1929. Believed to be a New Zealander. Joined Marshall from the RAF in May 1960. Flew the Ambassador, Canberra, Varsity, Viscount and MA4. A keen 'skydiver', he sometimes parachuted from a Tiger Moth onto Cambridge airport during the lunch break. He used a Singer sewing machine to service his own 'chute, laying it out on the ground outside the present Aero Club Flight Planning room. His last test flight before leaving the Company was in a Canberra B15 on 25th June 1962. He was killed flying a homebuilt aircraft in Africa.

PAGE Douglas Charles. Featured in Part 1.

PASCO Dennis. Featured in Part 2.

PICKAVANCE Mark. (Marshall 12). Born in January 1961, Mark's childhood interest in aviation matured after joining the Air Training Corps in 1974, and culminated in obtaining his PPL at Cardiff in 1979. From '79 to '83 Mark flew the Bulldog with Oxford UAS at Abingdon. After joining the RAF in 1984 he flew Jet Provost Mk 5s at Cranwell and then the Jetstream at the Advanced FTS, Finningley. Posted to Lyneham in 1987 Mark joined 30 Sqn as a co-pilot. The common thread for all Marshall test pilots, instructing, came along in 1990 when Mark moved to the Elementary FTS at Swinderby to instruct in the Chipmunk. In 1994 the RAF dispatched him back to Lyneham to join 70 Sqn as a captain. From there, in November 1998, Mark left the RAF and joined the Company.

PICKETT Raymond Edward. Born 13th November 1936. Joined Marshall in October 1966 from the RAF. His first test flight was with Bob Smythe in a Canberra B2. He made his final test flight in Canberra B2, WJ 627, on 3rd January 1968. During the previous flight in WJ 627 the port engine had flamed out. Ray left the Company in January 1968 to fly Boeing 707s with BOAC.

PREECE John Martin. Featured in Part 2.

RUDDER Colin David. Featured in Part 2.

SCATCHARD Leslie. Featured in Part 1.

SMYTHE Robert H, AFC. Featured in Part 1.

TAPPIN Herbert. Featured in Part 1, 'Tap' was awarded the DFC in September 1942 for leading his Flight in the first and three other sorties in the Dieppe raid. He was awarded a bar to the DFC in April 1944 for day and night operations with 157 Sqn.

WASS Brian Oscar. Featured in Part 1.

WHITTAKER Neville Stewart. Born 2nd July 1931. Ex-RAF instructor. Joined Marshall in June 1969 and left in October 1971. Flew as co-pilot in Hercules.

WORSDELL Leslie Victor. Featured in Part 1, Leslie was awarded the DFC in 1942 for leading attacks on enemy shipping in defence of Malta. In 1953, for services to the RAF, he was awarded the Coronation Medal. In 1965, for services in the air, he was awarded the Queen's Commendation. For services to military and civil test flying, he was awarded the Queen's Silver Jubilee Medal in 1977. Three years later Leslie was awarded the OBE for services to military and civil aviation.

YOUNG Iain. (Marshall 11). A Mancunian by birth, in October 1946, Iain became bored with his work in the semiconductor industry, saw and responded to an advert for the RAF in a magazine, and joined the Service. The Chipmunk was his first aircraft, at Church Fenton. A short hop north to Linton-on-Ouse to fly Jet Provosts Mk 3 and 5 was followed by a posting to Valley to grapple with the Hunter Mk 6. From swept fixed-wing aircraft Iain changed direction and moved to Odiham to fly helicopters. Newly qualified on the Wessex, Iain headed to the Far East to join 28 Sqn at Kai Tak, Hong Kong. Two years later he moved westwards to join the United Nations as an Air Liaison Officer. Home was now Nicosia, once a RAF station, but now astride the boundary between the Greek area of Cyprus and the Turkish, Northern Cyprus. In 1979 Iain returned to Odiham to fly the Wessex with 72 Sqn, a two-year tour that included detachments to Northern Ireland and Germany. A short drive took him to ETPS in 1981 for 19 rotary-wing course on which he won the Westland Trophy. He was then posted to D Sqn, A & AEE, for two years. With a wealth of rotary-wing experience behind him, Iain rejoined ETPS in 1984 as the Principal Tutor, Rotary Wing. Now a Sqn Ldr, he attended the RAF Staff College at Bracknell, Berkshire, in 1987. Iain's final military posting was to MOD in London.

In 1989 Iain said farewell to the RAF and joined Pilatus Britten-Norman as head of Flight Operations where eight years of development and test flying included four new Islander type-certification programmes. After a short spell as an Inspector of Air Accidents he joined the Company as Chief Test Pilot (Designate) in January 1998.

Appendix Two

Special Marshall Designations & Project Numbers

G52 Registrations are for Marshall flights under 'B' Conditions as laid down in the UK Air Navigation Order.

G52-1	BAC-111, originally G-ASJA, made its first Marshall test flight on 20 Jun 68 with Capt. Musgrove at the controls. Bought by Barwick, a US Company, it became N734EB.
52-2	Canberra B (I) 8, RAF serial WT 368. Became B (I) 68, serial 247, for the Peruvian Air Force. Doug Page made the first test flight on 23 Dec 74. Doug made first flights on all subsequent G52 Canberras, accompanied on all but one occasion by Dave Ryding as observer.
52-3	B (I) 68. Ex -XK 951; became 248. First flight 28 Mar 75.
52-4	WT 342; became 249. First flight 28 Mar 75.
52-5	WT 364; became 250. First flight 6 Jun 75.
52-6	WT 340; became 251. First flight 30 Jun 75.
52-7	XH 234; became 252. First flight 19 Sep 75.
52-8	XM 273; became 253. First flight 19 Oct 75.
52-9	XM 936; became 254. First flight 18 Dec 75.
52-10	XM 263; became 255. First flight 25 Aug 77.
52-11	XM 276; became 256. First flight 23 Nov 77.
52-12	XM 279; became 257. First flight 15 May 78

(Note. XM 278 was broken up for spares).

52-13	Belfast XR 368 became G-BEPS for HeavyLift. First test flight 20 Jun 79 with Bob Smythe and Mr Reynolds (HeavyLift).
52-14	Belfast XR 362 became G-BEPE. First test flight 27 Feb 80 with Doug Page and Peter Jobling (HeavyLift).
52-15	Belfast XR 367 became G-BFYU. First test flight 28 Sep 81 with Doug Page and Peter Jobling.
52-16	TriStar G-BBAI (BA). First test flight 20 Mar 84 with Bill Weaver (Lockheed), Captain Larkin (BA) and Dennis Pasco.
52-17	C-130H, N4247. First test flight 23 Feb 86 with Rob Butterworth and Colin Rudder.
52-18	C-130H, N4246M. First test flight on 23 Jul 86 with John Preece and Dennis Pasco.

Sample MCE Project Numbers

MA 4	Auster 7 conversion for boundary layer control experiments.
MB 4	Varsity fitted with K49 camera installation.

MC 5   Saunders Roe Type 177 work.
MD 5   Vickers Viking – installation of Mallinson floor.
ME 6   Vickers Valiant – Modification 1971 – Blue Steel.
MF 3   Canberra – Aries V – fuel tank installation & Green Satin radar.
MG 2   Viscount 702 – VIP bulkhead (BWIA).
MH 7   Shackleton – modifications to rear fairing.
MJ 3   Boeing 707 – fifth engine pod, to carry R-R Avon engine.
MK 3   Grumman Goose conversion for Grosvenor Estate.
ML 1   C-130K – RAF Hercules.

MT 1 and MT 5 – RAF L1011-500 TRISTAR AIRCRAFT

ZD 948   KC1, ex G-BFCA of BA, (Lockheed serial 193V-1157)
ZD 949   K1, ex G-BFCB (193V-1159)
ZD 950   KC1, ex G-BFCC (193V-1164)
ZD 951   K1, ex G-BFCD (193V-1165)
ZD 952   KC1, ex G-BFCE (193V-1168)
ZD 953   KC1, ex G-BFCF (193V-1174)

ZE 706   C2A, ex N503PA of Pan American Airways (193Y-1177)
ZE 704   C2, ex N508PA (193Y-1186)
ZE 705   C2, ex N509PA (193Y-1188)

Index

AIRCRAFT, GLIDERS & MISSILES

Airbus A300-B4 112
Albemarle 20, 78-80, 84
Ambassador 54,55, 66, 109, 143
Andover (HS 748) 164-167, 181, 184, 193, 194
Anson 20, 84, 107, 151-153, 181
Apache (PA 23) 24, 40, 56, 57, 67, 138, 139
Argonaut 25
Argosy 180, 181
Atlas 48
Audax 73, 83
Auster 24, 39, 40, 55, 65, 67, 76, 84, 94, 208, 218
Avro 504 28, 58
AW52 88
Aztec 40, 46, 67, 72, 127, 130, 139, 141-142, 147, 169, 171, 186, 208, 211
B-25 122, 123
BAC 111 111, 218
Barracuda 19
Baron 57, 111
Battle 16, 73, 81
Beagle Husky 127
    Pup 56, 137
Beaufighter 31, 33, 36, 40, 52, 53, 85, 100, 108
Beaufort 28-33, 52
Beech 99 130
Belfast 71, 89, 218
Beverley 116, 158, 159, 181
Blenheim 50, 81, 82
Blue Steel 43, 178
Boeing 707 219
    737 112, 127
    747 44
    B-47 114, 179
    B-52 180, 211
Boston 53
Botha 20
BP 111 59, 87
Breguet BR 121 125
Brigand 36, 54, 66, 108, 160
Bristol Freighter 180, 182
Britannia 181, 183
Buccaneer 95, 135, 186, 196, 207
Bulldog 58, 147, 148, 208
C-130 (see Hercules)
Cadet 48, 49, 81
Canberra 38, 54, 66, 67, 69, 70, 95, 99, 105, 106, 108, 109, 149, 173, 177, 180, 181, 186, 199, 207, 208, 218, 219
Cessna 150/152 44, 72, 89, 95, 103, 127, 130, 135, 137, 138, 149, 169, 170, 187, 191
Cessna 172 135
    182 139
Cherokee (PA28) 56, 111
Chipmunk 23, 24, 35, 56, 57, 65, 105, 111, 127, 132, 133, 136, 147, 148, 175, 208
Cirrus Moth 12
Citation 23, 46, 72, 89, 91, 126-128, 130, 141-143, 147, 149, 169, 171, 186, 195

Comanche 145
Comet 111, 132, 167, 183-184
Concorde 47, 57, 145
Constellation 67, 131
Dakota 34, 53, 67, 68, 78, 79, 84, 89, 132, 153, 185
Dash-7 132
DC-6A 160
DC-10/KC-10 89, 197
Defiant 77
DH 108 88
Dominie 147, 210
Dornier Do 17 81, 83
F-86 Sabre 94, 174
F-104 180
F-111 100, 200
Fairey IIIA 12
Falcon (Miles) 23,
Focke-Wulf 190 52, 62, 151
Fortress I 21, 60
Gipsy Moth 13-15
Gladiator 20, 77, 83
Gnat 119
Grumman Goose 219
Hadrian 78, 79
Halifax 53, 60, 64, 79, 92
Hamilcar 92, 93
Handley Page 0/400 12
    HP 42 16
Harrier 125
Harrow 58
Hart 16, 18, 20, 49, 73, 83
Harvard 23, 34, 73, 93, 105, 175, 186
Hastings 23, 133, 161-163, 176
Havoc 50, 52
Hawk 189, 203
Hawker 1052 87, 88
Heinkel 111 77, 122
Hendon 58
Hengist 92
Hercules (C-130) 44-46, 68, 69, 71, 89-91, 97-103, 126-130, 145-147, 149, 161, 167, 186, 189, 191, 192, 196-207, 218, 219
Hermes II 180
Hind (Hawker) 16, 18, 20, 49, 73, 80
Horsa 78, 79, 92, 93, 100
Hotspur 92
Hunter 106, 114-119, 125, 132, 133, 152, 176, 179, 181, 183, 184, 186
Hurricane 19, 50, 51, 58, 64, 122, 145
Jaguar 124-126
Javelin 180, 182
Jet Provost 119, 163, 164, 183
Ju 88 52
Kingair C90 69, 140, 141
Lancaster 60, 63, 64
Leopard Moth 27
Lincoln 176
Lightning 180
Lysander 19, 20, 49, 53
MA 4 38, 39, 68, 69, 95
Magister 19, 34, 49, 73, 80, 82, 113
Martel 185
Martinet I 86
Master 19, 28, 50, 64, 92
Messerschmitt 109 74-76, 114, 122, 123, 145
Meteor 88, 93, 94, 104, 105, 119, 151, 176, 181, 190, 210

Minerva (Rallye) 24, 25, 127, 186
Mitchell 174
M L Utility 54
Monospar 17
Mosquito 15, 20, 34, 52, 53, 65, 83-86, 100, 104, 106, 107, 151
Mustang 174
Nimrod 183, 196
Oxford 19-21, 28, 59, 64-66, 83, 105
Pegasus 6, 189, 190, 211, 213
Pembroke 182
Phantom 119, 185, 196, 200
Piasecki H-21 182
Pioneer 88
Piston Provost 66, 113, 132, 160
Prentice 88, 153
Proctor 34, 35, 54, 55, 66
Puss Moth 16, 23, 27
Queenair 40, 41, 68, 69
R101 58
Rapide 54, 55, 66, 67, 102, 109, 110
Roc 19, 20
Saunders Roe 177 219
Scimitar 133, 180
Seahawk 159
Sea Balliol I 88
Sea Devon 138
Sea Harrier 196
Sea Hornet 36
Sea King 135, 200
Sea Vixen 180
Shackleton 159, 181, 219
Shrike 185
Sia Marchetti SF 260 56
Sioux 182
Siskin 48
Snark 15
Spitfire 18, 19, 23, 49, 50, 58, 64, 65, 73-77, 80, 93, 100, 114, 120-123, 133, 145
SR-71A 200, 201
Stearman PT17 85
Stirling 20, 50, 60-64, 71
Supermarine S5, 6, 6B 47
Swift 87, 88, 106
Swordfish 131
T-33 175, 176
Tebuan (CL-41G) 123, 124
Tempest 53
Thor 67, 110
Tiger Moth 16, 19, 26-28, 34, 35, 38, 44, 50, 54, 55, 59, 66-68, 73, 75, 76, 84, 92, 93, 95, 98, 104, 108, 135, 186
Tipsy Nipper 68
Titan (Cessna) 72
Tornado 182, 194, 200, 207, 210
Tripacer 137
TriStar L1011 129, 130, 171, 186, 188, 197-207, 210, 211, Appx 2
TSR 2 119, 179
Tutor (Avro) 18, 28, 49
Twin Pioneer 123
Typhoon 20, 21, 84
Valentia 58
Valetta 54, 66, 95, 108, 109, 120, 153-160, 164
Valiant 6, 36, 38, 41-43, 54, 67, 68, 95, 108, 109, 219

Vampire 23, 24, 35, 36, 39, 54, 55, 65, 66, 93, 95, 107, 108, 114, 132, 150, 151, 160, 161, 176
Vanguard 57
Varsity 54, 66, 95, 108, 119, 120, 160, 167, 176
VC-10 44, 57, 189, 200, 206
Venom 36, 37, 54, 55, 66, 99, 108, 120, 158, 159
Victor 191-194, 197
Viking 131, 219
Virginia 47, 58
Viscount 36-38, 43, 54, 55, 66, 67, 89, 109, 219
Vulcan 177-180, 182, 185, 190, 191, 194
Vl (Doodlebug) 53, 151, 173
Waco CG-14A (see Hadrian)
Wallis Autogyro 68
Warwick 53
Wellington 18, 20, 32, 60, 64, 120
Whitley 18-21, 58, 78, 83
Wyvern 88
X-34 6, 189, 213

PERSONNEL

Abbott, Mr 56
Adeane, Lady 127
Aitken, Sqn Ldr N A 50
Alexander, Field Marshal Lord 79
Ambrose, Mark 187
Andrew, HRH The Prince 200
Ashby, Ken 90
Astor, J J 139
Bader, Gp Capt Douglas 100
Bairsto, Sqn Ldr 114, 116
Baker, Geoff 22
Balloch, Cpl 174
Banfield, Sqn Ldr Tony 197
Barclay, Jeff 108
Beadle, Ted Appx 1
Bentley, Sgt Jack 49
Berry, Sqn Ldr A E 52
Billière, General Sir Peter de la 159, 160, 210
Birch, Barbara (née Wass) 92, 95
Birch, Derek 95
Bishop, Mike 134
Blake, John 6, 130, 143, 145, 186, 207, 209, 210-213, Appx 1
Boothman, Flt Lt John 47
Boscawen, Judy & Simon 143, 145
Boyle, Marshal of RAF Sir Dermot 15, 207, 208
Boyle, Anthony 207
Bradley, Flt Lt 80
Bragg, Lady 34
Bramson, M L 76
Broad, Hubert 15
Brown, Sqn Ldr John 192, 199
Brownlow, Air Vice Marshal John 207, 208, 211, Appx 1
Burnett, Jack 21, 83
Bussey, Ben 187
Butlin, Billy 127
Butterworth, Rob 170, Appx 1
Bywater, Air Cdre David 190, 192, 211, Appx 1
Caine, Michael 122
Carpenter, David Appx 1
Chamberlain, Neville 19
Chapman, Karl 195
Charles, N A 20, 21

Cheshire, Gp Capt Leonard VC 17, 19, 49
Clark, Gordon 20
Cobham, Sir Alan 14, 15
Collier, Peter 139
Cooper, Cyril 83
Cousens, Ken 90
Cozens, Sqn Ldr H Iliffe 18
Crowley-Milling, Air Marshal Sir Denis 167
Cunningham, Gp Capt John 46, 86
de Bruyne, Dr Norman 15, 18
Dowding, Air Chief Marshal Lord 74
Duff-Mitchell, Peter 56
Eisenhower, General Dwight 79
Elizabeth II, HM The Queen 199, 211
Elizabeth, Princess of Toro 170
Elliot, Wg Cdr George 120
Else, Diana 73
Else, Peter 18, 73-76, 83
Evans, Mark Appx 1
Flight, Ron Appx 1
Fox, Bob 212
Foxley-Norris, Air Chief Marshal Sir Christopher 17, 49
Frans, Henri 138
Freeman, Mr 149
Frost, Ron 100, 104-112
Galtieri, General 165, 170, 185, 186, 191, 195
Garrod, Air Chief Marshal Sir Guy 17
Gates, Joe 139
Gates, Roy 197
George VI, HM The King 78
Goering, Herman 74, 117
Gooch, Tim 97, 99, 100, 188, 191, 192, 194, 195, 197, 206, 213
Goodyer, Air Cdre Gerry 179
Grace, Flt Lt E B 49
Green, Hughie 127
Greig, Flt Lt d'Arcy 47
Haig, General Alexander 193
Harry, Norman 195, 197
Head, Dr M R 39, 40
Healy, David Appx 1
Heap, Frank 203
Henson, Ron 195
Hinkler, 'Bert' 48
Hogan, Keith 89
Holme, 'Pidge' 181
Hubbard, Gordon 36, 39, 43, 54, 100, 108, 153, Appx 1
Hughes, David 187
Hughes-Rees, J A 49
Hussein, King of Jordan 143-145
Ignatowski, Flt Lt 'Iggy' 162, 163
Ingle, Keith 203
Jackson, Flt Lt 163
Jagger, Sqn Ldr 94
James, Daz 147, 209, 210, 212, 213, Appx 1
Jeffrey, Mr 208
Jenkins, Sqn Ldr 48
Jermyn, John (Lord Bristol) 127
Johnson, Air Vice-Marshal J E 17, 49, 75, 158
Jones, Robert Appx 1
Jones, Fg Off Mike 176, 177
Kalitta, Connie 211
Keable, Sqn Ldr John 176, 177
Kesselring, Field Marshal 73, 79
King, Pauline 97
Kinkead, Flt Lt Sam 47, 212
Krishnamurthy, Ramaswamiah 95
Legg, David 133

Love, Sgt 82
Loverseed, Bill 132
MacDonald, Flt Lt John 179
Macleod, 'Mac' 139
Mahaddie, Gp Capt Hamish 121
Mallorie, Wg Cdr 177
Manns, Wg Cdr 24
Margaret, HRH The Princess 129
Marsh, Captain 37
Marshall, Sir Arthur 6, 7, 12-23, 27, 34, 35, 40, 44, 69, 76, 82, 84, 89, 91, 95, 112, 126, 129, 143, 145, 186, 195, 207, 208, Appx 1
Marshall, David 6, 7, 12-15, 18
Marshall, Michael 6, 23-25, 127
Marshall, Lady Rosemary 21, 23, 77, 143
Mason, Angela, Jacque & Julie 182, 183
Mason, Penny 182, 186, 190
Mason, Timothy 130, 173-190, 201, 203, 210
May, Doreen 77
May, Peter 19, 21, 76-80, 82, 92
McLauchlan, 'Mac' 132
Miller, Glenn 52
Millett, Paul 125
Mills, Flt Lt Alan 49
Milne, Mick 89, 195
Mitchell 'Mitch' 114
Montgomery, Field Marshal Lord 32, 64
Morell, Frank 14
Moss, Fred 192
Mountbatten, Earl 127
Nasser, Colonel 154, 159
Newington, Sam 133
Nightingale, Dave 109
Nightingale Father 95
Nointy, Sgt 83
Northfield, Cdt 83
Northwood, Sqn Ldr Barry 161, 164
Nyabongo, Wilbur 170
O'Rourke, Kenneth Appx 1
Orlebar, Flt Lt A H 47
Orlebar, Chris 47
Osborne, Sqn Ldr Sammy 115
Page, Doug 44, 58-72, 89, 100, 129, 169, 195, 208
Parsons, Sgt 82
Pasco, Anna & Nicholas 167
Pasco, Dennis 6, 89-91, 129, 130, 150-172, 194-199, 201, 209, 211
Pasco, Judith (née Beake) 167
Pasco, Margaret (née Brown) 172
Pasco, Harry, Nell & Ron 150, 151, 154
Pemberton, Jeremy 137, 138
Pickavance, Mark Appx 1
Pickett, Ray Appx 1
Pitman, Lt 83
Pontin, Fred & Bobby 127
Preece, Audrey 117, 126
Preece, Clive & Roger 118, 119
Preece, John 113-130, 169, 170, 191, 193-196
Radina, Master Pilot Frank 163
Rimmington, Flt Lt 176
Robertson, Mr 110
Rose, Neville 97
Rosson, Keith 136
Rudder, Colin 97-103, 130-149, 196, 198
Ryding, David 69, 98-100, 128, 192, 194, 199, 200

Said, Sabah El 143
Scatchard, Jean 83
Scatchard, Leslie 21, 80-84
Scoular, Gp Capt David 186
Silk, Doug 93
Simmonds, David 142, 143
Smulian, Flt Lt Philip 80
Smythe, Marjorie 88
Smythe, Robert 23, 68, 83, 84-92, 126, 142, 145, 191, 192, 195, 196
Spinks, Ron 'Spike' 210
St Joseph, Dr 67, 110
Stainforth, Flt Lt George 47
Staples, Sgt 82
Strause, Sgt 81
Tappin, Charles Edward 47
Tappin, Herbert 17, 39, 47-57, 66, 77, 100, 110, 112, Appx 1
Tappin, Emily Martha (née Cotton) 47
Taylor, Hector 136
Taylor, Mr 149
Taylor, Flt Lt Len 157
Templar, Field Marshal Sir Gerald 157
Thatcher, Lady Margaret 170
Thomas Flt Lt I H 53
Thompson, Tommy 16, 20
Tranum, John 15
Trubshaw, Brian 41, 43, 44
Turner, 'Topsy' 102
Tuxford, Sqn Ldr 189, 201-203
Tydeman, Sqn Ldr Bob 206
Vickers, Sqn Ldr 69
Wadams, Flt Lt 'Curly' 160
Waghorn, Fg Off H R 47
Walker, Air Marshal John 115
Warburton, Sqn Ldr Adrian 32
Wass, Ann & John 95
Wass, Brian 40, 68, 89, 92-95
Watts, Air Cdre Ray 180
Watts-Phillips, Wg Cdr Jim 181
Weaver, Bill 200, 201
Webster Flt Lt 47
Wheeler, Wg Cdr V J 52
Whittaker, Neville Appx 1
Wilkinson, Air Cdre John 182
Wilkinson, Stephen 16
Williamson, Flt Lt Ron 150, 160, 161
Wood, Sir Kingsley 18
Woods, David 203
Worsdell, A V 26
Worsdell, Leslie 6, 17, 18, 22, 24, 26-46, 67, 68, 76, 88, 98, 100, 108, 120, 126, 129, 130, 140, 194, 208, Appx 1
Young, Sqn Ldr Graham 103
Young, Iain Appx 1
Zwayer, Jim 201

RAF SQUADRONS

1 (F) 94
2 88
3 (F) 50, 53
7 60
8 158
9 178
12 176
14 117
19 18, 28, 80
24 161
30 151, 167-169
35 178
39 30, 31
43 114

47 161
52 164-167
53 71
64 93
65 93
66 93, 94, 100, 115, 116
68 88
69 32
72 73, 77
83 177, 178
84 154-160
85 83, 86
88 69
90 60, 61
92 93, 94
108 53
109 106
114 81
137 22
139 106
148 53
157 50, 52, 53
202 161-163
208 117, 118
216 167, 186, 200, 210, 211
242 100
256 53, 85
264 94
295 79
296 78, 79
534 52
604 85
610 73, 75, 94
617 177
Experimental Flying Sqn 184
Ferry Comm Sqn 160
Malta Comms Sqn 181

RAF TRAINING & OTHER MILITARY UNITS

1 Air Signaller School 151-153
1 Parachute Trg School 153
2 Air Grading School 104
3 Air Observers' School 20
2 CAACU 65, 100, 107
2 FTS 105
3 E & RFTS 48
3 EFTS 81
4 FTS 93, 176
4 SFIS 19
6 FTS 58, 73
7 FTS 163, 164
8 FTS 105, 113, 114
12 Service FTS 81
15 E & RFTS 13
17 E & RFTS 13
22 E & RFTS 19, 73, 77
22 EFTS 19, 49
22 RFS 23, 35, 65
25 E & RFTS 80
26 E & RFTS 49
28 EFTS 59
29 EFTS 153
202 AFTS 23
204 AFTS 93
206 AFTS 105
A & AEE 192, 207, 208
Bomber Cmnd Instructors' School 105
Cambridge UAS 18, 19, 24, 58, 65, 76, 208
CFS 13, 16, 28, 49, 106, 119, 120, 133, 136, 163, 171, 177
DFCS 118

ETPS 87, 126, 179, Appx 1
Glider Pilot Regt 92, 93, 100
Heavy Glider Conversion Unit 78
Oxford UAS 17, 49
RAF Central Fighter Establishment 118
RAF College FTS 59, 208, 210
RAF High Speed Flt 47
226 OCU 93
229 OCU 114, 124
231 OCU 105, 208
242 OCU 145, 153
17 OTU 81
51 (Night-Fighter) OTU 52
52 (Hurricane) OTU 50
84 OTU 59
1651 HCU 60, 64
77 Sqn RAAF 94
232 Wing 85
322 Wing 53
334 Wing 53
11 Group Fighter Cmnd 49, 74
54 Maintenance Unit 77

AERODROMES, AIRPORTS, BASES

Abbotsinch 49
Abingdon 154
Acklington 115, 116
Akrotiri 116, 167
Aldergrove 161-163
Andover 78
Ansty 105
Aquaba 143
Ascension (see Wideawake)
Aston Down 83
Aviano 53
Azaiba 159
Ballah 53, 54
Bahrein 154, 159, 161
Bangor, Maine 140
Basra 25
Bassingbourn 105, 176, 208
Bedford 45, 52, 66, 68, 72, 99, 120, 137, 184, 190, 211
Beihan 159
Benson 160
Bentwaters 86
Biggin Hill 74
Binbrook 118, 119, 124, 176
Blackbushe 55, 61
Blakehill Farm 22
Bluie West One (see Narsarssuaq)
Bobbington (see Halfpenny Green)
Bombay 25, 167, 181
Boscombe Down 45, 67-69, 87, 125, 128, 148, 180-184, 189, 192, 195-198, 200, 201, 205, 206, 208
Bottisham 35
Bourges 137
Bourne 187
Bradwell 50
Brawdy 66
Brindisi 143
Brize Norton 78, 97, 99, 188, 206, 211
Brockworth (Hucclecote) 21
Butterworth 118, 166, 167
Cairo 143
Calshot 47
Cambridge 13-18, 21, 24, 27, 39, 41, 43, 45, 58, 65, 66, 77, 82, 89, 95, 97, 102, 108, 126, 141, 145, 160, 189, 200, 207-209, 213

Cape Greco 115
Caracus 70
Cardington 114, 151, 174
Castle Camps 52
Centralia Station 174
Changi 165-167
Chetwynd 132
Chivenor 28-30, 114, 119
Church Fenton 73, 163, 164
Church Lawford 34
Clermont Ferrand 137
Clyffe Pypard 23, 153
Colerne 103, 161, 164
Cologne 34, 141
Colombo 25, 167
Coltishall 94, 100, 101
Coningsby 176-178
Cranfield 52
Cranwell 59
Croydon 15, 35
Dakar 70, 89-91, 208
Dalcross 105, 111
Damascus 25
Debden 50
Defford 83
Desborough 59
Dhala 158
Digby 23, 104, 105
Dishforth 153, 161
Driffield 93, 105
Dulles 167
Duxford 18, 58, 77, 94, 120, 121, 145
East Fortune 33
Eastleigh 47, 48, 57
Edwards Air Base 180, 182
El Adem 116, 161
El Ayoune 145
Fairford 93, 103, 143
Farnborough 86, 87, 184, 186, 192, 208
Feltwell 23, 63, 93, 113
Fen Ditton (see Cambridge)
Finningley 64, 177, 210
Firq 159
Fort Chimo 127, 142
Frankfurt 141
Froha 79
Gander 167
Gatow 151
Gatwick 27, 74, 89, 111, 112, 137
Genoa 137
Gibraltar 30, 31
Gimli 23
Goodwood 57
Gourine 79
Goose Bay 40, 67
Grantham 28
Gravesend 73-75, 131
Gunter Field 85
Gütersloh 37, 117, 185
Halfpenny Green 20
Halton 48, 75
Hamble 47-49, 55-57, 81, 111
Hargeisa 158
Hatfield 13, 108
Hatley Park 139
Hawkinge 74, 75, 122
Headley Court 24, 181
Heany 93
Heathrow 43, 55, 66, 67, 111, 171, 188, 189
Hednesford 54
Hemswell 106, 110
Hendon 19, 76
Henlow 121, 122

Hickam Air Base 169
Hooton Park 13, 14
Hornchurch 104, 114, 151
Horsham St Faith 82
Hunsdon 50, 51, 53
Hurn 57
Idris 177
Iraklion 145
Istres 153
Jersey 128
Kai Tak 25, 118
Karachi 25
Kastrup 76
Keflavik 37, 38, 67
Kemble 167
Khartoum 161
Khormaksar 154-161
Kidlington 49, 57
Kinloss 183, 185
Kirton-in-Lindsey 105, 113, 114, 174
Korat 164
Kuantan 123, 124
Lagos, Nigeria 89
Lakenheath 63, 160
Langham 65, 85, 100, 104, 106
Las Palmas 91
Le Bourget 16
Le Touquet 137
Leeming 86, 183
Lee-on-the-Solent 57
Leuchars 185
Liège 140
Lima 70
Lincoln Air Base 179
Lindholme 176
Linköping 141
Linton-on-Ouse 93
Little Rissington 73, 119, 163
Little Snoring 100
Liverpool 19
Llanbedr 190
Lodar 157
London, Ontario 174
Love Field 142
Lulsgate Bottom 64
Luxor 143, 167
Lympne 15, 27
Lyneham 30, 53, 91, 123, 145, 153, 154, 167-169, 192, 196, 200, 203, 204
Macdonald Air Base 175
Malta 30-33, 54, 57, 77, 79, 116, 153, 154, 161, 167, 181
Manby 88
Manston 51, 151
Marham 120, 192, 194, 211
Marka 143
Martlesham Heath 50, 132
Masirah 155, 159
McClellan Air Base 169
Miami 140
Mildenhall 97
Montreal 66, 67, 78
Mount Pleasant 199, 200
Mukieras 157, 158
Nairobi 157, 158
Narsarssuaq 38
Netheravon 78, 93
Newchurch 53
Newmarket Heath 62
Newton 36
Nice 145
Nicosia 25, 116
North Coates 33
North Luffenham 88

North Weald 51
Northwood 33
Norwich 12, 13, 82
Oakington 105, 119, 120, 123, 167
Offutt, Nebraska 179
Okinawa 25
Oslo 112
Ottawa 167
Oulton 81
Padgate 23, 104
Pershore 180
Pisa 167
Prague 34, 151
Predannack 52
Prestwick 37, 67
Rearsby 39
Recife 70, 208
Renfrew 46
Reykjavik 142
Riyan 155
Rome 25
Saigon 25
Salalah 154, 155
Salmesbury 149
Santa Maria 141
Såtenas 147
Scampton 177, 180
Scorton 85
Seeb 159
Seletar 164-166
Sept Isles 142
Seria Anduki 165
Sewart Air Base 44, 68
Shannon 70, 111, 171
Sharjah 154, 159, 167
Shawbury 19, 77, 88, 132, 133, 139, 160
Shoreham 51, 52, 56, 57, 105
Søndre Strømfjord 38, 67, 127, 142
South Cerney 160
Speke (see Liverpool)
Spitalgate 81
Stanley 194, 199
Stansted 137
Stephenville 140
Stradishall 93, 210
Swanton Morley 151
Swinderby 65, 113, 114
Sylt 117
Sywell 27, 58, 137
Takhli 164
Tangmere 132, 133
Tern Hill 113, 160, 174
Teversham (see Cambridge)
Thorney Island 151, 153, 167
Thurleigh (see Bedford)
Tit Melil 24
Tokyo 25
Toronto 142
Tromso 103
Tuddenham 60, 62
Tuscaloosa 85
Twinwood Farm 52, 53
Udorn 164
Upavon 28, 49
Upper Heyford 100
Upwood 81
Valley 23, 119, 160, 161
Waddington 152, 194
Wahn 88
Waltham (Grimsby) 80
Warton 66, 69, 124-126, 141
Watchfield 22
Waterbeach 20, 36, 37, 93, 95, 108
Wattisham 100, 101

West Freugh 23
West Malling 53, 150, 151
West Raynham 60, 94, 152
West Wickham 60
Wheelus Air Base 181
White Waltham 107
Whitehill Farm (see Cambridge)
Wichita 126, 140, 142
Wideawake 191, 194, 197, 199
Wildenrath 151
Wisley 66, 67
Wittering 125
Woburn Park 64
Woolfox Lodge 64
Worksop 86, 176
Worthy Down 47
Wratting Common 60, 64

GENERAL

Aden Protectorate Levies 155-158
Aeroplane & Flight 12, 13, 49, 139
Air Canada 66, 67
Air Liban 131
Air Ministry 7, 15, 18, 19, 21, 26, 28,
    31, 37, 43, 88
Air Service Training 48, 49, 55
Air Training Corps 55, 76, 83, 92, 110,
    127, 136, 151, 171, 182
Air Transport Auxiliary 54
Allison 212
American Airlines 142
American International Airways 211
Aviation Hall 13
BAC & BAe 69, 70, 124
BAINS trial 185
Battle of Britain 17, 49-51, 73-77, 81,
    94, 104, 115, 120-122, 145
BEA 55, 56, 66, 110, 111
Berlin 74, 83, 111, 120
Birmingham University 131
Bismuth 161-163
Blue Parrot 95
Blue Shadow 95, 106
BOAC 25, 55, 56, 110, 111
Bramdean School 114
Brighton 12, 104, 112
British Airways 47, 56, 112, 171, 188,
    197
British Oxygen Corp'n 109
Caen 63, 64
Cambridge Aero Club 16-18, 26, 27,
    34, 58, 66, 76, 89, 103, 110, 127,
    130, 135, 139, 170-172, 207, 208,
    211
Cambridge Daily News 26
Cambridge Gliding Club 18
Cambridge County High School for
    Boys 92
Cambridge University 12, 15, 19, 28
Cambridge University Engineering
    Laboratory 19, 38, 40
CAA 16, 44, 55, 71, 127, 130, 143,
    171, 188-190
Clem Pike Trophy 17
College of Air Training 55, 57, 110,
    111
Crayford 150
Cyprus 115-117, 131, 167
Dacre Trophy 116
Daily Mail 79, 170
Dan Air 111, 112
Dartford Grammar School 151
de Havilland Co 13, 14

Denstone College 131
Dieppe 51, 75
Dowty 212
Eagle Airways 160
Elfleda House 12
Empire Air Day 48
English Electric 94
Exeter 113
Exeter Public School 114
Falklands War 128, 170, 178, 185,
    191-196, 198, 200
Flight Refuelling Ltd 193-195
French Foreign Legion 163
French Resistance 61
GAPAN 14-17, 55, 112
German Air Force 68
Gneisenau 51
GEE-H 177
GCI 65, 66, 107
GPS 208
Guildford Grammar School 173
Gulf War 45, 209, 210
Hack Trophy 133
Hampshire Aeroplane Club 48
Haslemere 173
HeavyLift 71, 72
Highball 84
Huntingdon 14, 26
Huntingdon Grammar School 26
Imperial War Museum 27, 58
Ipswich School of Flying 138
Italian Air Force 167
Itchen Grammar School 48
Jebel Akhdar 159, 160
Jesus College 12
Jungle Line 166
Korean War 93, 100, 105
Kuwait 45, 161, 209
LABS 95, 177, 207
Linton Primary & Junior School 92
Linton Haulage Co 92
Lockheed 44, 46, 89, 198, 206, 212,
    213
Marconi 154
MAROC 199, 200
Marshall Ab Initio Flying Instructor
    Scheme 16, 17
Marshall of Cambridge (Eng) Ltd 70,
    126, 138, 139, 160, 169, 186-188,
    198-201, 205, 208, 211
Marshall's Flying School 23, 26, 34,
    35, 42, 49, 54, 56, 73, 75, 82, 88,
    93, 94, 100, 106, 108, 110, 112,
    143, 153, 176
Mickey Mouse 29, 30
Minelaying Ops 61
Ministry of Defence 7, 39, 44, 46, 66,
    71, 89, 146, 184, 194, 212
Missionary Aviation Fellowship
    (MAF) 130
Misson range 176
ML Aviation 66
Munich 182
Murphy's Law 30
Newmarket 54, 73
Nigerian Air Force 89, 90
NASA 211
Norfolk & Norwich Aero Club 12
Operation Chestnut 80
                    Eve 79
                    Goodwood 64
                    Round Trip 208
                    Sealion 74
Orbital Sciences Corporation 189, 211,
    213

Oxford Air Training School 111
Pan American Airways 210, 211
Perse Preparatory School 12
Porchester Road Infants' School 48
Peru 69
Peruvian Air Force 70
Pete Clark Trophy 215
Polish Air Force 162
Rover patrols 30
Royal Canadian Air Force 34, 174, 175
Royal Jordanian Air Force 127, 129,
    143
Royal Malaysian Air Force 123, 124
Royal Netherlands Air Force 211
Rural Flying Corps 187
St Elmo's Fire 32
St Paulinus C of E School, Crayford
    151
SAS 80, 159, 160, 166
Sawston 58
Sawston Village College 58
Scharnhorst 51
Schneider Trophy 47
SCNS 209
Sholing 47
Sholing Boys School 48
Short Brothers & Harland 70
Sicily 32, 78, 79, 93
Singapore Air Force 166
Smallwood Manor School 131
Spanish Air Force 123
Spanish Armada 128, 129
Sri Lanka Air Force 212
Station Keeping Equipment (SKE) 198
Stroud School 173
Swedish Air Force 127, 147, 210, 212
Tirpitz 19
Tobruk 32
Tonbridge School 12
Trinity College 15
United Airlines 119
USAF 100, 164, 169, 170, 197, 198,
    200
Varndean Grammar School 104
Vickers Aircraft Co 41, 44, 66, 67
Wainfleet range 176
Westland 212
Weybourne range 104, 107
Woolwich 92
Wylde Green 131
Wylde Green School 131
ZZ/QGH Approach 81